# MAKING YOUR OWN
# MARBLED
# and Decorated
# PAPERS

### JANE H. REESE

**NORTH LIGHT BOOKS**

First published in North America
in 1996 by North Light Books,
an imprint of F&W Publications, Inc
1507 Dana Avenue
Cincinnati, OH 45207
1-800/289-0963

First published in the UK by
New Holland (Publishers) Ltd
24 Nutford Place, London W1H 6DQ

ISBN 0 89134 712 7

**Art director** Jane Forster
**Design assistant** Sarah Willis
**Photographer** Shona Wood
**Illustrator** Terry Evans
**Calligrapher** David Harris

Photoset by Ace Filmsetting Ltd,
Frome, Somerset
Originated by HBM (Pte) Ltd, Singapore
Printed and bound in Singapore by Kyodo
Printing Co (Pte) Ltd

The publishers would like to thank
Framecraft of Birmingham for loaning the
crystal jar on page 51 and the paperweight
on page 71.

# Contents

# Introduction

The human urge to decorate is probably as old as our visual history. As food and shelter became easier to obtain, our ancestors found extra time, some of which they spent in ornamenting tools, clothing and cave walls. These earliest fragile items may not have survived, but later artefacts reveal the development of the human desire to decorate and embellish.

Like most young children, I pursued this desire (not always in approved places, and I was soon corrected). However, once I became involved in an art degree programme, decoration techniques became part of my training.

I did not taste fully the joy of paper decorating until much later when I was preparing for my certificate in Craft Bookbinding. I have my lecturer, Alf Brazier, to thank for opening the door to the technique of carragheen moss marbling and the enjoyment of the simpler oil and glue size marbling as well as the lovely paste decorated papers.

The position of the professional marbler in commercial binderies at the turn of this century was an uncomfortable one, with marbled book covers and the hand edge marbling of account books going out of style. The preferred technique of carragheen moss marbling was understandably guarded, as marblers feared the loss of their jobs. Unfortunately, its demise came anyway and those bookbinders who had 'peeked' at the marbling became the ones to fulfil the occasional commission requiring the technique. They did not have first-hand instruction, so there were gaps in the knowledge of the specific technique and I believe this caused a lot of misconceptions, searching and experimenting. Now, thanks to the generosity of some marblers, information is being shared and we can preserve the craft for successive generations of marblers, whether professional or amateur.

My best reward comes after working with a student who has entered my workshop with no previous knowledge and leaves having grasped the technique so that they are able to accomplish a good result by themselves. It is therefore my hope in writing this book that a similar quality of instruction will prevail.

I have said nothing of the excitement and feeling of accomplishment experienced at the moment a print is achieved, but you see, that is because I know what enjoyment is waiting for you! Remember, decoration is in itself a form of celebration.

There is also the pride of joining the ranks of marblers and paper decorators through the ages. Just think, historians believe that by the year 2000, the Japanese art of paper decoration called suminagashi marbling will have been in practice for 800 years. I was introduced to this technique by Sukey Hughes' book, *Washi*.

It is my aim in writing this book to simplify the marbling processes, to demystify those techniques which have been shrouded in secrecy, encourage exploring other decorating techniques – and to enjoy them as well.

*Marbled papers left to right, suminagashi, carragheen moss, oil and glue size, carragheen moss, carragheen moss with soap spirit, suminagashi, oil and glue size, suminagashi, oil and glue size, carragheen moss, carragheen moss*

# Chapter 1
# Basic principles

For the most part, you will be able to produce decorated and marbled papers with good results in just a few hours, provided that you follow the instructions carefully. This is not necessarily true of carragheen moss marbling, which is notoriously fickle in its behaviour. However, experience and diligence to detail will earn full confidence. Keep your mistakes so that you can learn from them. Make notes on the backs so that you can progress and improve. Do the same with your good results to learn control.

It is lovely to get caught up in the excitement of the three marbling techniques: oil and glue size marbling, carragheen moss marbling and suminagashi marbling. However, it is wise to understand the *why* as well as the *how* things happen. These three marbling techniques are actually practical examples of the basic properties of surface tension. The reactions that happen are determined by properties of the earth's elements which comprise our natural environment. These properties of matter are very diverse and that gives us the opportunity of working with or against them. Science gets to understand or interpret our natural environment in an increasingly refined way. These principles will become clear to you as you begin to introduce the inks and paints on the surface of the size.

**Planning suggestions**
Plan your sessions so that if all is going well you could continue to work for several days. This is especially true of the techniques which require a lot of preparation beforehand, like carragheen moss marbling.

When you are nearing the end of a working session, the size is getting muddy and the colours are running out. Rather than quitting just then, use this time to experiment and use up the materials. This is often the best time to produce unusual results carrying you forward, because you will have a 'nothing to lose' attitude and be creatively relaxed.

Resist the temptation to make the project immediately after you have decorated the papers. Instead, let your papers rest, weighted down, and make the projects at another time.

## Materials

**Papers:** Handmade papers are excellent as they do not swell or shrink. Papers need to be strong, absorbent and somewhat transparent so that you can see unwanted air bubbles underneath when you lower the paper on to the size to take a print. If your budget is restricted to machine-made paper, avoid glossy, hard-surfaced papers and choose those intended for writing and drawing.

**Bath or size:** Each marbling technique varies, but you will need to create a solution on which to float your colours. For suminagashi, this will be a bath of tap water; for the other two marbling techniques, you will have to make up a size using soft water. See the introduction to each marbling technique for more details.

**Colours:** For marbling, two techniques use water-based colours and one uses oils. I suggest using proper sumi inks in stick form which depend on surfactant to float. For carragheen moss marbling, use inks sold in pots or bottles which depend on moss size to float. Oil paints diluted with white spirit of course float on water.

**Support materials:** Look for the descriptions of other materials at the beginning of each section. For example, alum – a mordent – is applied to the paper to grip the colour onto the paper so it does not wash away in rinsing. A surfactant is used in the sumi inks and on a separate brush to keep the inks separate and afloat on the water in suminagashi marbling.

*Below, a selection of suminagashi marbled papers. The pink example on the right is on heavy hand-made paper.*

**Storage:** As preparation time and materials can be costly, store equipment and materials for each technique together so they are ready to assemble quickly for another session.

If your carragheen moss size is a bit mucky, but still fresh, decant it into a large plastic container through a cloth filter inside a funnel. Add a few whole cloves and the size will keep for several weeks once refrigerated. When returning it to the tray for use, do not forget to remove the cloves and allow standing time so it returns to room temperature.

Clean your tools used for carragheen moss marbling in plain water with the aid of a stiff brush. Do *not* use soap or detergent to clean tools as the residue will reject the inks and disturb your patterns in your next session.

Oxgall will improve with age but it needs to be stored in a cool place, preferably in a dark glass bottle or in a cupboard away from the light.

If your marbling inks are not in regular use, give them an occasional stir, adding distilled water if they show signs of becoming dry. A little first aid will save money later.

Diluted oil colours will keep for a few weeks in jars with well-fitting tops.

Protect sumi ink sticks as oil from your fingers will cause damage. When handling them during the grinding process, keep a piece of thin paper or plastic around them. When they are ground to a short piece, extend their life with an inexpensive 'sumibasami', a tool made especially to grip the short stub.

If you have sumi inks left at the time

when you stop working, allow the inks to dry in the dishes before you begin again. They can be swiftly revitalised with a little water.

The surfactant which you add to the sumi inks retains its power when dry and loses its strength if stored moist.

## Equipment

*Vat:* For the three marbling techniques, a large tray or vat is needed in which to put the size ready for floating colours. See each technique for suggestions about the best type of tray or vat to obtain and the most suitable size for beginners to the crafts.

*Drying rack:* A clothes airer is useful for every technique, as wet printed papers can be hung over the rungs to dry.

*Press:* Two pieces of clean medium density fibre (MDF) board, slightly larger than your printed papers, will be needed to press the papers once they are dry. Place the papers between the boards and weight them down with heavy items like bricks or books.

*Key:*
 1  Fan for suminagashi
 2  Brush for paste decorating
 3  Drinking straws for suminagashi
 4  Lotus bowl for inks
 5  Ink sticks for suminagashi
 6  Suminagashi grinding stone
 7  Knitting needles for suminagashi, oil and glue size and carragheen moss marbling
 8  Oil paints for oil and glue size marbling
 9  Japanese brushes for suminagashi
10  Drying rack for all wet prints
11  Pressing boards for all marbling and decorating

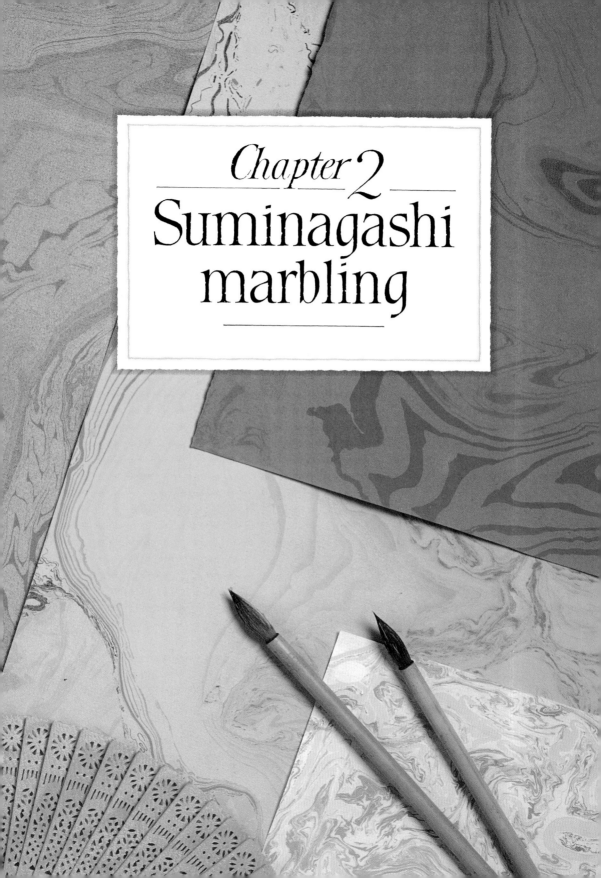

# Chapter 2
# Suminagashi marbling

Suminagashi, or Japanese marbling, is an art form delicately exquisite in both the process and product. It is said to emulate the flowing motion of windblown, white cloth and the patterns seen in slowly running streams coursing through fields.

This technique of decorating paper has been practised in Japan for close to nine centuries. It is suggested to have religious significance because of its association with paper, which has long-established spiritual importance. (I recall seeing little knots of prayer papers tied in trees near Shinto shrines. They were given as offerings to the gods.) The spiritual association of suminagashi is also linked to the impressive tea ceremony.

Suminagashi has been so well veiled in secrecy, it is only in recent years that the Western world has observed enough to successfully accomplish the process.

The Eastern philosophy imbued in suminagashi embraces an attitude which encourages interaction with the craft's components. Eastern artists endeavour to cooperate with the ingredients, being less concerned with tools and materials than with expanding their sense of what those components might include. The western concept of other decorative processes places the artist in the *prime* position, to *control* the medium and *direct* the action, whereas the Eastern artist *relinquishes* control, preferring to be seen as only one of many natural forces determining the final work.

Suminagashi is a good technique to share and enjoy with children. It is neat, clean and gives one the feeling of following Alice right down the rabbit hole into the Queen's garden. The aura of peace surrounding its performance instills a beneficial effect.

So, relax, clear your mind of worries, and assemble the equipment and materials in an orderly fashion. Unless you have a studio, the kitchen is probably the best place to perform this wonderful technique.

*'Slowly running streams coursing through fields'
– these gently flowing suminagashi marbled
designs live up to the Japanese description of this
ancient craft.*

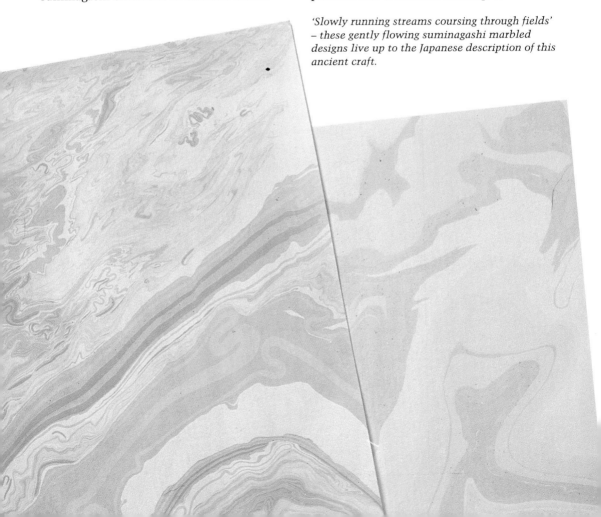

## Equipment

Japanese terms appear in italics.

**Vat** *(Fune)*: This can be any shallow tray roughly 5–8 cm (2–3 in) deep. As the bath is only tap water and the inks are soluble, there is no worry whether the vat is metal or glass. Ideally, place the vat on a sturdy table; this will ensure that vibration does not change your design.

**Brushes** *(Fude)*: Any small watercolour brush which will hold a fine point is acceptable. If you own enough brushes to have one for each colour, good; if not, then rinse the colour brush out each time you change colours. The brush for the surfactant should not be switched around but used continually for that purpose.

**Inkstones** *(Suzuri)*: Buy one of these at the same time as the inksticks. You will need one to grind the colours.

**Lotus bowls:** These small bowls are used to hold the liquid inks. They have an attractive petal-shaped edge, which can be used to hold the brush when not in use. You may, of course, substitute any small bowl or saucer.

**Skimmers:** These are merely strips of newspaper which can be cut as long as the width of the vat, and 10 cm (4 in) high. Their function is to break the surface tension and clear the vat of leftover colours.

## Materials

**Inks** *(Sumi)*: Look for inksticks from Japan (the list of suppliers on page 76 will give you stockists of these).

**Surfactant:** This is the chemical agent which causes the ink to float over the surface of the water. (See the list of suppliers for the one source of this material. It is a mail order item.)

**Papers** *(Washi)*: You can use any paper which is absorbent enough to take up the ink quickly from the surface of the water. *Unryu* or *Okawara* are good Japanese papers to try, but Western papers can work well too. Avoid papers with hard, shiny surfaces, as they will not absorb the ink fast enough and will not give a sharp image. If you use handmade paper, try to find some which is unsized (waterleaf) or only very lightly sized.

## Marbling

To enjoy yourself and gain exciting results, it is very important to relax into your work otherwise your tensions are likely to be reflected in the suminagashi. Do your best to enter into the spirit of the experience.

the surfactant brush in the other. When you feel adept at this, progress to holding three ink brushes in one hand, as shown below.

**1** First, grind your colours. Place a few drops of water in the deep end of the inkstone. Protect your inkstick from the oil on your fingers by wrapping a little tissue or plastic around the end you hold. Holding the inkstick in a vertical position, dip it in the water and drag some up on the grinding slope. Grind the stick in circular motions, not pressing too hard as that will result in a coarse mixture. Keep trailing the water up to the grinding slope until you have produced a dense paste. The time for this task will be about 10 minutes. Pour the resulting liquid ink into a lotus bowl or saucer and cover, letting the mixture stand for a couple of hours before using.

**2** Add one drop of surfactant. If the ink does not spread when you first test it on water, add another drop and so on until it is performing well. Prepare two or more colours in this way.

**3** Fill the vat with 2.5–5 cm (1–2 in) of water, and begin by holding the ink brush in your writing hand and the surfactant brush in the other. As you gain in confidence, hold two ink brushes in one hand like chopsticks, and

**4** Holding the colour brush vertically, bring the point to the water *very gently*. It will look as though the water is coming up to meet the brush tip. Allow the ink to flow out on to the surface. If you *jab* the brush in below the water line the colour will sink.

**5** When the ring of colour is a size you like, lift the brush and repeat the procedure with the surfactant brush which will chase a negative area into the centre of the ink circle. You are away!

**6** Alternate with colour and surfactant until you have a set of concentric circles. The amount of ink on your brush, plus the length of 'dwell' while the brush is in contact with the surface of the water, will determine the width of the bands of colour, helping to form the character of the design. You can now manipulate the ink circles using a variety of tools and techniques (see right and overleaf) until you have created a design you like.

Three colour brushes are held in the writing hand, the surfactant brush is held in the other. The colours are alternated with the surfactant.

The basic pattern begins to build up, each circle pushing against the previous one, so that the colours on the outer edge become slender rings.

Here, you can see clearly how the surfactant creates a negative area which pushes against the previous circle of colour. Continue alternating colours and surfactant in a rhythmic motion until the tray is filled with rings of colour.

**Note:** It helps to have one brush for each colour, but it is not essential. Instead, rinse the brush well between colours.

*Fill your tray with as many bands of colour as you want.*

*The rings form a fairly dense pattern. You are now ready to begin manipulating them.*

*By gently wafting a fan over the surface of the water and inks you can see the disturbance creates a design. Repeat the fanning from four sides.*

**Note:** *Once the colour rings have formed, tease them into a design by fanning, blowing or moving the surface with a stylus.*

**7** Now begin to coax the ink into pleasing patterns. Some of the traditional methods include:

* Blowing, with your mouth or through a drinking straw, close to the surface of the marbling (right).
* Fanning, using a proper Japanese folding fan (or if you do not have one, accordion pleat a piece of paper to make one). Do this very gently, or you could destroy the design.
* Stirring, traditionally, with a single human hair. However, I use a scrap of electrical wire or the tip of an old knitting needle.

You can see what results each method brings from the photographs, here and overleaf, and it is fun to experiment and try different combinations of treatments. The inks remain afloat quite a while.

*You can build up a number of colour bands on the surface of the water. As they spread, the bands on the outer edges become narrower. The design here shows how the pattern changes when the surface is gently blown with a drinking straw. Notice how the rings appear to fragment. Experiment by blowing from different angles to create intricate patterns. Or combine blowing with other methods of manipulating the design.*

Two drinking straws are used to blow the three colours into a swirling design.

Let the surfactant brush touch the surface and watch how it creates a 'hole' in the pattern.

A variation on the basic design, above, gives a different pattern when it is manipulated (below).

Instead of concentric circles, here, several sets of circular shapes are formed next to each other.

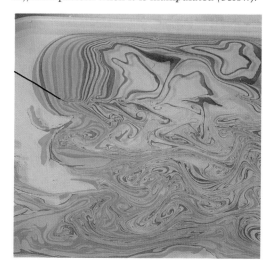

The basic pattern is now teased into a wonderful design using a scrap of electrical wire.

**8** You may take a print at any time when you are pleased with the design you have coaxed out of the medium.

**9** Look closely at your paper. There are two different sides. One is the 'wire' side which has a texture, the other is the 'felt' side which is smoother. Each will give a slightly different result (you choose). Holding the side you have chosen so that it faces the vat surface, grasp the paper by its diagonal corners and push the centre down into the middle of the water until the corners go down. This method should exclude air bubbles.

**10** Raise the paper, drain, and look to see if there are any air bubble scars. If there are, push that spot back on the size where there is a bit of design left and it should pick it up.

**11** Place the marbled paper over the bars of a drying rack. When the papers are completely dry, place them between clean boards and weight them down at least overnight, or perhaps longer, until they are pressed flat.

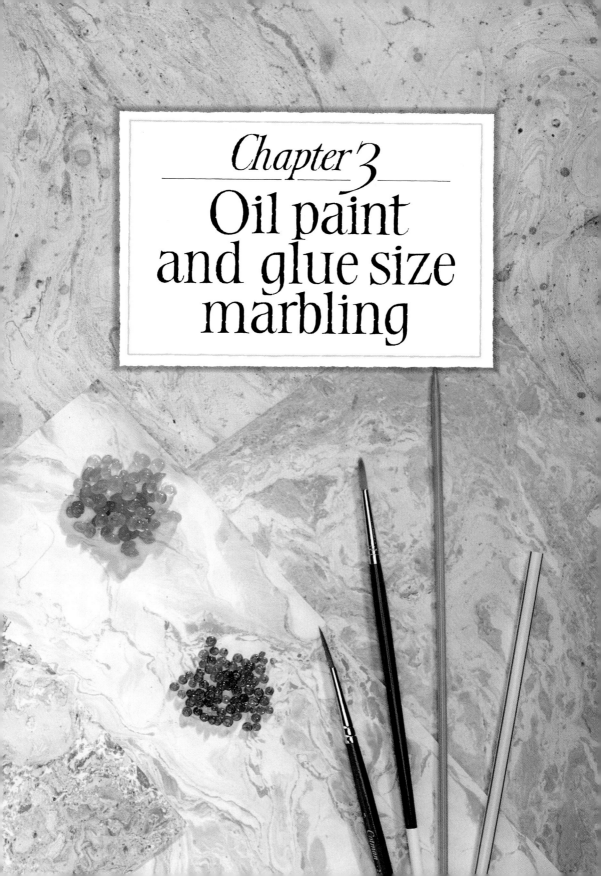

# Chapter 3
## Oil paint and glue size marbling

There are lovely associations with marbling techniques, probably because they have seemingly magic qualities. As surely as water runs off a duck's back, so oil and water do not mix, and that provides the fun which makes this type of marbling perform.

If you have a special projects room or a studio, fine. If not, the kitchen table will do nicely, provided you follow a few precautions (see safety note below).

Oil paint and glue size marbling is a relatively straightforward technique which will delight everyone from five years old and upwards. So, aprons on and let's get started!

You will need to allow roughly two days to undertake this type of marbling. The first day will be spent assembling your materials and making up the glue size. The second day can be spent setting up the design in the marbling tray and printing your papers. The paper will then need to dry and be pressed, which will take at least one more day.

## Equipment
Specifically for this type of marbling you will need the following easy-to-obtain pieces of equipment.

**Tray:** To hold the size, you will need a metal or glass tray with fairly deep sides, not less than 7.5 cm (3 in). Do not use plastic, as the solvent will dissolve it. The dimension is your choice. I suggest starting small and progressing to a larger pan later.

**Drying rack:** To dry the printed papers, an old clothes airer or washing line is ideal. (If it is good, protect it with plastic so it does not get stained.)

**Containers:** Collect small glass jars, or discarded aluminium pie dishes; these can be used to mix the artists' oil paints and solvent.

**Tools:** To form the designs and mix the colours, a selection of knitting needles and old teaspoons will be handy. Also collect old toothbrushes, drinking straws, some small paintbrushes, and a blunt table knife.

**Press:** Finally, to press the finished paper, you will need two boards, slightly larger than your papers, and weights – such as bricks or books – to place on the boards.

## Materials: consumable
*Artists' oil paints:* The least expensive.

*White spirit:* A solvent to dilute the oil paints.

*Bookbinders' pearl glue* or *wallpaper paste:* To make the size on which the colours will float.

*Paper:* Papers for drawing are recommended. Avoid glossy and rough surfaced papers as these will not hold a crisp design.

*Skimmers:* Strips of newspaper, 10 cm (4 in) wide and a length to fit the inside width of your tray bottom. They are used to break the surface tension.

*Gloves:* Good fitting, lightweight rubber gloves are essential to protect your hands.

## Method
*Bookbinders' pearl glue:* This is my favourite. (See list on page 76 for supplier.)

For a tray 25 cm x 20 cm (10 in x 8 in) put one heaped dessertspoon of pearls into a 1 litre (2 pint) glass container with 500 ml (1 pint) of cold tap water to soak overnight or until the pearls are swollen and milky in colour.

Measure 500 ml (1 pint) of boiling tap water and dissolve a heaped tablespoon of borax or water softener in it. Pour the mixture into the saucepan of pearls and mix to dissolve. If a few pearls will not completely dissolve, heat on low, stirring constantly. This is now a 'stock' solution. Fill tray a little less than half full with hottest tap water. Add stock and stir *gently* to avoid bubbles. Remove a small amount into a test tray. Cover with a board to exclude dust and leave to cool and settle until lunch time. Use this time between to prepare your oil colours, assemble all equipment and materials required.

*Wallpaper paste:* Follow the mixing directions on the packet and dilute the paste with warm water. Add dissolved water softener to the tap water.

When the glue size is lukewarm it is ready to use. If you are not going to use it right away, protect it from dust with a cover.

*Storage:* To store leftover size, skim it well and pour it into a clean glass container. Add a few whole clove spices to inhibit bacteria. Cover with a tight fitting top. Label and place in the refrigerator for up to one month. The glue will congeal. When you want to use the size again, set the jar in a pan of hot tap water until the glue size becomes fluid.

Glue size can be safely disposed of at the warm liquid stage by pouring it down a drain. It is bio-degradable.

*Once you begin oil and glue size marbling, you will not want to stop! You will discover ways of using combinations of colours and creating patterns to give you a host of wonderful designs.*

## Preparation

**1** Spread protective newspapers on the work surface. Pour two dessertspoons of solvent into a dish or jar and add 1 cm (½ in) of oil paint squeezed from the tube. Using a brush, stir well to dissolve. Keeping a separate brush for each colour, repeat with different colours (you will need at least three to create a good design).

**2** Spread newspapers on the floor and place the drying rack in the centre. Spread more papers around the floor and have newspapers ready for blotting the finished work.

**3** Using a skimmer, skim the size from one end to the other three times to break the surface tension.

**4** Take one of the small paintbrushes used to mix the paint and solvent earlier and, very gently, touch the tip of the brush on the size. The colour will flow from the brush on to the size.

**5** Repeat step 4, adding more of the first colour or a different colour. Drop it either next to the first colour or inside the centre of the first one. Experiment, try using the knitting needle to gently stir a pattern into the colour, or sprinkle a little colour on to the size by spattering it from a toothbrush. Try blowing the surface with a drinking straw to create movement and changes in the pattern. Play with the colours until the design pleases you. There is no rush, the oil colour will stay afloat for quite a while.

> ### Safety note
> ● *Do not use a plastic tray or indeed any plastic containers as the solvent will dissolve them. While working DO NOT put your fingers in your mouth, or touch your face or eyes. Supervise children closely with the same cautions.*

*Touch the brush on the size, the colour will flow, creating the beginning of the design.*

*More colour is added to the growing design. See how the colours are jostling for space.*

*Here, the colour is spattered on to the size from a paintbrush.*

*A stylus is used to move the colours into a pleasing design.*

As the green colour spreads, the outer edges fragment, creating a wonderful effect.

Blue is added to the centre of the green. Notice how it pushes out the first colour.

Gold is dropped on to the almost completed design. See how the spots of gold applied first (the lower part of the photograph) have spread.

These papers illustrate two quite different effects you can achieve with this type of marbling.

**6** When you are satisfied with the design, grasp your paper at diagonally opposite corners, letting it droop in the middle, and rest it on the centre of the size. Push the paper corners down towards the surface of the size to ensure a good contact to prevent trapped bubbles which will spoil your design. Let go of the corners and stroke the back of the paper from the centre outward.

*Top left, after the heavier gold paint is applied, wait a few moments and you will see it explode and expand. If colours are reluctant to expand, add one drop of spirit soap to help it expand. Below, a piece of wire is used to gently move the gold into a pleasing pattern.*

*Below, blowing through a drinking straw moves the colours around to create an interesting and quite different effect.*

**7** Pick the printed paper up by the two nearest corners to drain the excess size away, eventually moving to hold the paper by just one corner until it has stopped dripping. Place the printed paper, face upwards, on a piece of newspaper and cover it with another piece to blot it. If the print is still very wet, repeat with a piece of fresh newspaper. If you do not do this you will have a marbled print with unattractive shiny puddles. Leave the print on the floor until you make a second print and then drape the first print over the drying rack.

*Blue and green designs formed on white, blue and cream papers; the paper on to which you transfer your design will modify the colours.*

**8** When the print is completely dry, place it between the boards and weight the 'sandwich' with bricks or books to flatten it. This step may take overnight or even longer. You can keep a whole stack of printed papers flat in this way.

Now return to your marbling and see how many different designs you can invent. NEVER throw mistake prints away! Some of the best final prints I have made started as a bad try. Parts are often good as wrapping paper, or you can re-print them after pressing and create a double print.

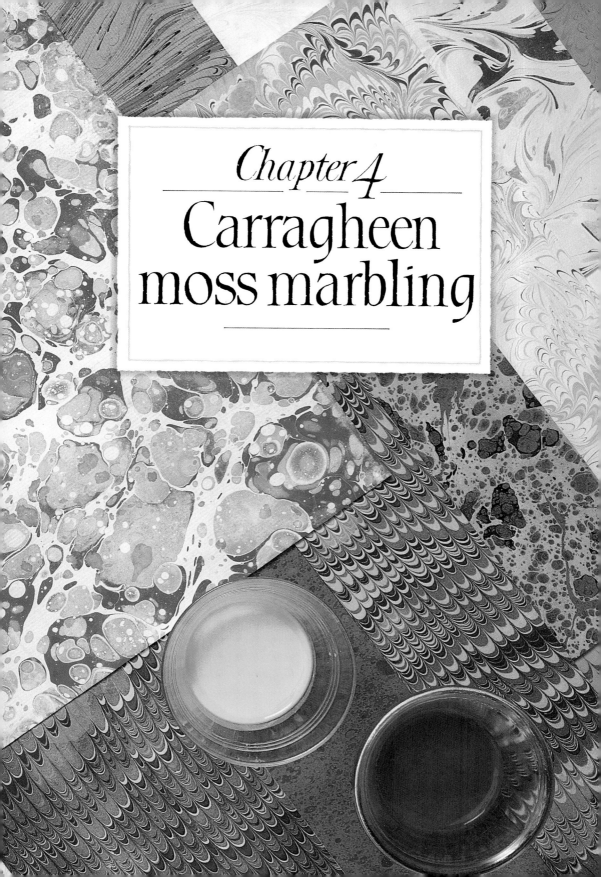

# Chapter 4
# Carragheen moss marbling

This beautiful technique of paper decoration as we practise it today is close to the 15th-century Persian marbling, called *abri*. By the 16th century, marbling had reached Turkey, and was called *ebru*. As time and space do not allow, I must leave its remarkable although small history to others as mine is a practical book. There are, however, some well-grounded facts which I believe should be set out and may interest both novice and experienced marblers alike.

Like oil with glue size, and suminagashi marbling, this technique is governed by the principles of surface chemistry. There is a tendency for those practising carragheen moss marbling to refer to a 'skin' on the surface of the size; however, this is not strictly true. Surface tension is a convenient way of describing the effects which actually result from the attraction between molecules of a liquid. This is best explained by the following teaching aid.

Think of yourself as a colour. Imagine that you and two friends (who are also colours) want to talk to a mutual friend from a public telephone kiosk (the type with a door that closes). You (colour number one) telephone the mutual friend and number two pushes in next to you. Number three friend is keen to enter the box, but has to push both of you aside to squeeze in as well.

This is a simple illustration of what is taking place on the surface of the size each time you add a new colour.

In this marbling technique, we overcome the crowding problem with the help of oxgall or photo-wetting agent by giving colour number three (the last colour added) the most drops of oxgall. This gives number three the power to push the other colours aside. (More of this later.)

As this technique requires considerable patience, I don't recommend using it with a young child. Do try it yourself though, as with continued effort, you will gain experience and should become adept with practice.

Unlike other marbling, this one can be closely controlled so that the patterns are nearly duplicated. Strange, that like suminagashi, it also originated in the East, but conversely, it places the practitioner in a position of firm control rather than practising suminagashi's philosophy of interaction.

There are two options in the preparation of the size. With the instant – non-cook, powdered extract – preparation takes only one day before marbling can begin. The traditional method, on the other hand, takes an extra day, as you must cook the moss and allow it to set overnight.

For beginners, I suggest starting with small sized trays, quantities of size, inks and paper. It saves time and reduces waste. You can advance to larger trays and quantities of materials when you are confident.

*Left, traditional combed marbling. Right, here the colours and 'sprinkling water' are just dropped and spattered on to the surface.*

## Equipment

**Tray or vat:** Slightly larger than a piece of A5 paper – 150 mm x 210 mm (6 in x 8½ in) will serve well to get started. It can be a seed tray, photographic tray, roasting or baking pan. Also set up a smaller tray in which to test the colours.

**Brushes:** 100 years ago, when marbling was commercially popular, specialist brushes were hand made and readily available. Now the tools needed for the specific tasks are no longer sold. Although you can use alternatives (see the list of suppliers on page 76), you can make your own marbling brushes quite easily (pages 38–39 give more details).

Basically, there are two types of brush:

1  Long, floppy brush to apply the colour. The soft bristles should be approximately 60 mm–80 mm (2½ in–3¼ in) long.

2  Small 'hallowe'en witches' broom', which I will call a bristle brush, and a larger one of the same style with stiff bristles to spatter ink and oxgall on to the size.

**Plastic bottles and one wide-necked jar:** Choose bottles with a nozzle top that dispenses liquid one drop at a time. Buy from a craft shop, a cosmetic counter or buy a few eye droppers from a pharmacy. You can also recycle old ones. They are ideal for dispensing either oxgall or ink, because you can count the drops or draw a line and make accurate circles.

A wide-necked jar with a lid will be needed for making a sprinkling mixture of oxgall and water.

**Metal rod/ruler:** Against which you can tap the brush to sprinkle colours on the size.

**Stylus:** A bodkin, scrap of electrical wire, steel or plastic knitting needles, a pencil, or meat skewer will do nicely to draw designs.

**Handle:** From an old toothbrush makes a good stirring rod to mix the oxgall and inks.

**Rakes and combs:** A marbling rake has widely spaced teeth while a comb has teeth which are closer together. Some can be bought, but it is best to make your own, (see page 40). Also an old hair comb is good for making swirling patterns.

**Large piece of glass/perspex:** To support the print during rinsing.

**Small, flexible shower hose:** To fit at the sink and provide a gentle spray for rinsing the finished print. Alternatively, use a jug or large cup.

**Cellulose sponge:** Approximately 10 cm x 12.5 cm (4 in x 5 in), to apply the alum to the papers. Or you can use a plant mister to spray alum on to the papers.

**Large plastic bag:** In which to rest damp alum-coated papers before use.

*Left, the design has been stirred with a fine stylus. Right, the colours have been combed and then stirred.*

**Plastic gloves:** Helpful when applying alum to the papers.

**Newspapers:** To keep the workspace tidy and to make skimmers.

**Skimmers:** To clear the surface tension and residue ink before each new design. Cut the skimmers from the newspaper; they should be 10 cm (4 in) wide by the width of the tray. Make plenty and have a pile ready beside the tray.

**Drying rack, pressing boards and weights:** (see page 15 for more details) These are required to dry and press your papers.

## Materials

**Carragheen moss (Chondrus crispus):** An Icelandic or Irish seaweed referred to as a moss. It can be purchased in art supply shops (see list of suppliers on page 76) and at some health food shops. Look for the instant powdered extract (no-cook) type which only needs warm water and a liquidiser for mixing. There is also dried carragheen moss, which needs to be cooked and prepared in the traditional way.

**Alum (Potassium aluminium sulphate; $K_2SO_4$, $Al_2(SO_4)_3$, $24H_2O$):** A mordant which grips the colours, holding them into the paper. There are other alums, but they do not work for this purpose, so make sure you ask for the correct one. It can be bought at an art supply store.

**Oxgall:** The refined bile from the gall bladder of an ox, this extract is available from art and craft shops. Alternatively, use a photo-wetting agent. Both reduce surface tension and allow colours to spread.

**Soft water:** Tap water must be softened with borax (see page 41) or save rain water and filter it through a clean cotton cloth; collect water drained from a dehumidifier or buy distilled water.

**Olive oil, soap spirit, pure turpentine:** These distort the designs. Each one causes a particular type of disturbance within the inks on the size. Apply one drop at a time.

**Sprinkling water:** Keep one jam jar containing softened water and a few drops of oxgall and another mixed with soap spirit. This can be splattered over the size.

**Inks:** I recommend jars of ready-mixed marbling inks from art and craft suppliers.

**Paper:** The most desirable is that which will absorb the inks quickly on contact and allow a sharp, clean line. Most commercial papers sold for pencil and charcoal drawing will be suitable. They all have some size in them (like a raincoat) but this should not prevent them from absorbing the colours quickly. Do not use very rough or glossy surfaced papers as they will not give a clearly registered print. Handmade paper with a fairly smooth surface is excellent.

## Preparation: tool making

As this is a centuries-old technique, both the tools and the craftsmen who made them are gone. We are left to find alternatives or make our own tools. Three natural bristle brushes are needed.

To buy: a whisk used in the Japanese tea ceremony, from a speciality shop; a long bristle brush – an angle cut brush used for a calligrapher's hand-drawn lines.
Alternatively, make your own tools.

## Witches' brooms
## Materials

You will need a large and small whisk or what I call a 'witch's broom' brush.
*a strong natural fibre sweeper's broom*
*strong hemp or linen cord*
*20 mm (½ in) diameter wood doweling*

**1** Using a sharp knife and cutting away from yourself, remove two or three 20 cm (8 in) long tufts of strong fibres from the broom. Keep together with a rubber band and soak in very hot water for one hour. For the small whisk, the binding cord at the top acts as a handle. Tie the cord with a knot.

**2** For the large whisk, drill a hole through the dowel 7.5 cm (3 in) from one end or cut a groove around the dowel to prevent the cord slipping. Thread the cord through the hole and leave 45 cm (18 in) for winding around.

Tie a reef knot, leaving a 10 cm (4 in) tail. Place the handle in a vice or clamp, or ask a friend to hold it.

**3** Remove the bristles from the water, blot dry, and arrange around the drilled end to make a bunch which, when squeezed, is

about 2.5 cm (1 in) in diameter. The cord ends should peep out 2 cm (½ in) from the head end. Wind the long cord end round and round for 7.5 cm (3 in) and return.

**4** Check that you have a tight winding job. If not, remove it and re-wind. On the return, tie the two cord ends in a double reef knot and trim the brush end with scissors.

## Long brushes

To make your own, it is probably best to acquire a hog's hair brush and then dismantle and remake it. I bought an inexpensive bookbinder's paste brush which had a plastic ferrule. This can be recreated using plastic tubing (available by the metre/yard from hardware stores).

REQUIREMENTS
*No 14 paste brush (buy the cheapest bookbinder's paste brush with hog's hair bristles)*
*Plastic tubing, 10 mm (⅜ in) in diameter*
*wood doweling*

**1** Cut the plastic ferrule on the brush with a sharp knife or smash it with a hammer. Remove it and the handle.

**2** Place the bristles with the hard adhesive centre on a strong surface and smash it into smaller sections of 10 mm (⅜ in) in diameter.
**3** Soak 4 cm (1½ in) long pieces of plastic tubing in boiling water for 5 minutes.
**4** Cut wood doweling into 20 cm (8 in) lengths and force a piece of softened plastic tubing over one end of each doweling handle (see the central brush in the photograph on page 39).
**5** Force the adhesive end of the bristles into the plastic tubing while the plastic is still hot and soft. When it has cooled, the plastic will hold the bristles tight. This is a rust-free brush construction.

## Patterning rake

This is a bold tool with widely spaced tines to be used for the first stroke through the inks. In the past they were made of wood doweling, but here I offer an expedient alternative.

REQUIREMENTS
*the longest aluminium alloy clout nails (roofing nails) you can find*
*strong corrugated cardboard with channels large enough for the nails*
*millboard (used by bookbinders), 2 mm (¹/₁₆ in) thick*
*PVA adhesive*
*polyurethane waterproof clear seal*
*bricks to weight down millboards*

**1** Trim one edge of the corrugated cardboard straight.
**2** To determine the width, lay a nail alongside a channel so that 4–5 cm (1½–2 in) on the point end extend beyond the corrugated cardboard. This dimension will depend on the length of nail purchased. You need enough nail in the channel for stability

and enough exposed to rake through the inks to make a pattern. To determine the length, measure the width of your vat or tray at the bottom and subtract 1 cm (⅜ in). You now know the correct width and length of the corrugated cardboard piece. Cut it with channels parallel to the short dimension.

**3** Push nails through the raised channels at about 3 cm (1⅜ in) intervals to make fairly wide pattern lines.

**4** Cut two pieces of millboard (the strongest material for this job) to a width just a tiny bit longer than the corrugated internal structure. The top where the nails emerge should be 14 cm (5½ in) or a width just comfortable for your hands to hold.

**5** Lay the internal structure on the millboard with the nail points protruding. Trace a pencil line around the top and the two ends.

**6** To make a good sturdy tool, cut a 'filler' piece of corrugated cardboard to fit from the top of the nails to the top edge of the millboard – a secure 'sandwich'.

**7** As PVA dries very quickly, proceed as follows. Apply PVA to the millboard section outlined for the internal structure so the nail section is straight across the bottom edge. Place the structure and press firmly. Apply PVA to the area above, place the 'filler' piece on it, press firmly. Dab PVA on any edges not coated, cover second piece of millboard with PVA, align and press. Top with bricks and let dry for 2–3 hours minimum.

## Preparing the size

***No-cook method:*** This very easy method is consistent and gives good results, as well as saving you time. It requires carragheen moss in powdered extract form.

Carragheen moss marbling requires patience but provided you are careful with measurements and follow directions, you should learn to balance the elements. However, it is not recommended for children as it can become frustrating. With continued practice you should gain experience and become accomplished with the technique.

## Preparing the moss size

If this is a new experience for you, I strongly advise using non-cook powdered extract (instant carragheen moss) – see list of suppliers. Prepare the size the day before it is required.

Mix about 2 tablespoons of powdered non-cook extract with 4 litres (7 pints) of distilled water, filtered rain water, or tap water with 1 tablespoon of borax dissolved into it (see box below). Also have a container of softened water ready to dilute the size.

Ensure the liquidiser is thoroughly clean and free from grease. Half-fill the liquidiser, turn to low speed and slowly add the powder. Repeat this routine until it is all mixed and is the consistency of milk. Pour into your 25 cm × 20 cm (10 in × 8 in) tester tray and the remainder into a clean container. Cover both to protect from dust. The size needs 12 hours to age and settle.

---

***Softening water with borax***
*Instead of distilled or filtered rain water, use borax to soften tap water. Dissolve 1 level tablespooon of borax in a cup of boiling water, then add to 3 l (6 pt) of tap water.*

---

**Preparing the alum:** Mix 50 g (2 oz) of powdered or crystalline alum with 500 ml (1 pt) of cold, soft water in a saucepan (not aluminium).

Bring to a boil, and stir well until all the alum is dissolved. Cool and store in a dark glass bottle or jar with a screw-topped lid in a darkened cupboard.

## Preparing the paper

To prepare the paper for marbling, you must first coat it with alum. This is a mordant which grips the colour, thus allowing you to rinse off the thin layer of size that lifts off with each print without losing the design.

No alum, no marbled print! The design will wash away with the excess size if you do not prepare the paper properly.

---

**Alum**

*If a large crystal appears later in the bottom of the jar or bottle, re-heat the solution to dissolve it. (The strength of the alum goes into the crystal, leaving the solution weak.)*

---

**Coating the paper:** Mark the papers you plan to alum coat by placing a small pencil X mark in one corner to identify the coated side, as afterwards, you will have no way of knowing which side was coated.

Pour some of the alum in a dish and, using the clean sponge (keep the sponge for this purpose only), dip it in the alum, squeeze out the excess. Work on top of the large plastic bag and carefully apply a damp, not sopping wet, coating of alum on to the paper. Put the paper to one side and coat a second piece in the same way. Place the second piece face down on to the first piece and place them right inside the plastic bag. Repeat this for all the other prepared papers.

Mature the papers inside the bag for a minimum of 15 minutes to allow the paper fibres to absorb the mordant.

Alternatively, allow the alum to dry completely and use the sheets dry.

## Preparing the colours

**1** Have ready your small testing tray of size. Use soft plastic bottles with nozzles. Place a strip of masking tape on the outside of each and number them 1 to 3. Put 2 tablespoons of marbling ink in each bottle.

**2** Put one drop of oxgall into colour number one. Shake to mix, skim the surface of the size and squeeze one drop of colour on to the surface. It may sink. If it floats, then you have a good beginning. If not, add another drop, shake, skim and make one drop again. It should spread to 5 or 8 cm (2 or 3 in) in diameter. (Have patience, this is the toughest part.) As soon as you get the colour to spread, mark on the label how many drops of oxgall are in the colour.

**3** Now move on to colour number two. Add as many drops of oxgall as in colour number one, plus two more. Shake the bottle and make one drop of colour in the centre of the first circle of ink. If it forms a rim about 2 cm (1¾ in) wide, then advance to number three colour. If not, proceed to increase the oxgall by one more drop until it makes the size rim you want.

Once again, record the number of oxgall drops on the label.

**4** Repeat this procedure again with colour number three.

## 'Fried egg' technique

Gather your materials and equipment together by the tray. In traditional marbling, there are set ways to make patterns which even have names. There are various ways of creating traditional marbled patterns. Probably, one of the most well-known methods – an ideal one for beginners – is the 'fried egg'. Here, three or four colours are used to create a series of concentric circles.

These are then gently moved with a stylus, comb or rake to create the waving patterns traditionally associated with marbled paper. This 'fried egg' method is shown clearly in the sequence of photographs below. Photos 1–4 show the fried egg pattern, to be done in the test tray first. Overleaf, there are · alternative suggestions for forming other types of patterns.

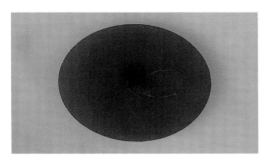

1 First drop colour number one to form a neat circle on the size.

2 Into colour number one, drop colour number two – see how it pushes the first colour out.

3 Into the first two colours drop colour number three – each subsequent colour has more oxgall.

4 A fourth colour is added which really pushes the other three colours out.

5 Begin to form the design: a scrap of electrical wire is used to glide through the colour.

6 By drawing the comb through the colours, you achieve the beginnings of a traditional pattern.

## 'Fried egg' technique

Skim the size and follow the directions on page 43 for adding the colours (photos 1–3, below). (In the design shown here, we have used two shades of blue and one of white.)

With a stylus or knitting needle, make random wavy lines up and down the tray (photo 4).

Now use the comb to create patterns in the opposite direction (photo 5).

If you wish, you can finish by spattering, using the 'witch's broom' or long brush, tapping it against your hand (photo 6).

*1 Create a number of dark blue circles on the size using a dropper bottle. Note the width of the colour band.*

*3 Drop a mid blue ink into the centre of the white circle; the size of the band determines the predominant colours.*

*2 Into the dark blue circles drop light blue ink using a dropper bottle or, as here, a long-bristled brush.*

*4 Take a knitting needle or scrap of wire – and move it gently through the 'eggs' to create a lighter, brighter horizontal pattern.*

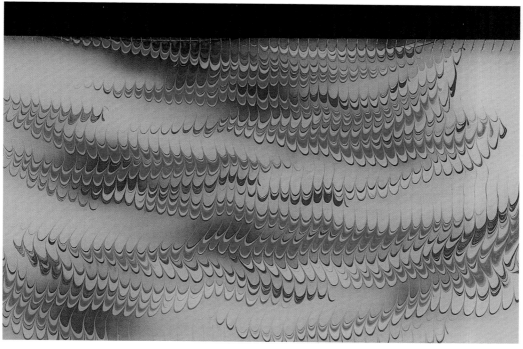

5 *Above, draw a comb across the horizontal pattern and a design begins to emerge.*

6 *Below, load the long brush with mid blue and gently tap it against your hand to spatter drops and bring the negative areas into balance.*

## Lines

Skim the surface of the size. Using the long brush, draw lines across the size. Now, carefully draw lines with another colour in between those you have just drawn.

Pull a stylus through the lines, then run the comb in the opposite direction.

If you wish, you can use the stylus once more to create a wavy pattern across the one you have just made. Or you can spatter with the sprinkling water or olive oil or turpentine to create 'holes'.

1 Run lines of colour across the size. First, work with one colour, then the next, then a third.

2 Using a piece of wire, draw lines at right angles to the colours applied with the brush.

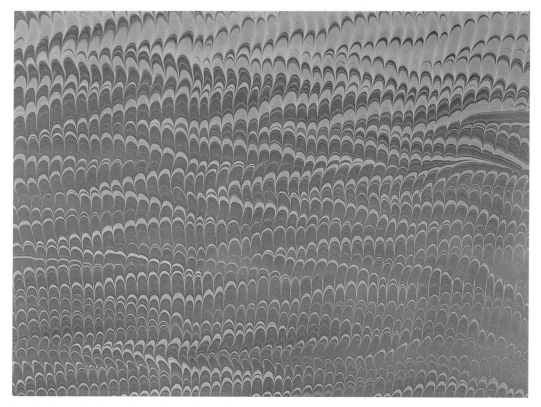

3 Pull the comb through at right angles to the lines formed with the stylus.

4 Tap a little sprinkling water or spirit soap onto the surface with the small whisk.

5 The result is negative areas from the tiny areas of sprinkling water or spirit soap.

6 For this design, follow steps 1–3 and draw wavy lines with a stylus to form peacock tails.

## Spattering

Spattering is less a problem of technique, rather more of restraint and planning ahead. Too much spatter means crowded design. Oxgall, spirit soap and turpentine object to mixing in the vat at the same time. Once used, they ruin the size for return to normal use. Plan ahead. When finished with normal designs, and the size is mucky, make yet another design.

Skim the size. Keeping your colours in the original sequence of testing, apply colours in a 1–4 sequence, as per the addition of oxgall. Once the colour is applied, you then have a range of options with which to distort the droplets into different patterns.

You can obtain further variations using different coloured papers. Try dark papers with light coloured inks for a beautiful contrast.

If you want to make two prints alike, you must repeat the method exactly for the second print.

1 Spatter spots of blue on to the size with the long brush.

3 Alternatively spatter light blue on top of the medium blue with the long brush.

2 Touch the centre of each blue spot with either spirit soap, thin oil or turpentine.

4 Additional colours can be spattered on with the small 'witch's broom'.

## Taking a print:

**1** Pick up an alum-treated paper. Turn it so that the side with the X is facing downward toward the size. Hold the paper by diagonal corners. Make a big curve in the paper by bringing your hands together a little and push it down in the middle of the tray.
**2** Push the paper gently and evenly on to the size until the whole paper is flat. See if there are any air bubbles. If so, carefully stroke the paper from the centre outwards using the backs of your fingernails.
**3** Lift the paper by the front corners and drain the size. Do not bump or touch the new design, it is fragile!
**4** Wet the perspex with water, so that the back of the print sticks in place. Rest the

> **Optional protective treatment**
> *Protect the dried papers by spraying artists' fixative on them. Alternatively, wax the surface using a clear crystalline wax. Apply the wax with your fingertips in a circular motion to achieve a most attractive matt finish.*

*5 Alternatively, after step 3, distort the spattered design with a stylus.*

paper on the perspex, leaning it at an angle with the bottom resting on the draining board and rinse off excess size with a gentle spray from a shower hose.
**5** Place the rinsed prints over a drying rack. When the papers are completely dry, weight them down between clean boards until they are flat and ready for use.

# Earrings

Oil and glue size paper or carragheen moss marbled scraps make wonderful, individual jewellery. Once you have made the earrings shown here, you can easily adapt the designs to create other shapes and colours.

Jewellery findings are available from craft and jewellery suppliers (see page 76). Small needle nose pliers are very useful when making jewellery.

REQUIREMENTS
*Earring findings*
*Two small beads*
*14 cm (5½ in) fine wire*
*Lightweight card*
*PVA adhesive*
*Acrylic spray or crystalline wax*

1 Trace an oval shape, the right size for your ear, using the templates shown below. If you're unsure of the size, try holding the paper shape up to your ear. Once you decide which oval is most suitable, transfer the tracing twice on to thin card. Cut these two shapes out carefully with sharp scissors.
2 Cut the wire into two pieces. Bend one piece in half and thread both tails through the bead. Push the bead up the wire until it is almost at the top. Twist the wire under the bead to hold it in place, and splay out the two legs of wire. Be sure wires are not too long. Repeat with the other wire and bead and set these aside.
3 Trace the shape on the back of your decorated paper twice. Cut out carefully. Apply PVA adhesive and paste the wire legs inside. Press with weights.
4 Hook the earrings on to the findings and protect the marbled paper with a coat of crystalline wax or acrylic spray.

*Convert pieces of marbled paper into earrings. The centre pair show carragheen moss marbled paper, the pairs on the outside use oil and glue size marbled pieces.*

## Crystal jar

These beautiful crystal trinket jars are available from craft or hobby shops, and can also be bought mail order (see page 76 for list of suppliers). The lid of the jar comes apart so that you can decorate inside it as you wish. Filled with a piece of marbled paper it can look simply exquisite. I have used a piece of carragheen moss marbling, the design of which has been coaxed into a flower shape.

REQUIREMENTS
*Crystal jar with lid which can be
    dismantled*
*Marbled paper design*

**1** Dismantle the lid of the jar according to the manufacturer's instructions.

*It is fun to try to form pictures with some of the marbling methods. Here a carragheen moss egg pattern has been teased into a flower shape with a stylus.*

**2** Use the backing card inside the lid, trace a circle on to the back of a piece of marbled paper. (Keep the design inside the lid margin, as here.) Cut this shape out inside the pencil circle.
**3** Push the marbled paper into the lid and reassemble the piece following the manufacturer's instructions.

# Chapter 5
# Paste
# decorated paper

Paste-decorated papers, with their shorter history than traditional marbled papers, flourished in the late 18th and early 19th centuries; although they were first recorded in central Germany towards the end of the 16th century and have been included among manufacturers' book end paper samples since the early 17th century. The best known practitioners were the Moravians from Hernnhut, eastern Saxony.

The earliest paste decorated papers tended to be rather subdued and monochromatic, favourite colours being indigo, carmine and burnt sienna.

Since the 20th century, there has been a marked revival of interest in this process. Fortunately, this easy technique is less surrounded in secrecy than other methods.

Traditionally, thick, coloured flour paste was brushed over dampened paper and, while still wet, it was patterned in a variety of ways: brushes, combs, fingers, sticks,

pressing wood blocks into the paste or using rollers into which a design had been cut. The simplest method involved laying two pasted sheets together and then peeling them apart. Sometimes string was inserted, the two sheets pasted together and then the string was pulled out, leaving a textured trail behind it. Likewise, the paste could be daubed or spattered on to the paper.

## Gold embossing

Gold-embossed papers were curiously known in Britain and the USA as 'Dutch gilt' or 'Dutch floral' papers. It is speculated that 'Dutch' was a corruption of Deutsch, as most of the papers are documented as originating in Augsburg about 1690. Others came from Nuremberg and Fürth. The only traceable English craftsman is Benjamin Moore in 1763, whose plates were signed.

The paper was first coloured by hand or stencilled. Thick, heated copper plates,

*Left: Lines of combing alternated with stamped blocks. Right: A blue strip covered with red coloured paste. Combs and blocks have been used to remove paste, thus creating the design.*

deeply engraved, were put through a roller press with imitation gold leaf together with the dampened, coloured and sized sheet of paper, plus a felt padding. The excess gold was brushed off, leaving the paper underneath exposed. The transfer resulted in an image in relief.

Many old gold embossed papers reveal an extraordinary range of designs, from exotic flowers, birds and animals to lavish pictorial scenes and landscapes.

Later, a different technique was employed. The brass was powdered, mixed with tacky varnish and applied to a wood block. This was then put on to a wooden hand press and an impression was made on to the paper. The result was sumptuous but not as detailed as embossing.

Variations of all these methods have been used, including letterpress printing. Whatever the variation or adaptation, I think it is important to understand the

original separate techniques. Here, I have decorated paste papers using tacky varnish and a gold powder dusting method.

This type of paper decoration is a good introduction to the subject. It is quite simple to undertake, uses readily available materials and equipment, can easily be done on the kitchen table, producing charming results.

Once you have applied the coloured paste to the paper, you can create designs using a variety of techniques which remove the paste from the surface, revealing the paler surface underneath: combing, dragging, using cut cardboard or even your fingers.

This form of paper decoration requires a fair amount of coordination. It's suitable for children if you provide some assistance and substitute food colouring for toxic paints, mixed with cornflour paste, making sure that any licked fingers do no harm.

*Left: A combination of combing and finger prints. Right, combed wavy lines and fan shapes created with a small scrap of hard plastic that has been given a half twist.*

## Equipment

**Brushes:** One about 15 cm (6 in) wide, to apply the base colour. I use a wallpapering paste brush; these are relatively inexpensive and readily available. The other brushes should be stiff bristled to make designs.

**Tools:** Apart from brushes, you can make the designs on the wet paste-covered paper with other tools. Many of these are easily made by yourself. However, it is wise to be on the look-out for applicable tools to buy, even though they may be designed for other uses. Ask for 'feather graining' tools used to decorate furniture. Also odd bits of perspex, broken combs, wine corks (to cut into stamps), pieces of bamboo, small whisk brushes or old wooden printing blocks.

**Sponge:** A large, clean cellulose sponge to dampen the paper.

**Base on which to work:** A firm rubber or firm piece of foam 12 mm (½ in) thick a little larger than your paper. You could also use a thick padding of newspaper.

**Plastic trays and yoghurt pots:** Recycle trays used to hold uncooked meat and use them to hold the coloured paste once it has been mixed.

**G clamps:** You will need two plus a strip of wood 12 mm (½ in) thick and as long as the width of your paper.

## Consumable materials

**Cornflour:** Is used to make the basic paste, also try wheat flour, or rice flour which has a coarse texture.

**Colours:** Use water soluble dyes or aqueous dispersed pigments. Food colouring is safest when working with children. It will fade.

**Paper:** Any smooth surfaced paper, but not plastic-coated.

**Newspapers:** Essential for keeping the work surface tidy.

**Whole cloves:** To act as a preservative if you want to keep the coloured paste mixture for several days. (Added at the end of the session.)

**Plastic spoons:** To mix colours and paste.

## Technique

This technique lends itself well to working in the kitchen where cooking the paste, creating the design and cleaning up are accomplished with little fuss.

**1** Dissolve 4 heaped tbsp of cornflour in 500 ml (1 pt) cold water. Cook in a double boiler until the paste is transparent.

**2** Divide the cooked cornflour into the yoghurt pots, add colour as you require and stir well. Spoon some coloured paste into a small plastic meat tray.

**3** Moisten the paper by wiping it carefully with the dampened cellulose sponge.
**4** Attach the paper by one end with G clamps and the strip of board to the work surface. Place the rubber mat on the table with one short edge flush with the table edge. Cover to the edges with newspaper. Leave no edges in the central area. Place the paper on top of the mat, lining up the edge with the edge of the table. Place the wood along this edge on top of the paper and secure with G clamps. If you are right-handed, keep the clamped edge to your left. Reverse this if you are left-handed.

**5** Apply paste in long, smooth strokes. The mixture will stay workable for about five minutes. On a dry day add water to the paste.
**6** Do an easy one first, all the same colour. Hold index and second fingers together and press them down on the paper. Wipe fingers, turn over and make a wavy line using the fingernails, removing some paste, revealing the lighter base. Stamping needs a soft under-pad; the sharp straight lines want a hard, smooth surface so only coat paste on the rows you will do.
**7** Remove the clamps and board and place the page on a drying rack or lay flat on newspapers. When completely dry, place between boards and weight overnight.

*Coloured cornflour paste is applied to the paper in long, smooth strokes.*

*An old wooden printing block is pressed into the wet cornflour paste to produce a repeat design.*

*Lift the printing block carefully and wipe it with a clean rag before positioning it for the next*

*impression. Rock the block slightly from side to side for a good register.*

Work briskly, while the paste is still wet. If the paste dries before you are ready, brush gently with clean water and wait a moment for it to be absorbed. Virtually complete, this print shows stripes of varying patterns.

Exert pressure and use a rocking motion. Remove rubber pad before making lines.

The areas between the motifs are 'combed' to form narrow stripes.

Green stripes made with a narrower brush are then over-brushed with a deep red.

The green picked up on the paste brush appears in the next brushstroke, creating an interesting effect.

Patterns are then combed and stamped into the stripes of still wet colour. Vary the design methods for a really interesting effect. Try stamping with printing blocks or wine corks cut into shapes, combing, drawing designs with a stylus or even your fingers.

1 Remove the rubber pad and draw the straight lines first.

4 Red paste is dragged up through the other two colours using a little piece of broken comb.

2 Wavy lines are combed in between the stripes; work in one direction.

5 Green and blue are added and combed together with a wavy motion.

3 Go back over the wavy lines to form a three-dimensional effect.

6 All feathered lines are drawn away from the G clamps to prevent rucking the paper.

7 First green paste is applied with a narrow brush and then a wide brush of blue paste is overbrushed to blend colours.

8 A small scrap of plastic is twisted to form a semicircle. Rows of these fill in the other design.

9 Don't forget to use your fingers! In between bands of combed scrolls, dab your finger tips to form little spots of design. Also, use your fingertip to draw a wiggly line.

*Using a paintbrush, apply coloured paste on to the printing block. Ensure that the colour covers all the block surface before trying to print.*

*Press the block down firmly on to the paper. You will need to apply considerable pressure for the pattern to transfer well.*

*The pattern begins to build. Apply coloured paste to the block each time you make a print, and*

*wipe the block after each register. Although time-consuming, the results render are worthwhile.*

## Simulated gold embossing

Here are two methods which do not require professional equipment to produce the gold embossed effect.

Imitation gold dry transfers are available from art suppliers. These can be rubbed or drawn on to the paste-decorated papers.

**8** When you are happy with your design, gently remove the paper. Hang the decorated paper over a clothes airer or lay it flat on sheets of newspaper to dry. When completely dry, place the papers between two boards, weight them down with heavy books or bricks at least overnight or slightly longer, so that they are flat and ready to use.

*Examples of simulated gold embossing on paste-decorated papers. The designs are stamped onto the paste base with adhesive and then the metallic gold powder is dusted on, and tapped off, back into its jar.*

Alternatively, use clear, all-purpose glue. Apply glue to a printing block or stamp and press on to the paper. Before the glue dries, put 'gold' dusting powder or powdered aluminium (from art shops) on to the glue and tap in several directions until the glue has been coated. Tap leftover powder back into its container, and repeat the procedure until all the design has been gold coated.

## Diskette box

To encourage good care of computer diskettes and create an attractive-looking work area, make this appealing and functional diskette box.

This attractive and stylish holder, with a contrast lining, has been designed to store and protect your diskettes. Both the lid and the base can serve as handy containers during the day when you are loading and unloading different disks and need to keep them in order.

REQUIREMENTS
*Strong cardboard (millboard)*
*Lining paper*
*Contact adhesive*
*Wheat paste*
*Decorated or marbled paper*

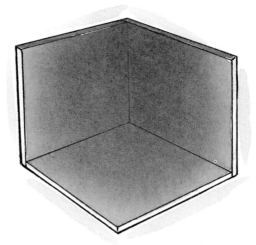

**1** Use the cutting plan here and transfer these measurements on to the cardboard with a pencil and ruler. Using a sharp craft knife or scalpel, cut out these shapes. Work on one side of the box at a time. The following steps make up one box. Repeat them to make the second box. Make the base first. Fit the lid over it.
**2** Apply all linings to the cardboard shapes and bring over the top edges. When dry, cut all round with a sharp knife.

**3** Make up the box bottom as shown, using contact adhesive to adhere side pieces and the base. Follow directions on adhesive tube.
**4** Measure all round the four sides of the box. Take this measurement, add 1 cm (⅜ in) to it, and cut out a strip of decorated paper to this length and about 1 cm (⅜ in) at the bottom edges of the box.
**5** Brush paste on the decorated paper and apply it to the box, neatly aligning the top edges, snip corners and fold the bottom allowance over. Cut a bottom piece, paste and apply. Repeat for the top.

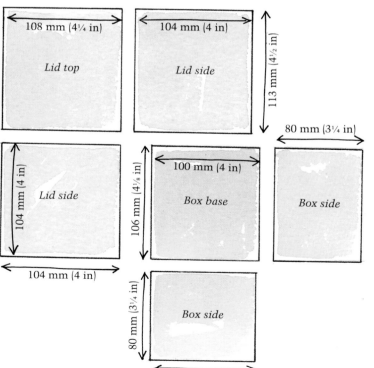

An old wooden printing block was coated in coloured paste and stamped on to plain and coloured paper. This folk-art-style paper was selected to line strong pieces of board, which are then glued together to form a functional and attractive desktop gift.

Lid top — 108 mm (4¼ in)

Lid side — 104 mm (4 in) × 113 mm (4½ in)

Lid side — 104 mm (4 in) × 104 mm (4 in)

Box base — 100 mm (4 in) × 106 mm (4⅛ in)

Box side — 80 mm (3¼ in)

Box side — 96 mm (3¾ in) × 80 mm (3¼ in)

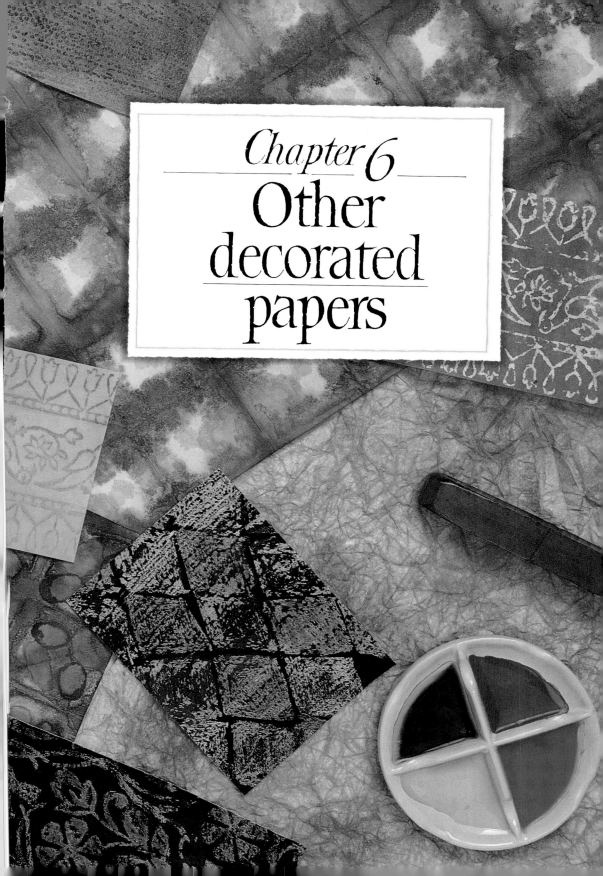

# Chapter 6
# Other decorated papers

# Tie dyed paper

As with fabric, you can fold, tie and colour paper in various ways, so that when it is opened flat you have an unusual pattern.

When you have finished decorating with this technique, you may want to turn the paper into a garment to wear – it is sheer, delicate and quite exquisite.

When planning a piece of work, try to include some stitchery, either by hand or on a sewing machine. Gather the sewn stitches and wrap the thread around tightly.

## Equipment

**G clamps:** To hold the paper.

**Brush:** Inexpensive watercolour brushes will be adequate.

**String:** Very strong fine nylon thread or fine copper wire can all be used to bind the paper and form a resisting negative design until the dried paper is opened.

*Patterns created by folding and binding the paper in different ways. Experiment and make notes how certain patterns are achieved.*

## Materials

**Paper:** It is worth investing a little money in fine, strong, handmade Japanese paper. You won't be sorry, the results are exquisite. If you cannot get hold of this, look around for synthetic, machine-made substitutes. You can try any size, but I suggest A4 as a good starting point.

**Transparent inks:** You will need at least three colours.

## Technique

Pressure excludes the ink. You can fold and clamp the paper to obtain one kind of design, or fold and wrap it with fine twine or wire to exclude the ink. Experiment, as different methods produce different designs.

**1** Accordion-pleat the paper until you have a long, skinny piece, roughly 5 cm (2 in) across.

2 Accordion-pleat again, the other way, until you have a 5 cm (2 in) square. Grip the centre tightly with two pads of wood and the G clamp.

3 Apply brush full of ink to the edge and 'feed' the ink to the edges. Now stop and do something else for half a day. Let it dry.
4 Open the G clamp and make a dot of colour in the centre. When dry, open out the paper for a delightful design. Next time gather paper, wind wire tightly around it, create different designs by altering the distance between bands. Open and press or leave crinkled.

The principle of pressure to exclude the ink will allow many variations on that theme. Until now you have made white or negative designs in straight lines but it easy to form circles by gathering a point or peak of paper. Tie a string around it and paint the parts not under pressure. Just remember the lines of pressure will always be negative designs the colour of the base paper.

It is also possible to re-die over a dried design to get a more complex pattern. Work the lines of design in opposition to the first ones applied. Imagine the result of a simple but effective pattern of straight lines in a chequered pattern. Or series of circles overlapping each other.

# Frottage

This is an incredibly easy technique which is a great favourite with children. You can achieve a very delicate, pretty result or you can find yourself on a bold dinosaur hunt.

## Equipment
*Brush:* An inexpensive watercolour brush for applying the paint.

*Newspapers:* To protect the worksurface.

## Materials
*Paper:* Ordinary typing or copying paper.

*White wax:* Use white wax candles for creating a 'negative' image.

*Wax crayons:* For rubbing a clear or coloured design.

*Paints:* Transparent watercolours are used to wash over the wax rubbed image.

## Technique
1 Select some interesting textured surfaces: try natural features such as leaves or bark, or look at architectural aspects, on fireplaces or interesting walls, etc.
2 Place the paper on the textured surface and rub all over it with a wax candle (for a 'negative' image), or use wax crayons. Make these form a picture, or just use them in abstract form.
3 Spread the newspapers over the work surface and place the rubbings on top. Cover the designs with a wash of watercolour. Use pastel colours or rich, contrasting ones depending upon the effect you want to achieve. The wax crayon or candle images will resist the watercolour paints and show through.

> *Note:* Your choice of what to use for rubbings is virtually endless. Try coins, relief designs on pieces of furniture, shells, textured wallpapers, weathered wood, wooden printing blocks.

## Stationery set

You can make a number of items to create a stylish and coordinated stationery set. Simple pieces, like the paperweight, take little time to assemble.

Glass paperweights, such as the one shown here, are available from craft suppliers (see the list of useful addresses on page 76). Look for a plain letter rack in gift departments in stores or stationers.

This set has been covered with a cream coloured drawing paper and frottage 'on-lays' of Kozo handmade paper. The edges are wetted with water from a brush and torn apart to feather them so they blend well when pasted down. These motifs created on handmade paper are gently torn to blend in with the base paper.

### Paperweight
REQUIREMENTS
*Glass paperweight*
*Decorated paper*

**1** Place the inner backing provided with the glass paperweight on to the right side of the decorated paper. Make sure that the motif is central, then trace round the shape.
**2** Cut out the decorated paper and place it under the glass. Put the backing liner in place and adhere the self-stick felt base last.

### Letter rack
REQUIREMENTS
*Plain letter rack*
*Coloured paper*
*Decorated paper*
*PVA adhesive and paste*

**1** First draw a pencil pattern. Trace the sides, front and back onto the decorated paper. Add 15 mm (⅝ in) on the bottom and right side of the shape for 'turn-in' margins.

**2** If your paper is too small, cut the four pieces separately but add a turn-in at the right of each piece. Cut out the paper.

**3** Apply a mixture of PVA and paste (half and half) to the back piece, position the top 10 mm (½ in) from the top edge, keeping the edge without a turn-in free so the next, a side piece with a turn-in, is tucked under. Press into position and smooth flat. Nip a cut with scissors at the bottom corners and fold those flaps over.
**4** Continue around until all sides are covered. Also cover the middle divider and back inside piece. To cut pieces for them, trace the back shape without the turn-in allowances, try them for size. Leave 5 mm (¼ in) borders at the tops, trim. Paste and position, then finger-press flat.
**5** Cut and paste and cover piece for the bottom to hide the turn-ins. Decorate the front, middle and sides with the frottage motifs, as here.

## Blotter

REQUIREMENTS
*Sheets of blotting paper*
*Piece of strong cardboard 2 cm (¾ in) larger than the blotting paper all around*
*Lighter boards for corner bases*
*Coloured paper*
*Decorated paper*
*50/50 mix of PVA adhesive and paste*
*Coloured tape*

**1** Paint the edges of the base or cover with a coloured tape wide enough to cover the top edges in a 2 cm (¾ in) border.

> **Note:** *If you want the blotter to have a really strong edge to each of the corner pieces, make the triangles a little bigger and fold under the long edge. Snip off the excess at each end and stick in place as instructed in step 5.*

**2** To make one of the triangular corner pieces, on the lighter weight card draw a triangle with two sides of 10 cm (4 in) which meet to form a right angle. Draw a line to form the third side. Repeat three times to make the other corners.

**3** Use these bases as patterns and trace around them on the back of your decorated papers, adding 3 cm (1¼ in) turn-ins all around.

**2** Curve a piece of paper to join these marks and draw a pencil line along it. Using a small saw or sturdy scalpel, cut through that line.

**3** Sand smooth. Place the cut holder on the back of the decorated paper and make a start mark on the paper and tube. Roll the tube

along until you meet the pencil mark. Go 1 cm (½ in) further to mark a turn-in margin and stop. Measure the holder height and add 1 cm (½ in) for a turn-in.

**4** Cut out two shapes like this, one on plain paper for the inside. Draw two circles for the bottom. Add 1 cm (½ in) turn-in on the decorated one and paste on the outer base.

**4** Spread the paste and PVA on the longest turn-in and fold over the matching base long side. Put the corner base on top of the blotter base, right sides facing you, and turn both over, matching the base support edges. Place one of the other base pieces plus a scrap of the blotter base board across the right angle point (to obtain the correct thickness) in a perpendicular position and draw a line. Cut off the tip marked. Paste margins and fold over. Repeat on other corners.

**5** Trim a little tip off the blotter corners and slip them into the corner pockets.

### Pencil holder

REQUIREMENTS
*Mailing tube*
*Sandpaper*
*Small piece of cardboard*
*Paper in two colours*
*Decorated paper*
*PVA adhesive*

**5** Cut and paste a plain bottom circle, snip the margin and place inside.

**6** Cut a plain paper strip the length of the circumference plus an overlap. Paste and place on top outer edge, snip little cuts and press the cut bits down inside. Paste inside piece, then the outside, keeping 5 mm (¼ in) away from top and bottom outside margins and top inside margin.

**1** From the bottom of the tube, measure the height you want for pens. Mark around the tube, about 4 cm (1½ in) apart.

# Trouble shooting

## Carragheen moss marbling

*Alum crystals:* If a layer of fine crystals appears on the surface of the paper after coating and drying, the solution may have been too strong or not entirely dissolved, the water not hot enough, or it was not allowed enough time to dissolve. A condition like this might cause the colour to come off when it is dried.

*Lumpy size:* Usually occurs when instant size is not blended long enough in the liquidiser. This condition is annoying but, as it will ruin your patterns, it must be dealt with. Although time consuming, you have several choices: pour the size through a fine sieve or cloth into another container and then return it to the tray, or if there are only a few lumps, pick them out by hand. Or, run the whole lot through the liquidiser again. Next time, remember to give the mixture longer in the liquidiser.

*Colours sink and do not spread:* This is very discouraging. It might be consoling to know that it is the most common of all carragheen moss marbling problems!
a) Probably the colours need more oxgall. This needs to be done one or two drops at a time. Test and continue until it works. If you accidentally drop too much in, add a bit more pure colour.
b) Possibly the size is too thick. The consistency should be like that of thin cream.
c) Perhaps the colour is too thick. The colours should be thin but not watery. Add distilled or other soft water.
d) Are you sure that you gave the colours and size sufficient standing time to reach room temperature? If the colour spreads, then shrinks and sinks, this means the size is colder than the colours.

Try adding a little warm, soft water to the size. Mix gently with your hand, re-skim and test.

**Blank spots with no pattern:** Trapped air bubbles are formed when the paper is lowered on to the size. Check to make sure that you lowered the centre of the paper down first and pushed the diagonal corners down last.

The paper was treated with alum, but **the colours wash off:** This could be one of several things.
a) perhaps you used the sheet too quickly. It takes a minimum of 15 minutes for the alum solution to penetrate into the paper fibres – when placed inside a plastic bag – and become fully effective. Leave the alumed sheet to dry completely and then use it.
b) Maybe your solution was too weak. Check your procedure.
c) Did you place a pencilled X in the corner marking the side which was treated? There is always the possibility of putting the wrong side down.

## Oil and glue size marbling
**The colour spreads too much:** It is probably too thin and a little pure colour should be added to the diluted mixture.

**The colour sinks:** When it goes straight to the bottom, it usually means the colour is too thick and requires more white spirit to be added. Try adding spirit soap – one drop at a time – to the oil colour and test until the colour floats and spreads.

**The colours spread and then contract:** This indicates a size which is too cold and the problem can be corrected by adding warm water or by making a warm water bath in a larger tray and setting the smaller one inside it. Spirit soap may also help cure this problem.

**There are ugly, shiny spots on the print:** Blot the wet print with newspaper to remove the excess glue size. The only thing you can do to rescue the already dried and damaged print, is to float it face down in a pan of warm water, drain, blot, dry and press. Next time do the blotting step and all should go well.

## Paste-decorated paper

***The cornflour base becomes lumpy:*** If the atmosphere is very dry, the cornflour forms a skin quickly after being cooked. Keep it covered, but if it goes lumpy anyway, you can rescue it by mixing it in a liquidiser. As long as you have not added the colour, it is still essentially a food and will not contaminate your food processor.

The path of coloured ***paste goes dry under the brush*** before it reaches the end of its course: Wet the paper first. Add water to the starch and colour mixture. This kind of problem happens most often on a hot summer's day, or in a centrally over-heated room.

## Suminagashi

***The image does not stay on the paper, but runs off:*** You have chosen a paper which is treated to reduce its absorbency. You need an absorbent paper to take up the inks and hold them.

***The colours are too pale:*** Each time an ink-filled brush tip touches the water it not only gives off ink but it also takes on water in exchange. This then dilutes the next colour application. One solution to this problem is to keep a soft, absorbent cloth at the ready and blot the excess moisture after each trip from the bath to the ink. Alternatively, perhaps too little pigment was placed in the ink?

# Further reading

Akers, Robert C., *Marbling*, (pamphlet), Dryad Press, Leicester, UK 1976.

Chambers, Anne, *The Practical Guide to Marbling Paper*, Thames & Hudson, London, UK 1986.

Cockerell, Sydney M., *Marbling Paper*, 1934.

Easton, Phoebe J., Marbling, *A History and Bibliography*, Los Angeles, USA 1983.

Guyot, Don, *Suminagashi*, (pamphlet), Seattle, Wa, USA 1988.

Hughes, Sukey, *Washi* (section on Suminagashi), USA.

Loring, Rosamond B., *Decorated Book Papers*, Cambridge, Harvard College Library, USA 1973.

Maile, Anne, *Tie-dyed Paper*, London, UK 1975.

Maurer, Dianne Philippoff, & Maurer, Paul, *An Introduction to Carrageenan and Watercolour Marbling* (pamphlet), Spring Mills, Pa., USA 1984.

Narita, Kiyofusa, *A Life of Ts'ai Lung and Japanese Paper-Making*, Tokyo, Japan, 1980. (Suminagashi).

Nevins, Iris, *Traditional Marbling*, Sussex, N.J., USA 1985.

Woolnough, Charles W., *The (Whole) Art of Marbling*, London, UK 1853, 1881.

# Useful addresses

Much of the basic equipment needed can be either found in your house or purchased from DIY stores, hardware and builders' merchants, chemists, health food shops, caterers' suppliers, stationers, etc. For special colours and art supplies, art and craft shops are the best sources.

I have made an effort to include as many sources as I could locate. If I have omitted any, I apologise. Please let me know of new listings at Nautilus Press for future publication.

## United Kingdom
**Faulkiner Fine Papers Ltd**
76 Southampton Row
London WC1 4AR
Tel: 0171 831 1151
(Carragheen moss, inks, books, fine selection of hand-made papers, Japanese ink sticks)

**Neal Street East**
5 Neal Street
London WC2H 9PU
Tel: 0171 240 0135
(Japanese ink sticks, lotus bowls and fans)

**TN Lawrence & Son Ltd**
119 Clerkenwell Road
London EC1R 5BY
Tel: 0171 242 3534
(Marbled papers, oil-based inks)

**Marbling, Ann Muir**
1 St Algar's Yard
West Woodlands
Frome
Somerset BA11 5ER
Tel: 019853 786

**Nautilus Press & Paper Mill**
Jane Reese
77 Southern Row
London W10 5AL
Tel: 0181 968 7302
(Hand-marbled papers, and tuition)

## Australia
**Artwise**
13 Wilson Street
Newtown NSW 2042
Tel: (02) 519 8234

**Wills Quills**
164 Victoria Avenue
Chatswood NSW 2067
Tel: (02) 411 2627

**The Paper Merchant**
316 Rokeby Road
Subiaco WA 6008
Tel: (09) 381 6489

**Oxford Art Supplies**
221 Oxford Street
Darlinghurst NSW 2010
Tel: (02) 360 4066

## New Zealand
**Faze Papers**
32 Alfred Street, Onehunga
Tel: (09) 622 2220

**BJ Ball Papers**
395 Church Street, Penrose
Tel: (09) 579 0059

**Rosehill Paper Supplies**
Bremmer Road, Drury
Tel: (09) 294 7506

**The Paper House**
7 Carmont Place, Mt Wellington
Tel: (09) 276 2683

## South Africa
**Art, Craft & Hobbies**
Contact: Ron Berkowitz
PO Box 9635, George, 6530
(24 hour service and a nationwide mail order service)
Tel: 0441 741337

**Art & Graphic Supplies**
Contact: Mrs Naude
7b Mutual Square
Rosebank , Johannesburg
Tel: 011 4429563

**Chemical & Industrial Marketing** Contact: Marcel
Unit 8, , Tungsten Park
Strydom Park, Johannesburg
Tel: 011 79255823
(Supplier of surfactant – minimum 25 litres)

**Schweickerdt Art Centre & Gallery**
Vatika Centre
Cnr Muckleneuk & Fehren Street
Brooklyn Circle, Pretoria
Tel: 012 455406

**Southern Arts & Crafts**
Contact: Sharon Webb
105 Main Street, Rosettenville
Johannesburg
Tel: 011 6836566

## United States

**Aiko's Import Art Materials**
3347 North Clark Street
Chicago, Illinois, 60657
Tel: (312) 404 5600
(Japanese paper, mail order)

**Andrews-Nelson-Whitehead
Paper Corporation**
718/937-7100
31-10 48th Avenue
Long Island City, NY 11101
(Large selection imported papers)

**Colophon Book Arts Supply**
3046 Hogum Bay Road NE,
Olympia, WA 98506
Tel: (360) 459 2940
(Don Guyot, complete supplies
for Suminagashi [especially
surfactant]. Technical support.)

**Color Craft**
14 Airport Park Road
E Granby CT 06026
Tel: (800) 243 2712
(Colours, powders, video)

**Kasuri Dyeworks**
1959 Shattuck Avenue
Berkley CA 94704
Tel: (510) 841 4509
(Decorative Japanese papers)

**Lee Scott McDonald Inc
Fine Hand Papermaking
Equipment**
PO Box 264
Charlestown MA 02129
Fax: 617 242 8825
(Marbling supplies, catalogue)

**Linder, Mary**
910 Knollwood Drive South,
Brainerd MN 56401
(Hand-marbled papers)

**Lost Link Bindery
Lost Link Papers**
103 The Bowery
New York NY 10002
(Paste, papers, custom design)

**Maurer, Diane**
Box 78, Spring Mills PA 16875
Tel: (814) 422 8651
(Hand-marbled paper, supplies)

**Miller, Ashley**
343 Iradell Road, Trumansburg,
New York NY 14586
(Hand-marbled papers custom
retail/wholsesale, include stamp
when requesting information)

**Jarmila Sobota Book Arts**
828 Firestone
Richardson TX 75080
(Hand-marbled, decorative
papers, catalogue, 40 samples,
$45, $35 deductible after a first
minimum order of 10 papers)

## Japan
**Tokyu Hands**
(creative life store)
Tokyo
(Sumi-liquid and solid ink
[sticks], grinding stones, papers)

# Index

# THE
# PRACTICAL
# BOTANIST

**Rick Imes**

All pictures supplied by
Photo/Nats

A FIRESIDE BOOK
Published by Simon & Schuster Inc.
New York   London   Toronto   Sydney   Tokyo   Singapore

A QUARTO BOOK

Simon and Schuster/Fireside
Simon & Schuster Building
Rockefeller Center
1230 Avenue of the Americas
New York, New York 10020

Designed and produced by Quarto Publishing plc,
The Old Brewery, 6 Blundell Street, London N7 9BH

**Senior Editor** Sally MacEachern
**Editor** Sue Condor
**Designer** Anne Fisher
**Illustrators** Valerie Hill, Sally Launder, Kevin Maddison, Janos Marffy,
Ann Savage
**Index** Hazel Bell
**Assistant Art Director** Chloë Alexander

**Art Director** Moira Clinch
**Publishing Director** Janet Slingsby

Typeset by Ampersand Typesetting Ltd
Manufactured in Hong Kong by
Regent Publishing Services Ltd
Printed by Leefung-Asco Printers Ltd, Hong Kong

1  3  5  7  9  10  8  6  4  2
1  3  5  7  9  10  8  6  4  2  Pbk.

Library of Congress Catalog Card Number: 90-45450

ISBN 0-671-69306-9
0-671-69305-0 Pbk.

# CONTENTS

# FOREWORD

It is important to understand plants, in part because they make all other life on earth possible. Green plants are the only known organisms able to produce their own food internally through photosynthesis. This enables them to feed not only themselves, but all the animals which feed upon them, and predators that consume the plant-eaters. Can you think of any creature which does not directly or indirectly owe its existence to green plants? Trace any food chain back far enough, and you will always arrive at the common provider, green plants.

In addition, virtually all the oxygen in our atmosphere is produced by green plants as a by-product of photosynthesis. Several billion years ago, the atmosphere of our young planet was composed of methane, ammonia, water, and hydrogen gases. Driven by the sun's energy, storms raged across the surface of this barren world, depositing rain which accumulated over the millenia to form oceans. The lightning which accompanied these storms also sparked changes in the atmospheric molecules, producing larger and more complex organic molecules that eventually fell with the rain into the seas. It probably was in this primordial soup that one day, quite accidentally, a molecule arose that was able to make crude copies of itself out of the surrounding molecules. The copies continued to replicate. Those that were more efficient produced more copies, and it was in these dense masses of self-replicating organic molecules that the first single-celled alga originated and began to photosynthesize, releasing oxygen in the process. As the numbers and diversity of plants grew, the oxygen content of the atmosphere increased, stabilizing as the world became cloaked in greenery. Should a large portion of the earth's vegetation suddenly be lost due to some catastrophe, scientists estimate that, even if an alternative energy source were miraculously found to feed the world's animals, they would all suffocate within eleven years without green plants to replenish their oxygen supply. You can see from this that plants are indeed critical to the survival of all life on earth.

**Right** A food web illustrates the interconnectedness of all life forms, and at its heart are green plants, providing food and oxygen. Like a spider's web, a food web is strong when intact, yet easily disturbed, each disrupted connection weakening the web until it collapses. We must recognize the value of all species and the hidden relationships between them.

**Left** Plants do much more than ornament spectacular scenes, such as this view of Laryn Lake in Banff National Park, Alberta; they are essential to all life.

carnivorous consumers

herbivorous consumers

photosynthetic organisms
(producers)

birds

birds

insects

mammals

mammals

crustaceans

insects

algae

molluscs

amphibians

decomposers

reptiles

# THE BASICS OF BOTANY
## WHAT ARE PLANTS?

What differentiates plants from other organisms? Early biologists classified all organisms into two categories, the plant kingdom and the animal kingdom. This was based on relatively simple criteria: animals moved about and plants did not, plants produced their own food while animals ate other organisms, and plant cells possessed rigid cell walls lacking in animal cells. These distinctions worked well for the more complex, multi-celled organisms, but as more and more simple life forms were discovered and investigated, the two-kingdom system broke down. For instance, there are more than 300 species of single-celled, fresh-water organisms called euglenoids that are able to swim by means of flagella, or whip-like tails, and consume small food particles. These traits led them to be classified as animals by many taxonomists. However, many euglenoids also contain chloroplasts which enable them to carry on photosynthesis, suggesting that they belong to the plant kingdom.

As exceptions to the two-kingdom system accumulated, the need for more categories became apparent, but exactly where to make the divisions was unclear. Most one-celled organisms constitute a gray area in which it is impossible to draw distinctions without creating as many problems as you solve. To compound this dilemma, many unicellular organisms have left no fossil record through which we could trace their ancestry and clarify relationships. Today, more than six different classification systems exist, recognizing up to five kingdoms including *Monera* (bacteria and blue-green algae), *Protista* (protozoans, algae, sponges), *Fungi, Plantae* (bryophytes and vascular plants) and *Animalia* (multicellular animals).

**Above** Though fungi are now categorized in their own kingdom rather than the plant kingdom, they possess a number of plant-like characteristics.

**Left** The lush vegetation surrounding this Vermont farm may incorporate hundreds of species. Each is unique, yet all share the similar characteristics of members of the plant kingdom.

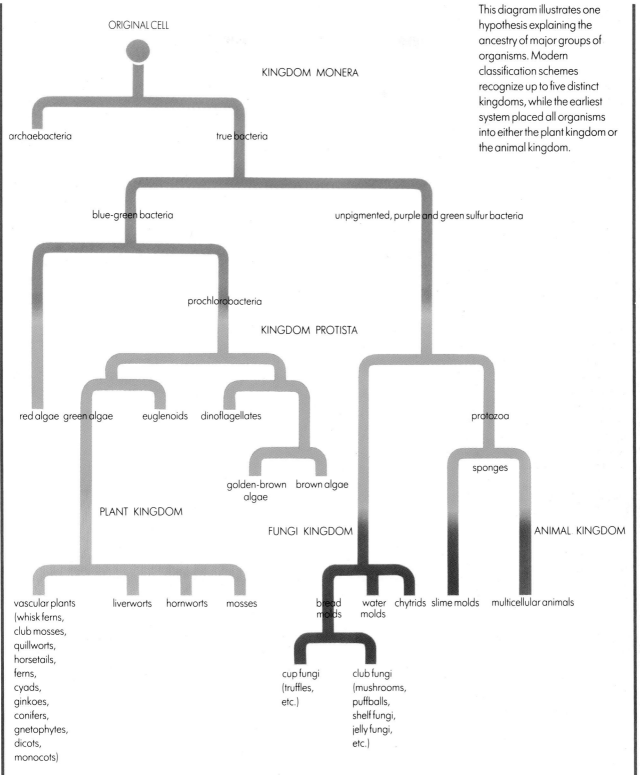

ORIGINAL CELL

KINGDOM MONERA

archaebacteria

true bacteria

blue-green bacteria

unpigmented, purple and green sulfur bacteria

prochlorobacteria

KINGDOM PROTISTA

red algae   green algae   euglenoids   dinoflagellates

protozoa

sponges

golden-brown   brown algae
algae

PLANT KINGDOM

FUNGI KINGDOM

ANIMAL KINGDOM

vascular plants
(whisk ferns,
club mosses,
quillworts,
horsetails,
ferns,
cyads,
ginkoes,
conifers,
gnetophytes,
dicots,
monocots)

liverworts   hornworts   mosses

bread
molds

water
molds   chytrids   slime molds   multicellular animals

cup fungi
(truffles,
etc.)

club fungi
(mushrooms,
puffballs,
shelf fungi,
jelly fungi,
etc.)

This diagram illustrates one hypothesis explaining the ancestry of major groups of organisms. Modern classification schemes recognize up to five distinct kingdoms, while the earliest system placed all organisms into either the plant kingdom or the animal kingdom.

# PARTS OF PLANTS

There is considerable variation in plant anatomy throughout the plant kingdom. As a practical botanist, you will be concerned primarily with the largest and most obvious group, the flowering plants, and so it is there that we begin our study. Even among flowering plants, anatomy varies significantly, but they generally possess four major parts: roots, stem, leaves, and flower(s). Each part has different primary functions.

## Roots

The root system anchors the plant and extracts water and essential minerals from the soil, transporting them upward into the stem. There are three major types of roots. Most *dicots* (dicotyledons, plants with two *cotyledons*, or "seed leaves") have taproots, while most *monocots* (monocotyledons, plants with only one "seed leaf") have fibrous roots. *Taproots* are large and fleshy, and often reach deep into the ground to obtain their needs. Taproots also store food, providing a distinct advantage to perennial plants starting into growth following dormancy. *Fibrous roots* depend upon branching filaments growing close to the soil's surface to collect precipitation before it sinks deeper into the ground. Many plants combine both types of root systems. *Adventitious roots,* the third type, are common to both monocots and dicots. These roots develop in certain plants, such as ivies, to facilitate climbing, and in plants with modified underground stems, such as corms, rhizomes and bulbs.

## Stems

Stems support leaves and flowers, positioning them in the best locations to accomplish their respective tasks. Stems and roots also house a vascular system of xylem and phloem, tube-like structures which conduct water and nutrients to various parts of the plant. *Xylem* transports water and dissolved substances upward in the plant. *Phloem* can move material both up and down, and primarily transports newly-synthesized organic molecules, such as amino acids and carbohydrates, from the leaves to the roots and stem for storage, or to growing parts of the plant for immediate use.

Stems may be simple or branched, upright, or creeping. Many modifications to the stem enable

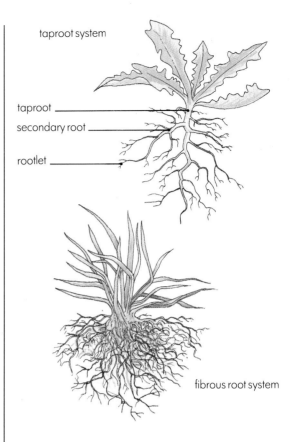

taproot system

taproot

secondary root

rootlet

fibrous root system

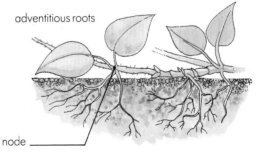

adventitious roots

node

**Above** The three root types are fibrous roots, adventitious roots and taproots. All the other structures shown are specialized stems.

**Below** The scientific community represents flowering plants with diagrams depicting floral parts; (**left**) monocot, (**right**) dicot.

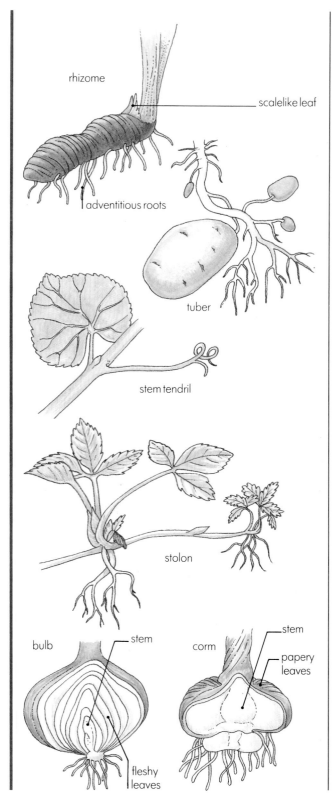

rhizome

scalelike leaf

adventitious roots

tuber

stem tendril

stolon

bulb

stem

fleshy leaves

corm

stem

papery leaves

**Above** The conspicuous flower of yellow trillium, a southern and midwestern species, attracts insect pollinators; the leaf whorls on the stem allow maximum solar energy gain.

different species to fit into a wide array of ecological niches. They may form underground food storage organs, such as *rhizomes, bulbs, corms,* or *tubers.* Some plants form colonies by sending up *suckers,* or shoots, from rhizomes, or by sending out *stolons,* or runners, which put down adventitious roots upon reaching a suitable new location. Certain climbing plants, such as grapes and Boston ivy, produce *tendrils,* modified stems which extend from the parent plant to grasp other plants or objects for support.

Plants are woody or herbaceous depending upon the amount of *lignin,* a strengthening material, in the cell walls of their stem tissues. Woody, long-lived plants supporting great weight such as oak trees, produce a great deal more lignin than herbaceous plants, which support only a light weight for just one season.

**Leaves**

Although any green part of a plant can carry on photosynthesis, leaves are the primary sites of photosynthetic production. They often grow in a broad, flat shape, called the *blade,* which presents the maximum surface area to absorb the sun's rays. On many plants, the leaves twist on their stalks, or *petioles,* turning from east to west throughout the

11

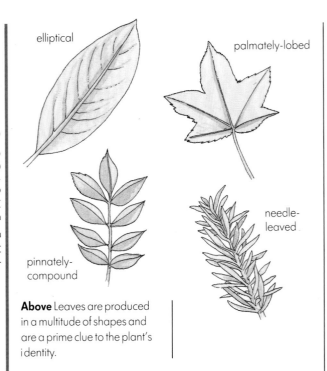

elliptical

palmately-lobed

pinnately-compound

needle-leaved

**Above** Leaves are produced in a multitude of shapes and are a prime clue to the plant's identity.

atmosphere, resulting in a lower osmotic pressure in the leaves. The leaves then act as a siphon to draw water from the roots, relying on the cohesiveness of water molecules to pull a column of water to the tops of the tallest trees. In leaves, water and nutrients travel through vascular bundles called *veins*, parallel to one another in monocots, and in a branching network in dicots. Dicots may have *pinnately veined* leaves, in which secondary veins branch from a central vein called the *midrib*, or *palmately veined* leaves, where several main veins fan out from the base of the blade, like fingers on a hand.

**Flowers**

Flowers are reproductive structures composed of modified shoots and leaves. Their sole function is the production of fertile seeds which, in turn, produce the next generation. Pollination is usually accomplished by enlisting the aid of wind or insects, although some species rely entirely on nectar-feeding birds or bats, and a few are pollinated by water.

A flower begins at the tip of its stalk, or *peduncle*. This swells into the *receptacle*, to which all other parts of the flower are attached. A typical flower consists of the following parts: *sepals*, the outer whorl of leaf-like protective coverings of the bud; an inner whorl of *petals*; one or more *pistils*, the female organ consisting of a sticky, pollen-receiving *stigma* connected to the *ovary*, where seeds will ultimately develop, by a *style;* and several to many *stamens*, the male parts each consisting of a pollen-producing *anther* terminating in a slender *filament*. Collectively, the sepals are known as the *calyx*, the petals as the *corolla*, and the sepals and petals together become the *perianth*. There are a great many modifications to this arrangement in the plant kingdom.

day to keep their leaves oriented toward the sun, returning to their east-facing position overnight to catch the first morning rays.

Leaves are usually arranged on the stem to take maximum advantage of the available sunlight. The largest leaves generally grow closest to the ground; leaves higher up the stem are progressively smaller, so they don't shade those below. Leaf arrangement may be *alternate*, with one leaf per *node* (point of attachment to the stem); *opposite*, with two leaves attached at the same node; or *whorled*, with three or more leaves per node. Leaves may be *simple* (undivided), or *compound*, with the blade divided into *leaflets*. *Pinnately compound* leaves have paired leaflets along a central stalk, or *rachis*, while the leaflets of *palmately compound* leaves radiate from a single point of attachment at the end of the petiole.

Leaves are important in the exchange of gases involved in photosynthesis and in *respiration*, an energy-releasing process. *Stomata*, tiny pores on the undersides of leaves, allow carbon dioxide to enter, and oxygen and water vapor, the by-products of photosynthesis and respiration respectively, to exit. Other waste products produced by the plant are deposited in the leaves and eliminated from the plant as its leaves are shed. Most water reaching the leaves evaporates, or *transpires*, into the

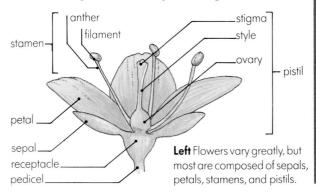

anther
filament
stamen
stigma
style
ovary
pistil
petal
sepal
receptacle
pedicel

**Left** Flowers vary greatly, but most are composed of sepals, petals, stamens, and pistils.

### Dissect a flower

Larger members of the lily family work well for this. Observe an open bloom and try to identify its various parts. Carefully clip off a bloom near its base and, using a razor blade or a sharp knife, remove the sepals, petals, and stamens, leaving only the pistil still attached to the stem. Arrange the parts on a sheet of paper and examine them. (You can make a permanent record of your dissection by following the procedure outlined on page 33.) Once separated into its components, you can see that, despite the profusion of flower shapes, colors, and sizes, the underlying principle of a flower is really quite simple.

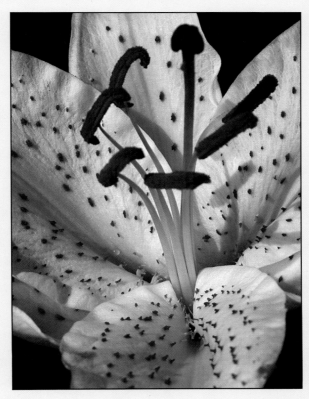

**Left** All flower parts are prominently displayed in this goldband lily, an Oriental species. Note the stamens with their pollen-laden anthers, the pistil, and the nearly identical petals and sepals.

### Investigate xylem

You can visually demonstrate the function of xylem tissue with an ordinary white carnation. Tint some water in a glass (no more than six drops of food coloring per 8 ounces is necessary). Make a fresh cut near the bottom of the stem, half-way between the stem joints, or nodes, and place it in the water without immersing the bloom. In a few hours the bloom will have taken on the color of the water. You can have some fun by splitting the stem lengthwise into two or more segments and placing each in a different color. You can also perform this experiment using a plant with a light colored stem, such as celery, and actually see the tinted water progressing through the stem after about an hour. Try two pieces, one with leaves and one without, to see which one works faster. Can you explain your results?

### Investigate roots and shoots

Roots orient toward gravity as surely as leaf stalks orient away from it. You can demonstrate both using easily germinated seeds such as tomatoes or radishes. Start the seeds between moist sheets of paper towel. When the roots are visible, mount several seeds between clear sheets of glass or plastic (lids from take-out salads work great), keeping a moist piece of towel between the seeds and one of the sheets. Use tape or a rubber band to hold the sheets firmly together. Stand the sheets on their sides until the roots elongate, then rotate the sheets 90° so that the roots and stem are horizontal. With further growth, you will notice that the roots have turned downward while the leaf stem has turned upward.

Plants accomplish this by means of *auxins*, chemicals which accumulate on the lower side of horizontal stems. Root cells are inhibited by auxins, and the faster growth of the upper cells forces the roots downward. Leaf stem cells are stimulated by auxins, so the more rapidly growing lower cells force the leaf stems upward.

# PHOTOSYNTHESIS: "EATING LIGHT"

We've mentioned that green plants are the only group of organisms capable of producing their own food, but how do they do it, and why can't we? Food is simply stored energy. More specifically, it is stored *chemical* energy. After we eat, our metabolism reduces the food to simpler forms and breaks certain chemical bonds, thereby releasing stored energy and nutrients and producing waste by-products. Energy released from food allows us to grow and also to carry on the activities necessary to maintain life.

Plants need not consume other organisms to obtain energy. Through their green pigment, *chlorophyll*, they are able to convert light energy to chemical energy and store it until needed. Through the action of chlorophyll and enzymes, a green plant can combine six molecules of carbon dioxide, six molecules of water, and light energy to produce one molecule of glucose, a simple sugar, and six molecules of oxygen, a by-product of photosynthesis.

Stored energy is of no use to an organism without some way to liberate it as needed. This is accomplished through *respiration*, a process taking place in all living cells 24 hours a day. *Aerobic respiration*, which occurs only in the presence of oxygen, is by far the most common form of respiration in both plants and animals. It is essentially the reverse of photosynthesis; one molecule of glucose and six molecules of oxygen are acted upon by enzymes to yield six molecules of carbon dioxide, six molecules of water, and energy. *Anaerobic respiration* occurs only under

**Above** and **right** In most vascular plants, such as this scarlet oak, photosynthesis occurs primarily in the leaves. They are veritable food factories, receiving raw materials through stems and leaf pores and shipping finished products via the same routes. Energy liberated through respiration allows the leaves to convert the simple products of photosynthesis into more complex compounds useful in growth, reproduction, and defense.

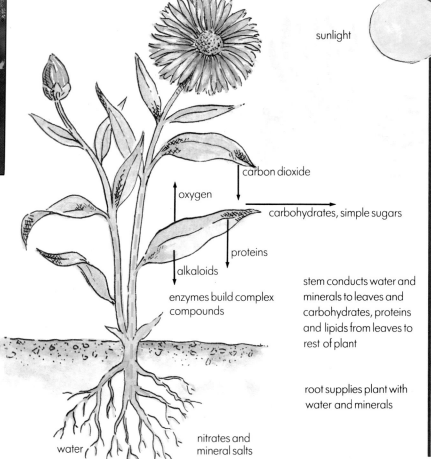

sunlight

carbon dioxide

oxygen

carbohydrates, simple sugars

proteins

alkaloids

enzymes build complex compounds

stem conducts water and minerals to leaves and carbohydrates, proteins and lipids from leaves to rest of plant

root supplies plant with water and minerals

water

nitrates and mineral salts

special circumstances in the absence of oxygen; the most familiar example is fermentation which yields the ethyl alcohol in alcoholic beverages. Respiration is analogous to throwing a log on a bonfire; the stored energy in the log is transformed into heat and light, consuming oxygen and producing carbon dioxide and other gases in the process. In cellular respiration, the "bonfire" is miniscule and rigidly controlled, converting fuel to energy in tiny amounts as needed.

Some sugars produced by photosynthesis are used directly in respiration, but often the rate of photosynthesis is much higher than the rate of respiration, and more sugar is produced than can be used immediately. Sugar not needed for respiration is transformed into proteins, lipids (fats) or other carbohydrates, such as cellulose, sucrose, and starch. At peak periods of photosynthesis, excess water-soluble sugar is transformed into insoluble starch, so as not to upset the osmotic balance of the cell, and some is stored in the *chloroplasts*, the chlorophyll-containing organelles (microscopic structures) of plant cells. It is later broken down into smaller soluble sugars, and transported out of the leaf for use or storage elsewhere in the plant.

# What you can do

## Demonstrate photosynthesis

We cannot directly observe photosynthesis, but we can observe its by-product. Collect a few submerged aquatic plants, such as pondweed, from a pond, or purchase some from a tropical fish store. Place a water-filled aquarium or a large glass container, such as a pickle jar, in a sunny location. Submerge the plants under an upturned glass, making sure no air remains in the glass. Over several days, you should observe an increasing accumulation of oxygen at the top of the glass; you may even observe bubbles rising from the plant. By marking the oxygen level at the end of each day and making careful observations, you can correlate oxygen production with the number of hours of sunlight each day. You can manipulate the amount of light reaching the plant by using an aluminum foil reflector, a special plant light, or by draping a dark cloth over the aquarium. Corresponding increases or decreases in oxygen production will be noted with such modifications.

## Demonstrate osmosis

Photosynthesis is possible in terrestrial vascular plants because water is absorbed by the roots from the soil through the process of *osmosis*. Osmosis is the movement of water through a cell membrane from a greater concentration of water to a lesser

concentration. You can make a device to demonstrate osmosis in roots using a carrot and a plastic drinking straw. Ordinarily, a carrot growing in the ground absorbs water by osmosis and transports it to the stems and leaves. If you remove the stems, hollow out the top of the carrot, and insert a clear straw, you can observe water rising in the straw by osmotic pressure. Simply seal the straw in the carrot with candle wax, drip a small amount of sugar water down the straw and mark its level,

support the carrot in a glass of water using toothpicks, and observe. After a short period, you will notice that the fluid level in the straw has risen as the water flowed toward the sugar water (the lesser concentration of water, since sugar occupied part of the volume). Tinting the water with food coloring or ink and then slicing the carrot lengthwise at the end of the experiment will reveal the veins through which water travels, as well as the untinted cells which store food.

# LIFE CYCLES

The lives of plants, like those of all other organisms, are finite, having both a beginning and an end. The interval in between ranges from days to centuries, depending upon the species. Plants hold the record for longevity on earth; the General Sherman, a 272-foot giant sequoia tree in Sequoia National Park, California, is more than 3,000 years old, an age surpassed only by a few bristlecone pines.

The more advanced groups of plants can be divided into three general categories based on their life cycles. *Annuals* complete their entire life cycle in one growing season. *Biennials* require two seasons to complete their life cycle; in the first season they are vegetative, and only flower and reproduce in their second year of life. *Perennials* continue to live and flower for some years after reaching maturity.

The beginning of a flowering plant's life cycle is preceded by the pollination of its parent. *Pollination* is the transfer of *pollen*, containing the plant's sperm, from the anther to the stigma. When this occurs between the flowers of different plants it is called *cross-pollination*, a process favored among flowering plants because it promotes a random mixing of genes within the gene pool of the

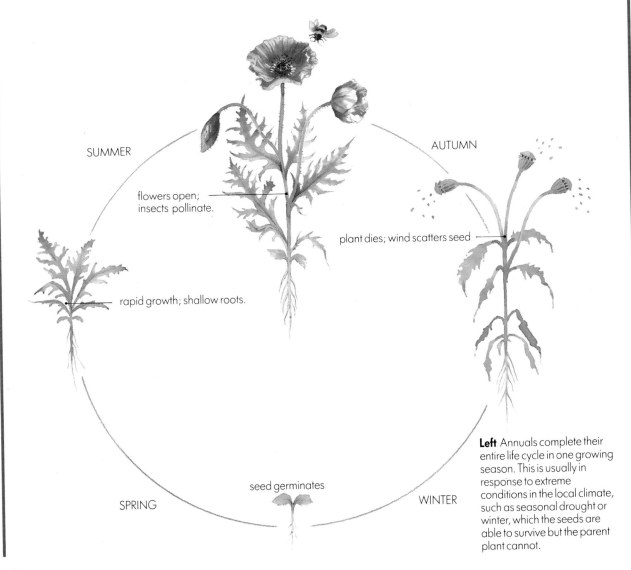

SUMMER

flowers open;
insects pollinate.

AUTUMN

plant dies; wind scatters seed

rapid growth; shallow roots.

seed germinates

SPRING

WINTER

**Left** Annuals complete their entire life cycle in one growing season. This is usually in response to extreme conditions in the local climate, such as seasonal drought or winter, which the seeds are able to survive but the parent plant cannot.

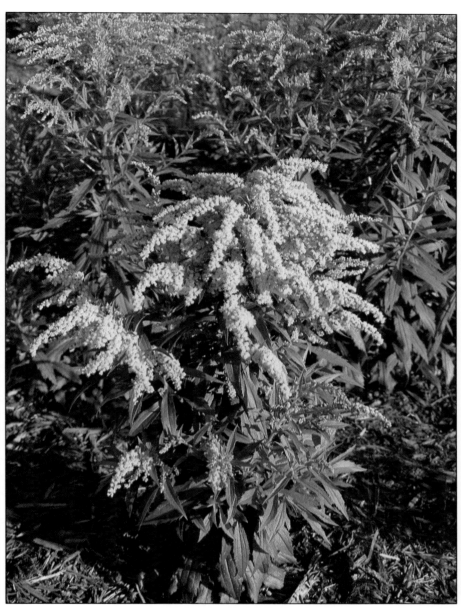

Wind-pollinated flowers produce copious quantities of light, airborne pollen and vast numbers of female flowers, relying upon the whims of air currents to unite the two. On the other hand, insect-pollinated flowers produce heavy, sticky pollen grains designed to adhere to a visitor's body. Insect-pollinated goldenrod (**right**) is often erroneously blamed as the cause of hayfever, but the real culprit is usually the less conspicuous, wind-pollinated common ragweed (**above**).

species. The resulting diversity of traits better enables that species to cope with changing environmental conditions, which is crucial to the process of evolution.

Plants employ many methods to ensure that cross-pollination occurs. Some produce plants of separate sexes, so that cross-pollination is inevitable. Others develop stamens first, and delay maturation of the pistil until the stamens have ripened and shed all of their pollen. However, many species produce both stamens and pistils simultaneously. How do they promote cross-pollination? Most plants in this category have flowers designed so that the pollinator, usually an insect or a nectar-feeding bird, comes into contact with the stigma before touching the anthers, so that pollen transferred is more likely to come from another plant.

Flowers are usually wind pollinated or pollinated by animals. Wind-pollinated flowers are inconspicuous, since they don't have to attract pollinators. Because wind is unpredictable, these

**Above** Plants have evolved a myriad ingenious ways of dispersing themselves to suitable new habitats. Many involve seed adaptations, such as the parachute-like appendages of dandelion seeds, allowing them to ride great distances on air currents.

plants produce pollen in astronomical quantities, relying on sheer numbers to get the job done. Their buoyant pollen grains are often carried great distances on the wind, and are responsible for the hayfever allergies suffered by millions of people. Animal pollination, on the other hand, requires the flowers to be conspicuous to potential pollinators, and there would seem to be nearly as many combinations of form, color, and fragrance as there are pollinating species. The greatest number of pollinators are insects, so many floral features, such as distinctive color combinations, bold markings called "honey guides," which lead insects toward the flower's nectar and/or pollen, and specific fragrances all lure potential pollinators. Insects perceive ultraviolet as a color, but most cannot see red, so, many insect-pollinated flowers incorporate ultraviolet features, while all-red flowers rely on hummingbirds and some species of butterflies to accommodate them.

Once pollination occurs, the next step is fertilization. Pollen deposited on the sticky stigma generates a fine *pollen tube* that conveys the sperm through the style to the ovary, where the ovules, or eggs, have developed. After fertilization, the rest of the flower parts wither and are shed as the ovary swells with seed development.

When seeds mature, they face the formidable task of dispersing to suitable sites for germination – no small feat for organisms without apparent means of locomotion. Dispersal is particularly important for seeds of long-lived plants which would face overwhelming competition from their mature parent if they were to simply fall and germinate at its base. Plants have, however, evolved a multitude of ingenious methods to ensure that at least some of their seeds reach locations where the seedlings can compete. Plants such as dandelions, milkweeds, and thistles rely on airborne dispersal, producing downy seed "parachutes" that ride air currents. Some plants hitchhike on animals to reach their destinations. The seeds of common burdock, for example, are equipped with hooks which cling tenaciously to fur or clothing until knocked or pulled off, usually some distance from the parent plant. Another means of hitchhiking is employed by seeds that develop inside a palatable fruit or berry, which is eaten by a bird or mammal, then passes through the animal's digestive tract, emerging some distance away. Seeds of many wetland plants float on water, while those of others, such as spotted jewelweed, are shot out of spring-loaded pods.

The interval between seedling and maturity varies greatly among species. Annuals grow rapidly, putting down only shallow roots and concentrating their resources on producing vegetative growth and flowers. In contrast, herbaceous perennials, trees, and shrubs, invest heavily in well developed root systems, often postponing flowering for several seasons. Some are opportunists. Many trees, for example, spend years as seedlings in a mature forest, patiently waiting for one of the old monarchs to fall, then race to fill the hole in the forest canopy with their own branches before their competitors can do so.

**Above** Another seed dispersal adaptation is the hitch-hiking technique employed by many plants, including common burdock. Hooked extensions snag the fur, clothing, or feathers of passers-by, and the seeds remain attached until they are worked free, usually at some distance from the parent plant.

## What you can do

### Discover hidden seeds

During the next spring thaw, put on your boots and take a walk someplace muddy. When you get home, scrape the mud from your boots and mix it with water to a semi-liquid consistency, and leave overnight. The next day, add the mud-and-water mixture to sterile potting compost, cover with a sheet of glass or clear plastic, and place somewhere warm and light, keeping the compost moist but not too wet. In two or three weeks, seedlings should emerge. As they grow, you can transplant them and raise them to maturity to identify them and observe their life cycles.

# SEASONAL CHANGES

Temperate-region plants must cope with extremes in climate through the year. To survive, they have evolved a great array of adaptations. Annuals simply limit themselves to one growing season, during which they sprout when conditions are prime, grow, flower and set seed. Seeds are quite hardy and can withstand the rigors of winter while awaiting conditions favorable for germination and growth. In fact, many species' seeds must undergo an extended period of freezing to germinate. This prevents their sprouting during a mild "Indian summer," when conditions often mimic spring.

Biennials must weather one winter, and usually spend it as a low-growing plant, sheltered from the elements under the debris of expired vegetation and a blanket of snow. Not until their second season do they rise to a mature height and flower.

Perennials are truly innovative when it comes to coping with the seasons. Herbaceous perennials often store food in modified underground stems before discarding their above-ground growth and entering a dormant period. Evergreen plants produce a resinous sap, a sort of botanical anti-freeze, so their leaves survive winter without freezing, and are ready to begin photosynthesis as soon as the ground thaws and water becomes available.

### Deciduous plants
*Deciduous* plants drop their leaves seasonally. Evergreen plants also shed their leaves, but much less conspicuously, dropping them sporadically throughout the year. The process by which leaves

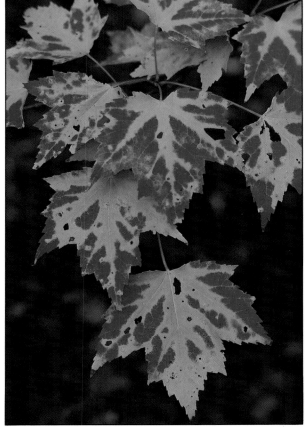

**Below** Herbaceous perennials, such as this wind-blown goldenrod, cope with winter by storing food in the roots and dying back above ground.

**Above** and **right** The shedding of leaves by deciduous trees, shrubs, and vines enables them to avoid the stresses of winter. As the green chlorophyll begins to diminish, yellow pigments are exposed. Sugar trapped in the leaf is converted into red, blue, and purple pigments which, when combined with the yellows and greens, result in the brilliant display of autumn colors familiar in the Northeast.

are shed is called *abscission*. In deciduous plants, hormonal responses to environmental changes such as decreasing day length, light intensity, temperature, and precipitation trigger the formation of specialized cells in the *abscission zone* at the base of the petiole. These cells are easily broken down by plant enzymes, leaving the leaf attached to the stem only by a few strands of xylem. Wind and rain easily sever this connection, and the leaf falls, leaving on its twig a *leaf scar* encircling several *bundle scars* where the vascular bundles of xylem and phloem once entered the leaf. A corky layer below the abscission zone prevents water loss from the leaf scar.

Preceding deciduous leaf fall is the color change that has become the hallmark of autumn. Chloroplasts, the cell structures in which photosynthesis takes place, contain groups of pigments including chlorophylls (green), carotenes (yellow or orange yellow), and xanthophylls (pale yellow). Chlorophylls are present in the greatest quantities in mature leaves, and their color masks other pigments. As cells in the abscission zone deteriorate and die, they begin to close off the vascular bundles that transport materials to and from the leaf. Without this influx of raw materials, chlorophyll is not replaced, and its diminishing concentration allows other pigments to show through.

The clogged vascular bundles also prevent the leaf's sugars and waste products from leaving. Trapped sugars are converted into anthocyanins, the deep-red pigments responsible for many autumn hues. The exact autumn color of a leaf often depends upon the acidity or alkalinity of the protoplasm, or sap, in its cells. Anthocyanins will turn red if the protoplasm is acidic, blue if alkaline, and purple if neutral. Such conditions vary from cell to cell, hence the kaleidoscope of colors.

A combination of bright, sunny days and cool nights, coupled with ample moisture, produce the most colorful autumn scenes. Bright sunshine stimulates the leaves to continue producing sugars at a rapid rate, and cool nights, around 40°F, cause the abscission zone to pinch off the vascular bundles quicker, trapping more sugar in the leaves. Dry weather diminishes the intensity of fall colors, because parched leaves produce less sugar, and therefore less anthocyanin.

Once deciduous leaves are shed and the sap has retreated to its root system, a woody plant becomes dormant. On the twigs, together with the leaf scars and bundle scars, are buds, the birthplace of the next season's growth. Buds are formed toward the end of the previous growing season. *Lateral buds* develop in the leaf axils, the angle between the stem and leaf petiole. On a winter twig they are located immediately above the leaf scars. The *terminal bud* forms at the end of the twig, and marks the end of last season's growth. Buds are covered by at least one, but usually two or more, protective bud scales. Larger buds enclose flowers or leaves and flowers, while smaller buds contain only leaves. In woody plants, all buds produce wood growth in addition to flowers and/or leaves. Also located within each terminal bud is the *apical meristem*, a region of actively dividing cells. Though dormant during winter, the apical meristem reactivates in spring and will produce the following year's growth. Below the terminal bud are several

blade

terminal bud

axillary bud

lenticel

node

petiole

internode

terminal bud scars

**Left** and **above** Buds enclose the tissues that produce the following year's growth. Encased within protective bud scales is the apical meristem, which produces new woody tissue, as well as a compact flower and/or leaf. In the spring, these tissues swell with new sap and force their way out of a bud, such as this sugar maple.

## What you can do

### Fool mother nature

Dormant tree twigs can be brought indoors to a warm room and their buds "forced" open by placing the twig in water. Wait until after December, since many Temperate-climate trees need a period of cold for their buds to open, ensuring that they do not mistakenly open during warm autumns. Many insect-pollinated trees such as serviceberry, apple,

and cherry produce impressive flowers, though the less conspicuous blossoms of wind-pollinated species, including oak, birch, maple, and willow, are also interesting, and the intricacy of unfolding leaves is a marvel to behold. You may wish to dissect an unopened bud with a razor blade, and try to recognize any of the structures within before they emerge.

scars encircling the stem, marking the point of attachment of last season's bud scales. Each interval between bud scale scars represents one year's growth. By counting these scars until you reach the parent branch, where the twig originated from a lateral bud, you can determine its age.

Another seasonal change illustrating periods of growth and dormancy are the annual rings on cut timber. Cambium, a layer of cells similar to those of the apical meristem, allows for the expansion of the trunk's girth to support the increasing weight resulting from stem elongation. New xylem tissue is laid down inside the cambium layer, and new phloem on the outside. When the cambium is first activated in spring, it forms relatively large, tubular *vessel elements* of xylem, the light-colored "spring wood." Later in the season, smaller vessel elements and more *tracheids*, a porous, non-tubular type of xylem tissue, are produced, resulting in darker-colored "summer wood." Both vessel elements and tracheids become impregnated with lignin and die soon after their formation, but they remain intact and functional as transport pipelines. The concentric circles of light and dark wood that result are called *annual rings*, each composed of one layer of spring wood and one layer of summer wood. Counting annual rings will accurately yield the tree's age when cut, and can often reveal much about the life of the tree. Events such as drought, fire, infestations, injury, and harvesting of surrounding timber all result in altered growth patterns.

**Above** Trees grow in girth as well as in height. A specialized layer of cells, the cambium, produces a new layer of vascular tissue each growing season, resulting in the annual rings visible on the end of cut timber. By counting these rings, you can determine the exact age of the tree.

# TAXONOMY: SIMPLICITY FROM CHAOS

Taxonomy is the science of identifying, naming, and classifying organisms. It is the discipline which puts order into an immensely diverse world and allows scientists to discuss any organism in the certainty that they are talking about the same one.

Common names are generally used in everyday conversation, but may not positively identify a particular species. Many plants and animals have more than one common name, and may be known by different names in different areas, and the same common name may be applied to different species. Clearly, the potential for confusion is great, with well over 350,000 plant species known and many more remaining to be discovered.

Contemporary scientists use a classification hierarchy to organize life forms into a series of categories arranged in order from general to specific relationships. They are, in order of increasing specificity: kingdom, division (or phylum, in the animal kingdom), class, order, family, genus, and species. Each of these is a collective unit composed of one or more groups from the next lower category. For example, a genus is a closely related group of species, and a family is a closely related group of genera.

While classification has always been a fairly simple affair, naming has not. By the beginning of the eighteenth century, the use of Latin in schools and universities was widespread, and it was customary to use descriptive Latin phrases to name plants and animals. All organisms were grouped into genera, and the descriptive phrase began with the name of the appropriate genus. All known mints, for example, belonged to the genus *Mentha*. The complete name for peppermint was "*Mentha floribus capitatus, foliis lanceolatis serratis subpetiolatis,* or "Mentha with flowers in a head, leaves lance-shaped, saw-toothed, with very short petioles." The closely related spearmint was named *Mentha floribus spicatis, foliis oblongis serratis,* which meant "Mentha with flowers in a spike, leaves oblong and saw-toothed." Though quite specific, this system was much too cumbersome to use efficiently.

In 1753, the Swedish naturalist Carolus Linnaeus introduced a two-word system of naming

*Caltha palustris* (**above**) and *Calta leptosepala* are both known as marsh marigold. Common plantain, *Plantago major* (**right**) is known by at least 45 other names in English alone.

organisms. It quickly replaced the older, clumsier method, and came to be known as the Binomial System of Nomenclature. It identifies individual species by linking the generic name with another word, frequently an adjective. All scientific names are Latin, although some have descriptive Greek roots. The first name is always capitalized, but never the second, and both are either underlined or italicized. When more than one member of the same genus is being discussed, once the generic name is given in full, it may be abbreviated when referred to again, as in *A. rubrum* for *Acer rubrum.*

# TREES AND SHRUBS

Technically, a shrub is a woody perennial branching at or near ground level, while a tree is a woody perennial with one main stem branching some distance above the ground. However, many contemporary field guides classify some small trees as shrubs, and some trees are naturally multi-stemmed, so the difference is somewhat arbitrary, but both have permanent woody frameworks that do not die back in winter.

The vast majority of trees and shrubs can be placed into one of two basic divisions. Division Coniferophyta, or conifers, includes needle-leaved trees that do not flower but produce their seeds in cones: pines, spruces, firs, hemlocks, cedars and redwoods, for example. The largest group of plants, Division Anthophyta, the flowering plants, includes most broad-leaved trees and shrubs. In addition, all

**Left** The quaking aspen is easily identified by its round, fine-toothed leaves which tremble in the slightest breeze.

**Top** and **above** The needle-like leaves of conifers, such as the eastern white pine and pitch pine, enable them to withstand extremes better than most deciduous trees.

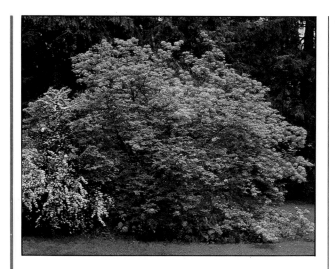

**Above** Shrubs, such as this flame azalea, are flowering woody plants, deciduous or evergreen, with several stems branching at or near the ground. Certain small trees with one main trunk may also be categorized as shrubs.

trees and shrubs in this division belong to Class Dicotyledonae, the dicots.

Like most plants, trees do not grow randomly, but need precise conditions to flourish, and when they find these conditions, grow profusely. Forest habitats are identified by their one or two dominant tree species, such as an oak-hickory forest or a boreal forest, which is composed primarily of black spruce, white spruce, and balsam fir. Naturalists know what type of conditions prevail in an oak-hickory forest, so they can also predict with some certainty the other plants, animals, climate, soil factors, and possibly even the landforms likely to be found there.

Trees and shrubs differ from herbaceous plants not only in their production of woody stem tissue, but also in their ability to produce bark, the protective outer "skin" that enables them to survive from decades to centuries. Inner bark refers to the phloem laid down by the cambium layer, while outer bark, the tough protective covering of cork tissue, is produced by a layer of cells immediately outside the phloem called the cork cambium. Bark reduces water loss and protects the stem against mechanical injury, bacterial or fungal infection, or infestation. In areas where fire is relatively common, some species have adapted to the threat by producing bark that is fire-resistant, and in some cases, nearly fire-proof.

## What you can do

**Take bark rubbings**
Making bark rubbings enables you to "collect" bark samples to study, and to compare the barks of different species, even those that do not grow near one another. You can add a bark rubbing to your record of a tree species, which may already include sketches, photographs, specimens of leaves and fruit, or notes on interesting or unique features. If possible, try to get a rubbing of one of the lower branches, which often have different patterns and textures to that of the trunk.

You need sticky tape, a large wax crayon, and strong but thin paper. Tape a piece of paper in position. Using the flat side of the crayon, rub slowly, making all strokes in the same direction. For future reference, label your rubbing with the tree's common and scientific names, your name, the date, and the tree's location.

# WILDFLOWERS AND GRASSES

Wildflowers are another arbitrary category of plants. All are, of course, members of the Class Anthophyta, the flowering plants, and include both monocots and dicots. By general definition, they grow without cultivation. Some have woody stems, but most are herbaceous. To complicate matters, certain shrubs are sometimes classified as wildflowers in field guides because of their blooms.

Wildflowers, like trees and shrubs, are a diverse group, with seemingly infinite combinations of flower and leaf shape, structure, color, arrangement, and other features. Flowers may be *radially symmetrical* (wheel-shaped, capable of

**Below** Black-eyed Susan and other members of the sunflower family produce composite flowers consisting of many disk and ray florets.

Radially-symmetrical or regular, flowers like purple trillium (**above**) are wheel-shaped and can be divided into two identical parts by numerous planes. Bilaterally-symmetrical, or irregular, flowers such as pink lady's slipper (**left**), can be divided into two mirror-image parts by only one plane.

being divided in half along more than one lengthwise plane), or *bilaterally symmetrical* (capable of being divided in half by only one lengthwise plane). The buttercup is radially symmetrical; the lady's slipper is bilaterally symmetrical. Some produce only one bloom, while others produce hundreds in one compact cluster. Their leaves may be *simple* (undivided), or *compound* (divided into *leaflets*). A large number of leaf shapes occur, such as *ovate* (egg-shaped), *lanceolate* (lance-shaped), *linear* (long and narrow), and others. Leaf *margins* (edges) may be *entire* (smooth), *lobed*, *undulate* (wavy), *serrate* (toothed), or a combination of these.

How does one put order into such an eclectic group of plants? A good field guide helps in identification but the real key is to become familiar with plant families. Families are handy divisions for learning about wildflowers because they are large enough to include plants with general similarities, yet small enough not to be vague and cumbersome.

**Left** One of the taller members of the grass family, giant reed is common in wet areas, especially in or near brackish water. Like all grasses, it flowers and produces seeds, but its primary method of reproduction is via spreading rootstocks.

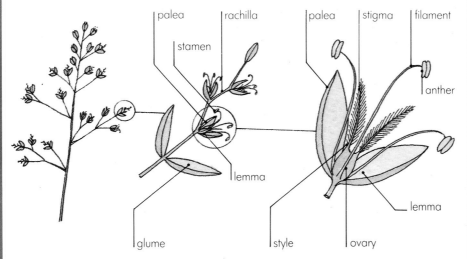

palea · rachilla · stamen · lemma · glume · palea · stigma · filament · anther · style · ovary · lemma

**Left** Many people do not recognize grasses as flowering plants because their flowers are often small and inconspicuous. Being wind-pollinated, they do not need large or showy blooms to attract pollinators.

More than one hundred families of wildflowers exist in temperate North America, but most species fit into about two dozen or so families. Learning the family traits listed in your field guide allows you to examine a flower and narrow the possibilities from many thousands to a small handful.

One family of flowering plants stands above the rest in terms of its significance to humanity: the grass family *Poaceae*. Although there are only about one-quarter the number of species in the grass family as there are in the sunflower family, *Compositae*, grasses are by far the most widely distributed family and the largest in terms of individual plants. They include all the cereal grains, such as corn, wheat, oats, rice, barley, and rye. In fact, nine of the ten most economically important plants in the world are grasses. More than one billion tons of cereals are harvested annually to supply more than half of the food needs of the world's human population.

Grasses are monocots, a class that represents approximately one-quarter of all flowering plants and also includes rushes, sedges, orchids, lilies and irises. They exhibit typical monocot traits, including parallel-veined leaves and flower parts in multiples of three. Grass flowers are highly specialized, unlike the rushes, another grass-like family with a more conventional flower structure. The calyx and corolla of grasses are reduced to tiny, inconspicuous scales, and the feathery stigmas effectively sift air-borne pollen from the wind. Grass leaves sheath the stem at their bases. Grass stems are cylindrical and hollow, major features distinguishing them from sedges, which are similar in appearance but have solid stems, triangular in cross-section.

# MOSSES, LIVERWORTS, FERNS, AND CLUB MOSSES

Mosses and liverworts belong to the Division Bryophyta. Bryophytes are the most primitive members of the plant kingdom. With no vascular system to supply water to their extremities, they must absorb water directly through their surface from their environment, and are hence low-growing plants of moist places never more than a couple of inches high. Most are soft and pliable, since they lack xylem and phloem tissue. Bryophytes are like amphibians, in that water is essential for fertilization to take place. However, only a thin film of water is needed for the plant's sperm to swim and find the egg.

### Liverworts

"Wort" means plant or herb. Liverworts are so named because some members of this group, the Class Hepaticae, grow as flattened lobes called *thalli*, somewhat resembling a human liver. Such lobes are common in only about one-fifth of the liverwort species, however. The rest are more "leafy" and superficially resemble the true mosses, except that liverwort "leaves" are scaly, and grow in two rows on a prostrate "stem", whereas the "leaves" of mosses grow spirally around an upright "stem". The lower surfaces of thalloid liverworts have numerous single-celled *rhizoids* that resemble tiny roots and function as anchors. Liverworts are particularly abundant in moist places where the light level is too low for competing flowering plants. Identification of individual species can be quite difficult.

### Mosses

Mosses are members of the Class Musci. Like liverworts, mosses only grow in moist places, or in areas that are damp part of the year. Moss "leaves" are attached to an axis, the "stem," which is anchored at the base by rhizoids. Mosses, like liverworts, must absorb water directly through their surfaces. Since the upright stems possess no xylem, they depend on water flowing up the outside of the plant by means of capillarity, the ability of a thin film of water to flow up a surface due to the tendency of water molecules to cling together.

Mosses are divided into three subclasses: peat mosses, true mosses, and rock mosses. By far the best known of these is a remarkable group of peat mosses belonging to the genus *Sphagnum*. Sphagnum mosses grow in very moist areas such as around the perimeter of lakes and on floating mats of vegetation in bogs. Like all mosses, they act as environmental sponges, absorbing water quickly and releasing it slowly, thus reducing flooding and erosion. Sphagnum mosses are particularly adept at this; a pound of dry peat moss will absorb 25 pounds of water. This property makes it an excellent soil conditioner in gardening, and it also adds *humus*, or organic

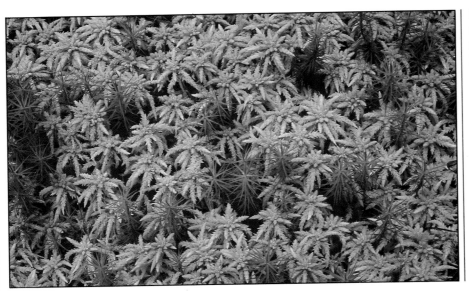

**Left** Common throughout northern North America, sphagnum mosses are found in bogs, along the shorelines of lakes and ponds, and on damp forest floors.

**Right** Liverworts are another non-vascular plant. With no xylem tissue to transport water throughout the plant, liverworts are confined to damp locations where they can maintain a thin film of water over the plant's surface.

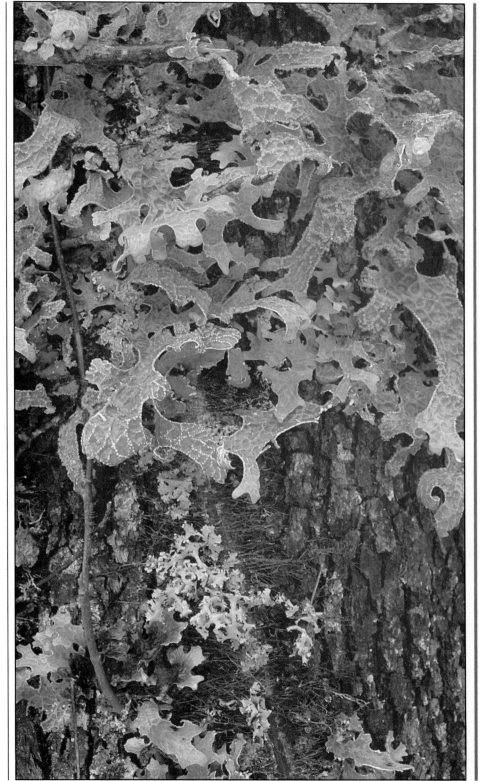

matter, to the soil. Also known for its antiseptic properties due to its natural acidity, sphagnum moss has been used as a poultice on wounds at least as far back as the Crimean War of 1854-1856.

## Club mosses

Club mosses are not really mosses. They belong to the Division Lycophyta, primitive non-flowering vascular plants, and as such differ from true mosses, which have no xylem or phloem. The two major genera are *Selaginella* and *Lycopodium.* Species of *Lycopodium* are also known as ground pines because they grow in forests and look superficially like tiny conifers. Their upright stems, less than one foot tall in temperate regions, grow from branching rhizomes which put down adventitious roots as they go. Club mosses reproduce asexually from spores produced on *strobili*, cone-like projections on the tops of plants, but they also have a sexual generation that is usually hidden below ground level.

## Ferns

Ferns have an undeserved reputation of being difficult to identify, and so are often ignored by novice naturalists in favor of wildflowers and trees. Though there are more than 11,000 fern species, the vast majority grow in the tropics, and it is simpler to learn the few dozen fern species found in temperate North America than the 10,000+ species of wildflowers in the same region.

Ferns are fairly advanced among non-flowering plants, having true roots, stems, and leaves. Their

**Left** Ferns begin their asexual (spore-bearing) generation as a tightly coiled structure commonly known as a fiddlehead. A familiar spring sight in many areas, fiddleheads arise from underground rhizomes, gradually unfurling into a frond. Certain ferns are evergreen, while others produce new fronds every year.

stems possess xylem and phloem vascular tissue, enabling them to grow to substantial heights. Many ferns spread by underground rhizomes, resulting in dense colonies of a single species. Fern leaves, called *fronds*, are often divided into leaflets, or *pinnae*, which themselves may also be divided, resulting in a lacy appearance. Henry David Thoreau, the nineteenth century author and naturalist, once stated that "God created ferns to show what he could do with leaves." Fern fronds first appear as tightly coiled "fiddleheads," which then unfurl and expand into the blades.

Like mosses, liverworts, and club mosses, ferns alternate between sexual and asexual reproduction and depend upon a thin film of water for the sexual portion of their life cycle. Mature fronds produce spores asexually in clusters called *sori,* which in many species are protected by individual flaps of tissue called *indusia.* Their pattern of development on the frond is often a key to identification. A wind-borne spore that lands on a favorable site produces root-like hairs anchoring it to the soil, and proceeds to grow into a small, flattened, heart-shaped plant known as a *prothallus*, the sexual portion of its life cycle. Regardless of the number of eggs fertilized, only one spore-bearing plant will grow from each prothallus, thus completing its life cycle.

**Left** Club mosses are common inhabitants of North American forest floors, and are usually found poking through the leaf litter.

**Above** Many ferns produce sori, or spore clusters, in patterns that vary according to species, on the undersides of fronds. Each sorus may be covered with a protective flap of tissue, called the indusium.

## What you can do

### Preserve mosses and liverworts

Mosses and liverworts contain lots of water, and must be dried thoroughly to preserve them. Place the specimen in a cheesecloth sack and hang it in a warm, dry area. At room temperature, the plant should be dry in 7-10 days. Store in a box or display case to prevent damage to delicate structures such as spore capsules. Place a small muslin bag of silica gel in the same box to help preserve your specimen. Dry the silica gel in an oven periodically to maintain its effectiveness. Label your specimen with its name (if known), location, and date. Mosses and liverworts may also be pressed, as described on pp52-3. They require less pressure, more changes of paper, and more time than wildflowers.

31

# ALGAE, FUNGI, AND LICHENS

Algae, members of the Kingdom Protista (which also includes protozoans), are among the most primitive organisms that can be considered plants, though they are no longer classified in the plant kingdom. Most are photosynthetic. They are single-celled or multi-celled, and often occur as filaments or colonies. Many are mobile, usually moving by means of whiplike "tails" called *flagella*. Long strands of kelp and other seaweeds cast up on the beach, green pond scum, and greenish or brownish film on the side of an aquarium are just a few forms of algae.

Aside from their infinite value as the base of most freshwater and marine food chains, algae also have human uses. One of the most extensively used products of algae is algin, produced from giant kelps and other brown algae. Algin is employed in the manufacture of many food products, beer, pharmaceuticals, latex paint, paper, and textiles. Another algae-derived material with wide applications is diatomaceous earth. This powdery, abrasive substance is quarried from massive deposits of these aquatic organisms where past geological events raised them above the sea level. Its abrasiveness is due to the glassy shells of diatoms, a type of golden-brown algae, which are composed of up to 95% silica, an ingredient of glass. Diatomaceous earth is used extensively in filtration systems, as high-temperature insulation,

**Above** Many species of microscopic algae grow in large colonies. Here, long strands of filamentous algae were left by receding floodwaters of a river polluted by fertilizing agents.

and in the manufacture of metal polishes, toothpaste, light-reflecting paint, and prefabricated construction panels.

## Fungi

Though not classified as plants, members of the Kingdom Fungi are nevertheless plant-like in many respects. Unlike most plants, however, fungi are not photosynthetic, but absorb their food in solution from their surroundings. They are members of a general group of organisms known as *saprophytes*, which gain their nutrition by decomposing dead

**Left** Mushrooms, such as this species of *Amanita*, are the visible spore-bearing parts of fungi. One of the two major groups of decomposers in nature, fungi absorb their food in solution, which requires that the major portion of the fungi grows inside its host or underground.

## What you can do

### Identify fungi

Fungi are much more difficult to identify than wildflowers, which have characteristic leaf shapes and floral types, with consistent arrangements and numbers of floral parts. You cannot always compare fungi with illustrations to determine their identity, since many species have look-alikes, and no single field guide has pictures of them all. If, however, you make careful observations regarding the fungus and record them in a field notebook, this information can then be compared with a reference book to narrow the possibilities. Here is a standard form you can fill out and keep for each new fungus you find. Doing so will sharpen your powers of observation and build your knowledge of fungi.

Name (once identified) _____
Location _____ Date _____
Nearby vegetation _____
Substrate (soil, wood, etc.) _____
Growth pattern (single, cluster, etc.) _____
Stem: Shape _____
     Size (length and diameter) _____
     Texture _____
     Shape of base _____
     Annulus _____
Cap: Shape _____
     Size _____
     Color _____
     Texture _____
     Odor _____
     Underside (gills or pores) _____
Gills: Color _____
     Attachment to stem _____

### Take spore prints

The color of spores and their arrangement in a spore print may provide a valuable clue to the identity of a mushroom. Permanent spore prints of mushrooms you've identified are useful additions to your field notes.

Cut the stem off a mature open mushroom and place the cap gill-side or pore-side down on a 3 × 5 index card (larger if necessary). You may need to use dark paper for light-colored spores. Cover with a bowl to exclude drafts and leave it for several hours or overnight. Afterwards, lift the bowl slowly and carefully remove the cap. The print will smudge easily, so to create a permanent record, spray with clear lacquer or artist's fixative, keeping the nozzle at least 18 inches from the print. Apply three coats and label the print with the name of the mushroom (if known), the location where found, and the date. Store your prints in envelopes for added protection.

organic matter. Fungi, along with bacteria, are nature's recyclers, without which continued life on earth would be impossible.

Most species of fungi familiar to the practical botanist belong to the Class Basidiomycetes, the club fungi. These include mushrooms, puffballs, shelf or bracket fungi and stinkhorns. The structures often recognized as "fungi" are just the fruiting bodies of the organism protruding above the surface in order to release spores into the atmosphere. The bulk of the fungi, a mass of thread-like *hyphae* known as a *mycelium*, remains hidden from view, embedded in the material from which the fruiting body protrudes. The mycelium secretes enzymes into its surroundings in order to break the material down into soluble substances which can then be absorbed directly into the cells of the hyphae.

Mushrooms, also called toadstools, are composed of tightly interwoven hyphae, forming a stalk and an umbrella-like cap. The stalk may have a ring, or *annulus*, the remnant of a membrane that once extended from the stalk to the cap but tore as the cap opened. In some species, the underside of the cap consists of membranous *gills* radiating from the center. These gills are covered with

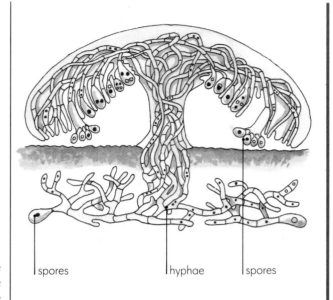

**Below** An emerging mushroom often leaves a ring of tissue, called the annulus, as the cap tears away from the stalk. Spores are produced in either gills or pores.

**Right** Spores fall from the gills or pores on the cap's underside, to be dispersed to suitable sites by wafting air currents.

button

developing basidiocarp

cap
gill
annulus
stalk

spores   hyphae   spores

tiny structures called *basidia*, which produce *basidiospores*. A large mushroom may produce several billion basidiospores over a few days, to be carried away on air currents. Some mushrooms produce their spores within miniscule pores instead of gills.

Another familiar type of fungi, shelf or bracket fungi, grows horizontally on dead wood. Bracket fungi shed their spores through gills or pores. Puffballs, which have no stalk, produce their spores internally. When disturbed, the puffball is compressed, expelling air and spores through a pore in the top and through breaks in the outer covering.

**Lichens**
These are a prime example of mutualism, a type of symbiotic relationship, for lichens actually consist of two different organisms. An alga and a fungus are combined in a spongy body called a *thallus*, which ranges from a fraction of an inch up to several feet in diameter. The alga produces food for both organisms, and the fungus absorbs and retains water and minerals for both, and protects the alga from harmful light intensities. The fungus also secretes a chemical that accelerates photosynthesis in the alga, so it can feed both organisms.

Lichens are loosely grouped into three categories based on their growth forms. Crustose lichens frequently form brightly colored crusty patches, firmly attached to rocks and tree bark. Foliose lichens have leafy, often wrinkled, overlapping thalli, loosely attached to trees or rocks. The thalli of fruticose lichens are cylindrical and branched, often resembling miniature shrubs.

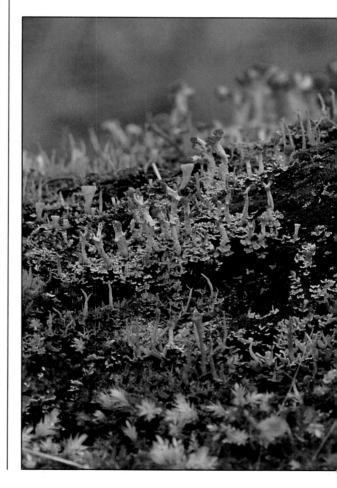

Their mass is attached to the ground or to vegetation only at one point, and sometimes hangs from branches. Although lichens are frequently attached to other plants, they do not parasitize them in any way.

Lichens are incredibly hardy, and grow under some of the most extreme conditions on earth. They can withstand prolonged periods of drought interspersed with wet spells. When dry, the upper layer of the thallus becomes opaque, effectively shutting down photosynthesis in the alga and plunging the lichen into dormancy. Lichens grow quite slowly, at a maximum rate of one-half inch per year. Some have been estimated to be 4,500 years old and are still growing. One condition they cannot tolerate, however, is air pollution, particularly sulfur dioxide. It is possible, in fact, to calculate the amount of sulfur dioxide in the air above a given area simply by mapping the occurrence or absence of certain lichen species.

**Above** The cup-shaped, spore-bearing structures of pixie cup lichen depend on a direct hit by a raindrop to dislodge their spores and disperse them in all directions.

fungal cells     algal cells

thread-like fungal cells

**Left** British soldiers, a lichen named for the red fruiting body, similar in color to the uniforms worn by British soldiers during the Revolutionary War, is common east of the Rocky Mountains.

**Above** Lichens are fine examples of mutualism, a relationship in which both organisms benefit. This is a cross-section of a typical foliose lichen, showing the algal cells underlying a layer of fungal cells which protect the algal cells and regulate the light reaching them.

# ECOLOGICAL SUCCESSION

Ecological succession is the process by which vegetative communities develop. It is also the land's way of healing itself following a disturbance. All disturbances, whether logging, fire, glaciers or volcano eruptions, eventually come to an end. As soon as they do, the process of ecological succession begins. The stage at which it begins and the time needed to re-establish a stable community both depend on the severity of the disturbance.

Succession is an orderly transition from one plant community to another. The entire series of communities is called a *sere*, and each intermediate step is called a *seral stage*. In each seral stage except the final one, the dominant plants thrive, but at the same time alter the local growing conditions, making them more favorable for their successors than for themselves. As this occurs, *pioneer species*, the first plants of the next seral stage, begin to move in through their individual means of dispersal, further altering the habitat. The rate of succession slows with each stage, until a stable, self-maintaining stage, or *climax community*, is achieved. At this point, the area undergoes no more major changes until another disturbance takes place.

*Primary succession* begins in areas devoid of and unchanged by other organisms, such as bare rock exposed by glacial scouring or geological upheaval, new rock formed by volcanic eruptions or newly formed sand dunes. In these cases the initial stage is called a *xerosere*. Primary succession also occurs at the edge of a lake or pond as it gradually fills with sediment, and is then referred to as a *hydrosere*. Soil formation occurs on bare rock through the process of *weathering*, in which rock is broken into increasingly smaller pieces. Physical weathering is caused by forces such as

alternate freezing and thawing of water in tiny fissures in the rock's surface. As water freezes, it expands, acting as a wedge to widen the crack and also forming new ones. When the ice thaws, water seeps farther into the cracks, and the process is repeated again.

Chemical weathering also aids soil formation. Lichens are typically the first plants to colonize a rock. Their acidic secretions slowly dissolve the rock, widening fissures, creating depressions, and liberating small particles. Chemical weathering also results from rainwater which may become mildly acidic because of atmospheric conditions or from draining over soluble materials. Lichens also help trap debris washed or blown over the rock, or debris may settle in cracks and depressions on its own, creating little pockets of sediment that retain moisture for short periods, encouraging the growth of small annual plants.

Soil, however, is more than pulverized rock. A very important component is *humus*, organic material derived from decaying plants and animals. Humus greatly increases the water retention of soil, and also provides a rich source of nutrients for plant growth. Each generation of plants adds more humus to the soil. In primary

**Below** A classic example of secondary ecological succession is the transformation of an abandoned field to a mature climax forest. Each seral stage, excluding the climax community, alters the habitat by increasing humus, water retention, and shade, thus creating conditions more suitable for plants of the succeeding stage than for the current inhabitants.

bare field | grassland 1-10 years | grass-shrub 10-25 years

**Left** Sumacs are common pioneers of the shrub-sapling stage of ecological succession. This staghorn sumac is abundant in the Northeast. Smooth sumac and shining sumac are more widespread, occurring throughout the eastern United States.

**Right** Red maple and gray birch are two common pioneer trees in abandoned fields. Red maple is found throughout the eastern half of the continent, while the range of gray birch is limited to the Northeast.

succession, the increase in soil depth is very gradual; it may take up to 10,000 years for an inch of topsoil to form. In the meantime, increasing soil depth and the accompanying increase in soil moisture and organic matter favors the germination of certain annual species, followed in time by perennial grasses, mosses, and herbaceous perennials, each making their own contribution to the soil buildup. Under the best of conditions, these will be followed by shrubs, small trees, and finally a mature forest.

Obviously, primary succession is a very long process. In contrast, *secondary succession*, which occurs following a disturbance to an area that already supported an advanced seral stage, is much quicker. In most cases, soil is already well established in the area. One familiar example is an abandoned farm field. Once the farmer ceases to work the field, grasses and annual plants quickly

invade during the next growing season. Typically these are the so-called "weeds," exotic species that have adapted over thousands of years to take advantage of human environmental disruptions in Europe and Asia. Following the annuals are perennials, many of which are also exotics, then shrubs, shade-intolerant trees, and finally shade-tolerant trees form a climax forest.

There are many variations on the theme of succession, some of which are examined in greater depth later in this book. Generally, however, species composition changes continuously until a climax community is reached, but the change is usually much more rapid in the early stages of secondary succession. Also, the total number of species present increases in the earlier stages of succession, but tends to stabilize in the later stages. Finally, the end result is a climax community that is stable and self-maintaining.

pine forest 25-100 years                    oak-hickory forest climax 100 plus years

# BOTANY IN ACTION
## THE TOOLS

The sage advice that one should use the right tool for the job applies to scientists as well as to carpenters and mechanics. You can study botany without tools, but you will advance much farther and faster by using a few basic ones. Some specialized items may have to be purchased through a biological supply house, but most of what you need can be had sooner and cheaper from retail stores. On the right is a basic list of those items a practical botanist will find most useful.

### Field guides

Field guides providing clear illustrations, which include characteristic identifying features, are invaluable in identifying and learning about new plants. Guides also limit the number of possibilities by listing the plant's likely geographic range and habitats. Finally, they give a clear physical description of the plant, and include an illustrated glossary to explain unfamiliar terms. Any field guide you purchase should have these features. There are many good field guides, although none can cover North American botany in its entirety.

Unfortunately, learning often ceases once a plant is identified, but it doesn't have to be so. After identifying a plant, read the text for that species again. Field guides often contain fascinating details about folklore, medicinal uses, historical associations and edible parts of the plant. Also, visit your local library regularly and look up your newest botanical acquaintances. Knowing plants' cultural and natural histories reveals the many ways in which plants interact with the rest of their world.

### Keys

Identification keys, sometimes known as dichotomous keys, are excellent companions to field guides, but harder to obtain. "Dichotomous" means divided or dividing into two parts. At each step, the key presents two, or sometimes more, characteristics, only one of which will apply to the organism under scrutiny. Depending on the option selected, you are directed to another section of the key to repeat the process until, finally, the plant's or animal's identity is revealed. Because keys only reveal the identity, you should follow this up by

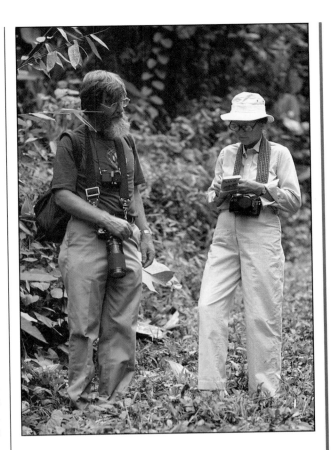

**Above** Copious note-taking in the field is an invaluable practice. Personal observations stick with you much longer than anything you read.

reading about the plant in a field guide.

Keys are normally available only for higher plants, such as trees, wildflowers, and ferns. They are sometimes found in bookstores, but you can often obtain them from the botany department of your local university, from university bookstores, or from a nature center. The "Finder" series is a practical set of keys in booklet form available in many bookstores, or from Nature Study Guild Publishers, Box 972, Berkeley, California, 94701.

### Field notebook

A medium-sized, unlined notebook, about 4 × 7 inches, is a good compromise between convenience and size. It should be strongly bound, and have high-quality paper that will not tear easily. Ziploc bags make tough, waterproof storage cases for your notebook in the field. (Use them for maps, field guides, and identification keys as well.)

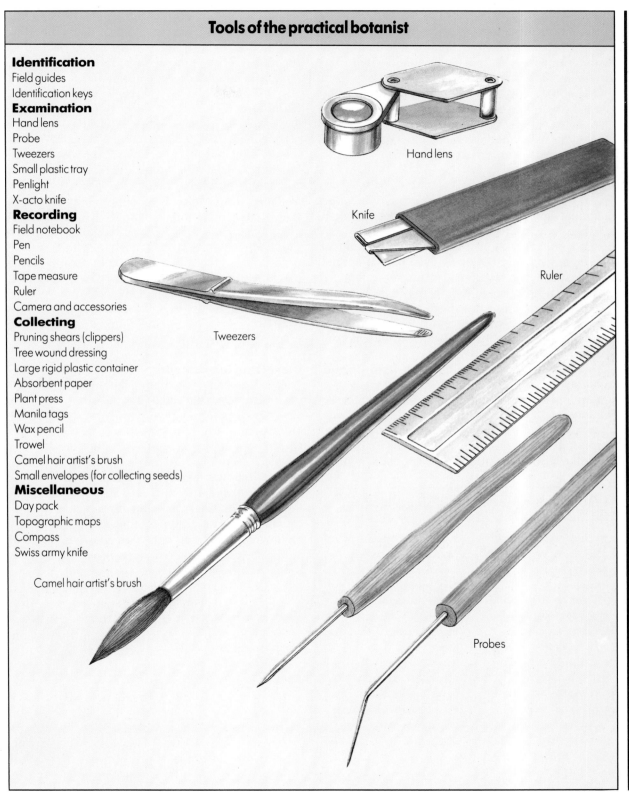

## Tools of the practical botanist

**Identification**
Field guides
Identification keys
**Examination**
Hand lens
Probe
Tweezers
Small plastic tray
Penlight
X-acto knife
**Recording**
Field notebook
Pen
Pencils
Tape measure
Ruler
Camera and accessories
**Collecting**
Pruning shears (clippers)
Tree wound dressing
Large rigid plastic container
Absorbent paper
Plant press
Manila tags
Wax pencil
Trowel
Camel hair artist's brush
Small envelopes (for collecting seeds)
**Miscellaneous**
Day pack
Topographic maps
Compass
Swiss army knife

Camel hair artist's brush

Hand lens

Knife

Tweezers

Ruler

Probes

## Photography

Probably the best way for practical botanists to "collect" specimens is to photograph them. It is faster, simpler, and, most importantly, more environmentally sound than removing plants from their habitats and preserving them. Photography is not the daunting endeavor it once was, especially with today's auto-everything cameras. The 35mm single-lens reflex models are the most versatile and have the most accessories (see pp46-51).

## Collecting

When collecting wild plants, you must use good judgment and follow ethical guidelines. Humankind has long since passed the point where we can do as we wish without regard for environmental consequences, and removing even part of a plant may destroy it or interfere with its reproduction. Obviously no ecological Armageddon will befall us for simply removing a few daisies and butter-cups from a meadow. However, the rules listed below ensure that your actions will have minimal consequences.

To carry specimens home, use a rigid plastic container, such as those sold in the housewares department of supermarkets or department stores. The large, rectangular, airtight models work best. Layer specimens between sheets of paper, and tie a manila tag to each one with the collection date and specimen number written in wax pencil, which remains legible even when wet. Record the specimen number and date in your field notebook, together with the plant's name, if known, plus location, soil type (moist, dry, sandy, loamy, rocky, etc.), and other pertinent information.

## Hand lens

A good-quality hand lens is indispensable to the practical botanist. It aids identification and reveals minute details that help you understand the function and admire the beauty of structures that you might otherwise overlook. They are usually available from a biological supply house, though they are occasionally sold elsewhere. A magnification of 8× to 10× is optimal, but some models have several glass elements that can be used independently or combined to obtain varying magnifications. To view an object with a hand lens, hold the lens about two inches from your eye, then slowly bring the object into focus. Hand lenses are invariably dropped in the field, so tie brightly colored yarn to them so you can find them again.

## Dissecting instruments

These are useful in separating minute structures for observation and for sketching. Ordinary, narrow-jaws tweezers from a pharmacy work well. Probes are available from biological supply houses, but you can make one by taping a stout needle to a six-inch section of quarter-inch wooden dowel, sold in hardware stores. A small plastic tray is useful for examining and dissecting specimens. In low-light situations, a small pocket flashlight is valuable for examining details. An X-acto hobby knife makes clean cuts for viewing internal structures. Use an old toothbrush holder to transport the probe and X-acto knife safely.

### Guidelines for responsible collecting

- Unless you are building a collection for serious study, take only the most common species.
- Collect only plants you can positively identify in the field. It is your responsibility to avoid taking threatened or endangered species. Your state or provincial conservation department can provide lists of the endangered species in your particular area.
- Do not remove the whole plant if part will suffice.
- When removing part of a plant, use sharp pruning shears to minimize trauma. Seal wounds on woody plants with tree wound dressing, available at hardware stores and garden shops.
- If you must remove an entire plant, replace the soil as well as you can.
- If you collect seeds, take only a few from one or two plants.

**Right** Hold the lens about two inches from your eye and bring the specimen to about the same distance from the lens.

# STARTING AROUND HOME

One of the best ways to fuel your new-found interest in botany is to examine the botanical goings-on around your home: the "weeds" you ignored for all of these years, the trees whose identities you always meant to learn but didn't, and the mosses and lichens you just plain didn't see before.

## Taking inventory

Some educators deplore listing species as counter-productive to learning, assuming that interest wanes once you attach a name to an organism, but the opposite can be true. Each new addition to the list of plants around home reinforces your interest, and just when you think that you've listed every plant, what a joy it is to discover a new species! You can then investigate how it got there, when, and why; whether it is an annual, biennial, or perennial; or even find a possible parent plant by venturing a little farther afield. If it is a flowering plant, you can discover when it will flower and for how long, what the fruit looks like, and what insects, birds, or mammals it might attract. These questions and many others may come to mind with each new discovery you make.

## Where to look?

An abandoned vegetable garden is a prime location for exotic wildflowers seeking disturbed soil in which to quickly put down roots before their competitors do. The waste soil along the roadside is another favorite habitat of theirs. A well maintained flower garden is also a challenge, but since you planted the flowers and presumably know their names, the challenge is not to identify them but to place them in their proper families. This can be formidable when dealing with selectively bred domestics, but the family descriptions in a wildflower guide may help. Trees are obvious subjects. Interesting moss is often found in the protected niches between exposed tree roots. Moist, shady, undisturbed places harbor moss, and maybe ferns or liverworts. Lichens colonize tree bark and exposed rocks and bricks, but they are slow growers and intolerant of air pollution, so they may be entirely absent. Even a puddle under a rain spout is likely to host a thriving colony of algae.

Ironically, the largest expanse of vegetation likely to be around your home, the lawn, is also

**Above** Your own yard or a nearby city park both offer more botanizing opportunities than you might think. Even the ubiquitous dandelion proves a fascinating specimen.

41

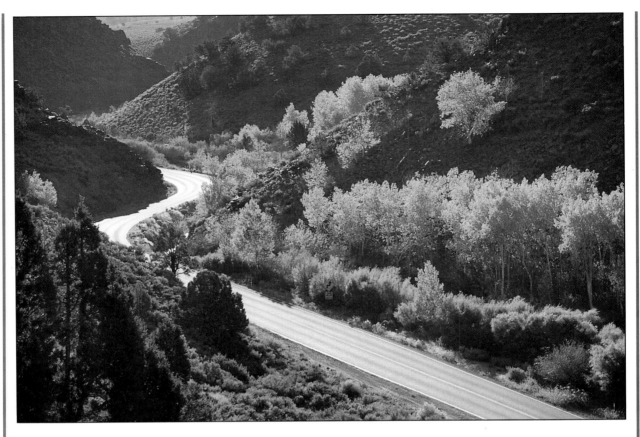

botanically monotonous. It is a monoculture, an artificial habitat composed primarily of one dominant plant type that is expensive to maintain in terms of time and energy. Monocultures are unstable, and invariably diversify once the forces maintaining them are eliminated. To demonstrate this, leave a small patch of lawn undisturbed for a season and observe. Not only will you notice that the grass grows tall and flowers, sometimes confirming the existence of more than one species of grass, but that members of other families become evident as well. Some, like common dandelion, bluets, and common plantain, may have been there all along but were held in check by the lawn mower. Others are pioneer species, able to establish themselves only in the absence of herbicides and the motorized whirling dervish.

### When to look

Any time is the right time. Spring reveals new growth, buds open, leaves unfurl, flowers blossom, and shoots elongate. Summer is the season of maturity, when late bloomers flower and the fruits

**Above** Many seasonal changes occur in autumn as plants prepare for winter. Here, the brilliant fall foliage of quaking aspens decorates a mountain road in California.

of early bloomers begin to ripen. As seeds develop, examine them and try to guess their method of dispersal. In the fall, plants begin preparing for their dormant period, and deciduous leaves change color. You can record when the first leaves begin to change, whether the same plants change color first every year, whether the foliage of one plant turns the same color every year, and what conditions produce the most brilliant colors. In winter, you can focus on woody plants and evergreens, but the dried stems and seed heads of last season's herbs also beckon, as do lichens on rocks and bracket fungi on dead trees.

It's fascinating to observe the same plants on a daily basis and note the changes in your field notebook; referring to these notes in future seasons will remind you of upcoming events and you can then look in the right place at the right time to witness them.

## Your field notebook

Field guides and identification keys aid identification and provide excellent background information, but *you will learn more about plants, and retain more of what you learn, from your own detailed observations than you will from reading about them!* Notes on anything you find interesting or significant serve you for the rest of your life. Basic information on each page should include the date, departure and return times, weather conditions, temperature, and locations and habitats visited.

Always record observations on the spot. If you trust them to memory, important details are lost. Even a short note with a few key words will jog your memory, and you can expand upon it later. Always include sketches with your notes. However crude, sketches are great reminders of exact details, such as leaf shape and arrangement, sizes, and flower structure.

A field notebook's value is enhanced by keeping a loose-leaf diary or logbook at home, into which you can transfer your notes, reorganize and expand them, and co-relate them with your readings and past observations. Do this religiously after each excursion, and you will amass a body of knowledge that is unique; some of it will not be found in field guides, and may never have been recorded before.

Don't expect to learn everything about a particular species on your first encounter. Think of each one as a jigsaw puzzle with the pieces askew; with each rendezvous, you can put a few more pieces in place. Gradually, over weeks, months, or even years, a picture begins to emerge. The background of the picture, too, becomes more distinct as you learn more about how the plant interacts with its surroundings. Keeping a field notebook allows you to do this; without it, many of the puzzle pieces are displaced before you chance upon that species again.

## Cataloguing

As well as a notebook and in place of a logbook, you may find it useful to start an index card file on the species you come across. Use one card per discovery and record its name, date found, relevant information, and the page number of your notebook on which you refer to it. Number each card and use the corresponding number to identify photographs, specimens, and notebook entries. It is easier to have notes on file this way than to search through notebooks for information.

**Above** and **right** The combination of a meticulously-kept field notebook and a detailed index card file is invaluable to the botanist.

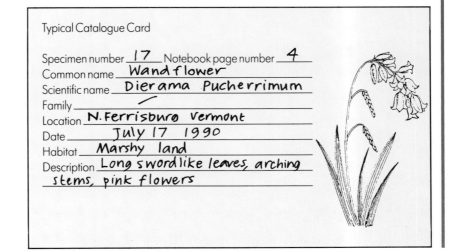

Typical Catalogue Card

Specimen number __17__ Notebook page number __4__
Common name __Wandflower__
Scientific name __Dierama Pucherrimum__
Family _____
Location __N. Ferrisburg Vermont__
Date __July 17 1990__
Habitat __Marshy land__
Description __Long swordlike leaves, arching stems, pink flowers__

# SKETCHING

Sketches should become an integral part of your field notebook, since your mind relates to pictures better than it does to words. Even the crudest sketch takes you back to the time you made it, and your mind will fill in the details. Drawing skills, luckily, improve with practice. The value of a sketch is not measured aesthetically; its value lies in what you remember from it.

Sketching trains you in precise observation, a skill critical to any naturalist. If you overlook details while drawing from a model, you will realize quickly that something is absent and, almost subconsciously, begin searching the drawing for the missing features. Again, quality is not important, but attention to detail is. A sketch does not have to include the entire plant. Often, detailed illustrations of different parts of the plant, together with a rough diagram to show how the parts are arranged, are more instructional than a rendition of the whole organism, especially if it is large.

Before drawing a plant, try to answer five basic questions about its construction.

### What are its roots like?

Some plants have fibrous roots, some have taproots, and some have both. Adventitious roots may be present and some plants have no true roots at all. Some plants have individual root systems, while others share a spreading root system. Anchor each plant in your drawings in the way it grows in nature. Draw roots from the top down to portray their tapering and probing nature.

### How do its stems grow?

Stems can be straight or branched, long or short, erect, arching, or trailing. Some plants have stout stems, others are slender and willowy. Depict these qualities in your drawings, recording, too, the shape and location of buds. Draw stems from their base upward to capture their tapering shape.

### Does it have leaves, and if so, what are they like?

Look at their shape, margins, texture, position, and vein pattern. Leaf arrangement may be alternate, opposite, whorled, or basal.

### How are flowers, fruits, or seed pods attached?

Note whether they are solitary or grow in clusters. Observe their location on the stem. Examine the flowers with your hand lens and move their parts around with a probe in order to see their exact shapes and arrangement.

### Are there any obvious tropisms?

Plants move as surely as animals do; they just move differently and for different reasons. Observe these movements and try to convey the impression of

**Right** To achieve an accurate representation, study a plant thoroughly before sketching and try to discern the direction in which each part moves or grows. Start at the base of that part and sketch the lines running in the same direction.

**Left** True to the maxim, "a picture is worth a thousand words" sketching sharpens your powers of observation and helps you recall important details later. A useful sketch can be rough, or well finished.

them in your sketches. Growing plants move when stimulated by light, gravity, or touch; such movements are called tropisms.

Geotropisms are movements stimulated by gravity. A root growing down into the soil is an example of positive geotropism. New shoots reaching up out of the soil demonstrate negative geotropism. To illustrate these, use downward strokes of your pencil when drawing roots, upward strokes when drawing sprouts.

Once above ground, plant stems and leaves move in response to the presence or absence of light. Such movements are called phototropisms. Herbaceous plants and young woody plants in semi-shaded areas move every which way to reach light, both stems and leaves bending toward the light source. To show this, draw the stem in the direction of the light source, then sketch the leaves at right angles to the light. Crowded trees grow straight and tall, reaching for a sunny spot in the forest canopy. Use upward strokes to depict the effect of reaching for light. Conversely, in open areas, a plant's stems and leaves tend to spread out evenly in all directions.

Plant movements in response to touch are called thigmotropisms: tendrils of bean plants and grape vines, for example. Draw free tendrils with a random, wandering line, as if they were feeling for an anchor. Once they touch a stationary object, tendrils wrap tightly around it, which can be depicted with a tight spiraling line. The twining climb of some vines, best illustrated with a weaving or spiraling line, is due to the stem's bending in response to the touch of its support while also bending toward the light and away from gravity.

# PRACTICAL PHOTOGRAPHY

For practical botanists, there is only one group of cameras to seriously consider; the 35mm single-lens reflex (SLR) models *with interchangeable lenses* offer the best compromise between quality, versatility, convenience, ease of operation, and cost. They are the overwhelming choice of nature photographers, including top professionals, around the world.

The quality of photographs taken by a competent photographer using a 35mm SLR camera is difficult to beat. In terms of versatility, 35mm SLRs are second to none, and possible subjects range from the microscopic to the astronomical. Simply by changing lenses, you can go from shooting close-ups of a buttercup to taking telephoto shots of a skittish songbird in a matter of seconds. They are also light enough to go anywhere. Ease of operation varies, but the newest auto-focus, auto-exposure cameras are literally as simple as point-and-shoot, although this by itself does not guarantee a good photograph. Finally, the cost of 35mm cameras and basic accessories is well within most budgets. Second-hand cameras in good condition can often be found in camera shops or through classified ads, but always have any second-hand equipment examined by a qualified camera repairman before purchasing it.

The choice of brand is largely a matter of personal preference. For background information, write to the major photography magazines and request their field test reports on models you are considering. These magazines also publish annual buyer's guides, which show what's available. Note the quality and variety of lenses and accessories available for different brands, but you needn't buy top-of-the-line equipment to achieve quality results. Remember the story of the photographer and the writer who met at a party. "I saw your exhibit at the gallery last week," said the writer. "You must have a very good camera!" To which the photographer replied, "Why, thank you. By the way, I really enjoyed your latest novel. You must have a very good typewriter!"

Certain accessories are quite useful to the practical botanist, others are less so. Lenses are labeled by their focal length, which in turn determines their perspective. Most cameras come with a standard 50mm lens, though you can purchase the camera body alone and select your own lenses. A 50mm lens gives roughly the same perspective, or angle of view, as the human eye.

Wide-angle lenses have a focal length of less than 50mm. These provide a wider field of view than seen by the human eye, and consequently subjects appear smaller, although the difference is negligible until you get down to a focal length of 35mm or less. Wide-angle lenses are useful for photographing landscapes, habitats, and large subjects at a close distance.

At the other extreme are telephoto lenses, with focal lengths from 50mm to 1,000mm or more. Only medium-length telephoto lenses, up to approximately 200mm, have any practical application in botany. Good quality longer lenses are

## Features to look for when selecting a camera

| Mandatory | Optional |
|---|---|
| Single-lens reflex | Auto-exposure with manual override |
| Interchangeable lenses | |
| Depth-of-field preview | Auto-focus with manual override |
| Built-in light meter | |
| Self-timer | Motor drive |
| | Dedicated TTL flash capability |
| | Auto-rewind |
| | Lock-up mirror |
| | Interchangeable focusing screens |

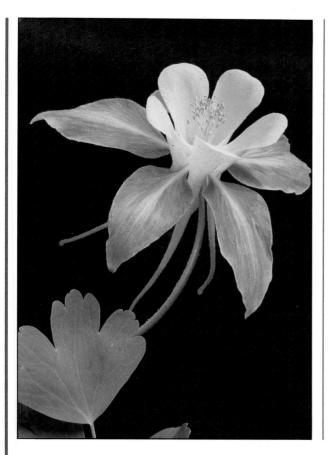

prohibitively expensive, heavy to carry and nearly impossible to hold still enough for a clear image without using a tripod. Telephoto lenses provide a narrower field of view, and subjects appear larger than when seen by the unaided eye. They are used primarily when you cannot get as close to your subject as you wish; or in order to isolate it and remove a cluttered foreground.

High-quality zoom lenses, providing variable focal lengths, are extremely practical for field work. The entire range of focal lengths from about 24mm up to 210mm can be covered with just two lenses, and in some cases even one lens suffices. This leaves you relatively unencumbered and able to carry other gear. By adjusting the focal length, you can compose a photograph exactly as you want it without having to move the camera closer to or farther from the subject.

Close-up equipment is highly useful in botanical photography, revealing a whole world of minute and fascinating detail. Macro-lenses can be used at their designated focal length, but you can also continuously focus down to close distances, usually a few inches. They do double duty, and many photographers prefer to purchase a 55mm macro-lens instead of the standard 50mm lens offered with the camera body. Macro-lenses come in a variety of focal lengths, the major difference

**Above** A macro lens can focus closer than a standard lens of the same focal length, so that the image of the subject on the film is larger. The same effect can be achieved by mounting extension tubes or a bellows between any standard lens and the camera body.

**Right** These two photographs, taken at the same distance from the subject, illustrate the difference in perspective between a 50mm lens, left, and a wide-angle lens (24mm in this case) at right. As the focal length decreases, image size decreases and range of focus, called depth-of-field, increases at any given aperture, and vice versa.

47

being how close you must be to the subject to achieve maximum magnification. The best macro-lenses give 1:1 reproduction; the image on the frame of film is the same size as the actual subject. The same results possible with macro-lenses can be achieved with standard lenses by adding dead air space between the camera body and the lens, usually by means of extension tubes or bellows. Extension tubes are much less expensive and more practical to use, but offer somewhat less versatility in achieving a specific image size. Regardless of the close-up equipment used, your image quality will be greatly improved with the use of a tripod.

## Film types

Film types are nearly as varied as camera models. What's right for you depends on how you want to use your images, the conditions under which you are shooting, and budget. Print films are developed into negatives, from which a print is made on light-sensitive photographic paper. Prints are easy
· to display and view, either in an album, or framed on a wall. Black-and-white prints produce an accurate representation of form and texture, but with such a rich spectrum of colors in the plant kingdom, you cannot achieve a complete portrayal of a plant in black and white. Color prints are more aesthetically pleasing and more accurately portray natural subjects than do black-and-white prints, but they are also the most expensive film to develop, thus limiting botanists on a tight budget.

Color-slide films, also known as color reversal films, are the workhorse of professional nature photographers, especially those shooting for publication, since transparencies (and black-and-white, to a lesser extent) are used almost exclusively in publishing. Transparencies cannot be viewed easily without a projector, slide viewer, or a hand lens and light table. Their major application, aside from publishing, is in illustrating lectures. Slide film is much less expensive to develop than color print film, a boon to the botanist on a budget. You can also have prints made from slides at a custom photo lab, and although it costs more per picture than print film, you can afford to experiment with different exposures and compositions and print only those you like.

The other major variable associated with films is light sensitivity, better known as film speed and denoted by an ASA (American Standards Association) number. The higher the ASA number,

the faster, or more light sensitive, is the film. Faster films require a faster shutter speed *or* a smaller lens opening under a given light intensity than do slower films. Greater light sensitivity is achieved by making the grains on the film emulsion larger, consequently photographs produced with faster films are more grainy than those produced with slower films; the lower the ASA number, the sharper the image. For this reason, publishers generally will not consider using images produced on film rated higher than 100 ASA. High-speed films are most useful under low light conditions without a flash, or when you want to use a very fast shutter speed to freeze movement.

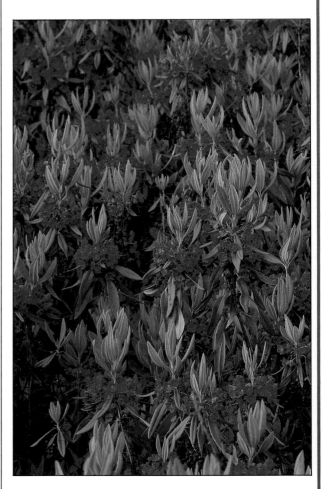

**Above** Slower films, designated by a low ASA number (which range from 25 to 1000) are less sensitive to light than fast film, but yield photographs of superior clarity, highly favored for publication. This sheep laurel was photographed with 25 ASA Kodachrome.

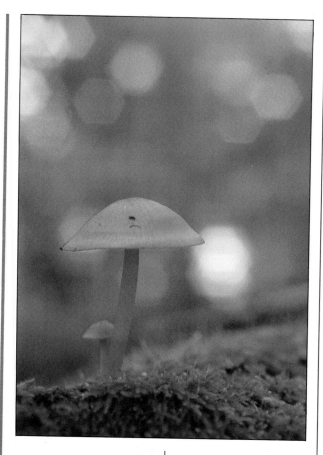

slow trickle takes longer than opening the faucet all the way. If too much water is added, the bucket overflows; if too little, it is not as full as you wish. Correspondingly, correct exposure requires the use of a longer shutter speed with a small aperture than with a large one, and vice versa. Too much light results in overexposure with washed-out highlights, and too little light results in an underexposed image.

Whether or not to use electronic flash depends on several factors. For a natural-looking photograph, try to use the natural light available. Bright overhead sunlight creates harsh, unappealing shadows, but on smaller subjects, shadows can be softened by using reflectors made of cardboard covered with crinkled aluminum foil. Shadows may also be softened by constructing a light-diffusing lean-to from translucent sheets of plastic, such as those used to cover fluorescent light fixtures. Low natural light requires a large aperture, a slow shutter speed, or

**Below** This side-flowered miterwort was photographed using natural light, right, and electronic flash, left. An electronic flash lets you use a smaller aperture, thus increasing the range of crisp focus, or depth-of-field. The smaller aperture, in turn, darkens the background and isolates the subject, often a desirable effect.

**Above** Faster films are useful in low light conditions, where electronic flash is impossible or undesirable. The large grains in the film emulsion that enhance light sensitivity also result in grainy photos, as this image of a mushroom, photographed with 400 ASA Ektachrome, shows.

## Exposure

Whether you use natural light or electronic flash depends on the effects you wish to obtain, the amount of natural light available, and on how much your subject is moving. A photograph records light. To achieve proper exposure, the correct amount of light must reach the film. This is a function of the combined shutter speed and size of the lens opening, called the aperture or f-stop. Modern 35mm cameras have built-in light meters that measure the amount of light reaching the film. Most cameras can use this information to calculate the correct aperture for a given shutter speed, or vice versa; some will calculate both.

Getting the correct exposure is like trying to fill a bucket exactly to the top with water from a faucet. A

**Above** These photographs of puffballs illustrate the effects of natural light, left, versus electronic flash, and the resulting greater depth-of-field, right.

both. Slower shutter speeds require a tripod to attain sharp focus, but any movement of your subject effectively prohibits slow shutter speeds, even with a tripod. In these cases, or to darken the background and emphasize the subject, electronic flash is the best method. Flash also fills in harsh shadows, freezes movement, and lets you use a smaller aperture to increase depth-of-field.

## Focus

Another function of aperture size is depth-of-field, the area in focus within a certain range of distances from the camera. Using a given lens, a smaller aperture yields a greater depth-of-field than a larger aperture. To emphasize a subject by focusing on it but not the background or foreground, use a larger aperture and a faster shutter speed. For more depth-of-field, to portray a plant in its natural habitat, for instance, use a small aperture, and a correspondingly slow shutter speed. Focal length of a lens also affects the depth-of-field. Shorter focal lengths yield greater depth-of-field than longer focal lengths. Most lenses have a scale showing your depth-of-field in feet and meters from the

## Recommended photographic equipment for the practical botanist

| **Option 1** | **Option 2** |
|---|---|
| 35mm SLR camera body | 35mm SLR camera body |
| 28mm lens | 28-70mm zoom lens |
| 55mm macro-lens | 70-210mm zoom lens |
| 105mm macro-lens | Extension tubes |
| 200mm lens | Warming filters |
| Extension tubes | Polarizing filters |
| Warming filters | Electronic flash |
| Polarizing filters | Tripod |
| Electronic flash | Cable release |
| Tripod | Reflector |
| Cable release | Diffuser |
| Reflector | |
| Diffuser | |

camera, so you can calculate exactly which parts of your photographs will be in focus.

A sturdy tripod is the most effective accessory for improving the quality of your photographs, since most blurred images result not from poor focusing, but from camera movement. Although a tripod can improve sharpness at any shutter speed, the universal rule of thumb is not to hand-hold a camera when shooting at less than the reciprocal of the focal length of the lens. Put simply, when using a 50mm lens, you should use a tripod or other steady support if your shutter speed is less than 1/50 of a second. Hand-holding a 200mm lens requires a shutter speed of at least 1/200 of a second, and so on.

**Above** Depth-of-field, the zone of sharp focus in your photographs, is an important consideration in composition and in capturing the details you wish to record. These two photographs of the same day lily illustrate the effects of using a small aperture (f32) to achieve maximum depth of field (**left**) and a large aperture (f2.5) which yields a shallow depth of field (**right**).

## Guidelines for purchasing a tripod

● Buy the sturdiest, not fanciest, tripod you can afford. Before you buy, set up the tripod and lock everything in place, then wiggle, twist, and turn every part of it. Nothing should move, not even one millimeter.

● Select a tripod that lets you shoot at or near ground level, so you can photograph low-growing plants. Avoid tripods with reversible center columns, which let you shoot at ground level, but have a tripod leg between you and an upside-down camera – nearly impossible for most of us to do.

● Buy a tripod that extends to eye level *without* the center column extended, otherwise your tripod is converted into a much less stable, three-legged monopod.

● Make sure the tripod and camera are light enough to carry without undue strain. The strongest tripod in the world is completely useless if left at home because it is too heavy.

● Buy and use a cable release with your tripod, to prevent camera movement caused by depressing the shutter button with your finger.

# PRESERVING PLANTS

The most practical and environmentally sound method of collecting plants is photography. You can "acquire" new specimens without disturbing them and without spending time and effort preparing and preserving them properly. However, if you want to establish a collection of plants, there are several methods of preservation.

### Herbaria

A herbarium (plural, herbaria) is a library of dried and pressed plants organized into families, with genera and species arranged alphabetically within each family. This arrangement allows them to be easily located for reference, just as one would look up a book in a library. Properly preserved and maintained specimens have remained usable for more than 300 years, and herbaria are standard botanical references of universities and museums. Creating your own herbarium is fairly easy and

involves making or buying a simple plant press and following a few elementary procedures.

A plant press consists of heavy blotting paper and cardboard sandwiched between two sheets of 12 × 18 inch plywood. It is usually held together by a pair of nylon webbing compression straps, but you can use 14 × 20 inch plywood and secure it with bolts and wingnuts at the corners. The dimensions should be slightly larger than standard herbarium sheets.

Proper handling and storage of specimens in the field is vital for successful preservation. Transport specimens in a rigid holder such as a large plastic food storage container, to avoid crushing. Keep them as moist as possible, but provide some ventilation. If you cannot press them immediately, gently wash the plants to remove any remaining soil and place them in a vase with fresh water.

When ready to press the plants, blot off excess water and arrange each one on an open sheet of newspaper so that the leaves and flower parts are not folded or overlapping. *Remember to keep the*

wing nuts and washers

plywood

newspaper

blotting paper

bolts

cardboard

newspaper

specimen

blotting paper

HERBARIUM OF THE CONCORD FIELD STATION
HARVARD UNIVERSITY
Sheet 1
Plants of Middlesex Co., Mass.
Fagaceae
Castanea dentata (Marsh.) Borkh.
AMERICAN CHESTNUT
Habitat: Dry sterile woods
Locality: Concord, Mass.; near Goose Pond &
town dump
Collectors: Ray Angelo & Mary Walker
Date: July 7, 1978
Notes: Diseased tree about 30-40 feet high.
VIII 540

**Above** and **left** Establishing a herbarium is a rewarding activity for the serious botanist. When properly assembled and maintained, it will be a valuable reference for future generations.

*identification tag attached that corresponds to the information recorded in your field notebook.* Fold the newspaper over, place it between two blotters, and sandwich this between two sheets of corrugated cardboard. The air spaces in the cardboard allow ventilation to aid drying. No more than ten items should be pressed at a time. The wingnuts should be finger-tight. Keep the press and plants in a warm, dry room for two to four weeks.

The faster specimens dry, the better the color retention. Change papers every two or three days, replacing damp paper with fresh and tightening the press. (The blotting paper can be reused after it dries.) Large, fleshy plants require more paper and more frequent changes than those with a lower water content. You can use a microwave oven for super-fast drying, but you need a small press with *no metal parts.* Drying times vary, but two minutes on medium power is a good starting point.

When pressing bulky items, such as taproots and fruits, pack wads of paper around them to prevent crushing; larger fruits may have to be cut in half. Arrange aquatic and weak terrestrial plants for pressing by floating them in a tray of water, sliding a stiff piece of cardboard or parchment underneath them, and lifting them out of the water. (Soak saltwater species in fresh water overnight to remove the salt.) Allow the plant to air dry for about an hour before pressing it lightly in the plant press with extra sheets of paper. With large plants select key parts and press them in the normal fashion.

Try to use 100% rag-content paper for mounting dry specimens, since pulp-content paper deteriorates with age. The standard paper size for herbaria is 11.5 × 16.5 inches. Use good-quality, white library glue at strategic locations to mount the specimen, leaving the lower right-hand corner free for the identification card, which should also be 100% rag-content paper. Transfer all relevant collection information from your field notebook to this card, including common and scientific names, collection date, and geographic location, habitat type and soil type where found. Include your name as collector, in case you should ever wish to donate your work to a museum or university, and assign an identification number to each one for your cataloguing system. Place the mounted specimens in the freezer for three days to kill any pests, and use mothballs in the storage area to prevent insect damage. Encase each specimen in a clear plastic bag and store in manila envelopes.

**Above** Creating dried flower arrangements is an enjoyable hobby for the botanist with an artistic streak. Use cultivated varieties or the *most* common, non-native wildflowers.

## Three-dimensional preservation

Three-dimensional specimens present some storage problems, but you may want to preserve some plants in this fashion, for study or just decoration. Each of the methods given below has its own advantages and drawbacks.

## Air drying

Air drying is the simplest method of preservation, but air-dried flowers may not retain their shape and color as well as those preserved by some other methods. Air dry plants in a warm, dry, dark, well ventilated place, but not near a heat source, which causes increased brittleness. Check the humidity level with a hygrometer, available in most hardware stores; the humidity should be less than 50%. Leave space for air to circulate around the material; avoid overcrowding.

Many species dry well when hung upside down. Gather the fresh material in small, loose bunches with the heads at different levels to prevent crushing, and to allow air to circulate freely. Hang large flower heads individually. Tie the bunches with rubber bands, which will keep them secure as the stems dry and shrink, and hang them where they will not be disturbed.

You can also air dry some plants, such as grasses, in an upright position, using a tall, empty juice can. Weight the can with sand or stones so it

**Right** and **below** Air-dry flowers upside-down or upright in a warm, dry, well-ventilated location.

doesn't tip over. Cover the top of the can with chicken wire, available at hardware stores, and insert the stems through the chicken wire, avoiding overcrowding. If some species wilt before they dry, try fresh specimens and put one inch of water in the bottom of the can before inserting the stems. The water will eventually evaporate, and the plant material will continue to dry without wilting.

Store air-dried material in cardboard boxes, loosely wrapped with a thin layer of silica gel in the bottom, covered by paper. Individual flowers or small bunches should be loosely wrapped in tissue or newspaper.

## Drying with desiccants

A desiccant is material that absorbs moisture from the air. Silica gel, sand, borax, and cornmeal are desiccants used to preserve plants, so they retain their natural shape and color. Specimens are placed in an airtight container, covered with desiccant, and sealed. By cutting holes in the bottom of the container and covering them with tape before filling it with desiccant, the tape can be removed at the end of the process, so the drying agent trickles out without disturbing fragile specimens. For a container without an airtight lid, plastic wrap and waterproof tape will form a suitable seal. Use newly opened flowers collected on a dry day. Cup-shaped, tubular, or many-petaled

flowers are best dried face-up, others, face-down. Tall flower spikes may be dried vertically in a tall cup or horizontally in a long container. To shut the container, you may have to cut the stems, leaving two inches to mount the dried blooms with floral tape and wire, available from florists' shops. Once dry, remove desiccant adhering to flowers, using an artist's brush or a photographer's lens brush.

Silica gel is available from hardware stores, pharmacies, hobby and craft shops, and chemical supply companies. It is a crystalline substance available in several textures, but the finely ground, sandy form is best. It is expensive, so buy in bulk if you can. Buy at least 5 pounds; it can be reused indefinitely by drying it in an oven between uses. White or pink granules indicate that the silica gel contains moisture; spread them on a shallow baking sheet and bake in an oven for 20-30 minutes at 250°F (120°C). When they turn bright blue, they are completely dry and ready to reuse. Store silica gel in an airtight container when not using it. Flowers dry in 2-5 days in silica gel.

Fine, washed sand is also effective, but too heavy to be used alone except with sturdy, heavy-petaled flowers. A mixture of 1 part sand to 2 parts silica gel, borax, or cornmeal is more useful. Plants may take up to 3 weeks to dry in sand mixtures.

Borax cannot be used alone because it cakes when damp and flowers left in it too long form burn

Stem bent with wire, box to be filled with desiccant.

Flowers with a single layer of petals, dried in silica gel.

Dry tall flower spikes in a paper or plastic cup filled with desiccant.

Cardboard bent into corrugations to support flowers, container filled with desiccant.

Bake sand in oven and pour over fungus in tray. When cool remove sand with paintbrush.

spots. It may be mixed with 1 part sand to 2 parts borax, or mixed in equal parts with corn-meal, a lightweight combination useful for delicate specimens. Flowers in borax mixtures will dry in 2-7 days.

Store flowers dried in desiccants in airtight containers, with a layer of silica gel on the bottom covered with paper. Use opaque containers, or place them in a dark cabinet, and seal the box with freezer tape for added protection.

**Glycerine infusion**
Glycerine infusion is excellent for preserving branches of mature foliage or individual leaves, but generally does not work well with flowers. Material preserved by this method lasts indefinitely and is much less fragile than living or dried plants, but its natural color is usually replaced by various brown tones. Glycerine is sold in pharmacies, but can be bought more cheaply in bulk from chemical supply companies.

Prepare a solution by mixing equal parts glycerine with boiling water, or 1 part glycerine with 2 parts water, which is cheaper but takes a bit longer to work.

Cut foliage for preserving in glycerine in late summer or early fall. Cut material at midday after several sunny days, so it is as dry as possible. Use branches up to 24 inches long. If the leaves droop, put the branch in warm water; if they do not become turgid within a couple of hours, they won't take up glycerine, and should be discarded and replaced with fresh. Strip the bark from the lower 2 inches of woody stems or crush them with a hammer. Place the branches upright in a narrow bottle, jar, or vase containing 4 inches of water/glycerine solution. If top-heavy, anchor the containers in a larger container with sand or gravel. Store in a cool, dark place, adding more glycerine solution as needed; never let the glycerine run out. When absorption is complete, in 4-28 days, leaves feel supple and oily, their veins are dark, and their color changes to shades of brown or bronze. Any remaining glycerine solution can be reused.

Store glycerine-preserved material in a dry, well ventilated spot, out of direct sunlight. It may be stored between layers of tissue paper in cardboard boxes, with air holes cut for ventilation and a few mothballs to deter insects. If beads of glycerine form on the foliage, carefully wipe them off, then wash in warm water and dry with a soft cloth.

# URBAN BOTANY
## PLANTS OF DISTURBED SOILS

A freshly dug garden does not stay that way for long. Small green shoots begin to appear within a few days; after another week, they evolve into recognizable plants and more shoots sprout between them. If left unchecked, by the end of the season the soil surface will be covered in greenery without a seed ever having been sown. Where did they all come from?

They are "weeds," the scourge of gardeners everywhere, and their attack on a garden is no accident. Weeds are the Boy Scouts of the plant kingdom, for their motto is "Be prepared." In the example given, some weed seeds were already in the soil, awaiting their opportunity. Others moved in afterwards; dispersed from their parent plants by a variety of means, they found conditions to their liking. Still others sprouted from the rootstocks of their deposed predecessors. They struck fast, putting down roots and sending up shoots as quickly as possible in an attempt to beat the competition.

While this scenario may sound anthropomorphic, it is not far from reality. Certain plants are particularly adapted to take advantage of disturbed soil, whether the result of human activity or some natural event. Disturbed soil is a clean slate; it provides a fresh seed bed with no established competitors for available water, sunlight, and nutrients. But competition is never far behind, and exposed soil becomes a racing ground on which plants vie to become established first and ultimately reproduce and pass on their genes to the next generation.

The practical botanist thinks of weeds, not as pests, but as plants growing where they are not wanted. While weeds seldom pose serious problems, they are often among the most readily available subjects for practical botanists to study, especially as they tend to congregate around areas of human activity.

Look for "weeds" along roadsides, field edges and railroads, and in or around fairgrounds, meadows, construction sites, lawns, embankments, playgrounds, and gardens.

### Some common species of disturbed areas

| | |
|---|---|
| common dandelion | daisy fleabane |
| Asiatic dayflower | bluets |
| red clover | bachelor's button |
| crown vetch | common burdock |
| Japanese honeysuckle | meadow goldenrod |
| field mustard | common mallow |
| black mustard | catnip |
| teasel | jimsonweed |
| common mullein | Queen Anne's lace |
| butter-and-eggs | tall buttercup |
| birdsfoot trefoil | bouncing Bet |
| rocket larkspur | white campion |
| dame's rocket | scarlet pimpernel |
| charlock | mouse-ear chickweed |
| shepherd's purse | common morning glory |
| lady's thumb | tiger lily |
| yarrow | coltsfoot |
| spotted knapweed | oxeye daisy |
| periwinkle | curly dock |
| Deptford pink | New England aster |
| common St. John's wort | common milkweed |
| common chickweed | sheep sorrel |
| rugosa rose | black-eyed Susan |
| day lily | common sunflower |
| common barberry | fireweed |
| orange hawkweed | butterfly weed |
| chicory | field bindweed |
| bull thistle | purslane |

**Above** Butterfly weed is a native species adapted to disturbed areas.

**Right** Queen Anne's lace quickly colonizes abandoned areas.

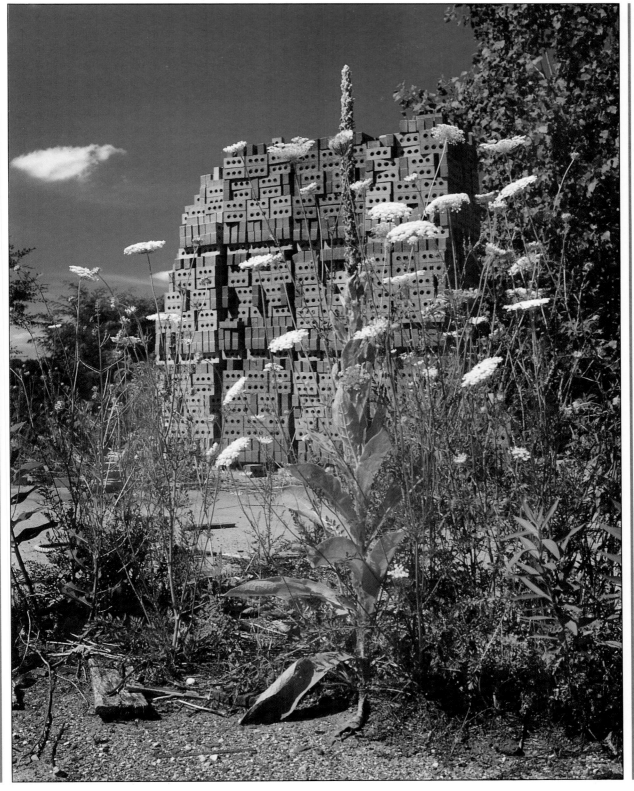

57

# LAWN AS HABITAT

Lawns pose particularly difficult problems to plants seeking to put down roots there. Consequently, only a few plants other than grasses are able to establish themselves in this hostile environment. A lawn's major defense against invaders is the sod layer formed by the dense fibrous root systems of grass. Many grasses spread by rhizomes, underground runners that emerge far from the parent as a tuft of grass that puts down its own roots, and sends out more rhizomes. The typical lawn is laced with miles of roots and rhizomes so tightly interwoven that they are nearly impenetrable to most other plants.

Another barrier to invaders is the complex mat of living and dead grass blades which prevent soil moisture from evaporating but also prevent most seeds from reaching the soil to germinate. Most seeds that breach this obstacle are thwarted by the sod layer below. Lawns are also mown periodically, so any plant that establishes itself must be able to survive at or below the mowing height and also reproduce vegetatively, or quickly bloom and set seeds, between mowings.

Many successful interlopers in lawns produce leaves in a basal rosette, a wheel-shaped arrangement of overlapping leaves that radiate outward from the plant's base. This configuration provides the plant with several advantages over the surrounding grass. Leaves in a basal rosette tend to arch over neighboring blades of grass, depriving them of sunlight while receiving maximum exposure themselves and staying low enough to avoid mower blades. Rosettes may also funnel rain striking them toward the center of the plant, from which the water soaks into the soil and is absorbed by the plant's own roots. Dandelions, plantains, and hawkweeds are lawn plants with basal rosettes.

Another strategy invoked by would-be invaders is the production of taproots. These tough anchors can penetrate the sod layer and obtain nutrients and moisture from deeper in the ground, thus avoiding competing with the well established network of grass roots.

Plants that spread by runners or rhizomes can play the same game as grasses, snaking their way through the maze of grass blades or roots until they find a chink and putting down their own roots. Wild strawberries and violets employ this method successfully in lawns.

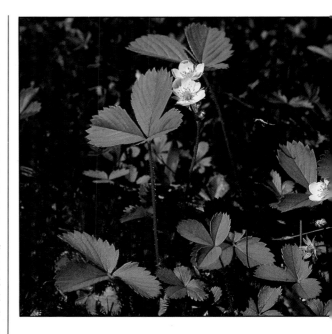

Fungi successfully colonize lawns because they do not compete directly with grasses. Fungi mycelia intermingle freely with dead roots and grass blades, decomposing them and deriving nourishment from them. A fruiting body can be quickly erected to release spores before the next pass of the lawn mower. Mosses also may find a niche in a manicured yard, although not in the midst of the grass. Moss needs a moist environment in which to grow, but not necessarily a lot of soil, since they do not possess true roots. They often find suitable niches between the branching roots at the base of a tree, or on the lower tree trunk itself, if conditions permit.

## Some common lawn visitors

| | |
|---|---|
| white clover | Many pioneering plants |
| common dandelion | attempt to colonize lawns, |
| common blue violet | but cannot survive periodic |
| common chickweed | mowing or flower between |
| orange hawkweed | mowings. To demonstrate |
| scarlet pimpernel | this, allow a small patch of |
| selfheal | lawn to grow for a month, or |
| bluets | summer, and observe. How |
| red clover | many new plants are you |
| wild strawberry | able to identify? |
| common plantain | |

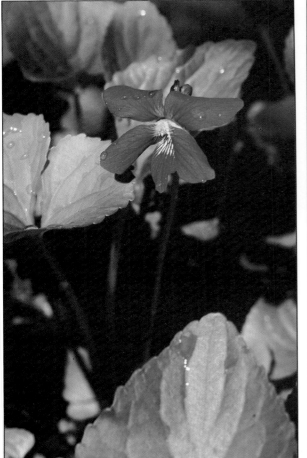

Less-manicured lawns may host a surprising variety of botanical visitors. Four examples are, clockwise from upper left: common strawberry which spreads by above-ground stolons; four sky-blue petals and yellow centers identify the flowers of low-growing bluets, which spread by creeping underground rootstocks to form dense colonies; common plantain thwarts competing grasses by shading them with a dense basal rosette of broad, spoon-shaped leaves; common blue violets are a favorite find — their edible leaves are sometimes used in salads, and delicious jelly and syrup can be produced from their blossoms.

# PARKS

Parks are excellent places for botanizing. Most state parks and all national and provincial parks contain the same plant species that inhabited the area before the creation of the park, and accurately portray the flora in that region. National forests and national wildlife refuges are also valuable public resources for the botanist.

City and municipal parks are often rich in plant life, but vary considerably in terms of diversity and in their use of ornamentals (selectively bred species which may or may not resemble their wild relatives). Many parks are formally landscaped, while others strive for a more natural look through the use of indigenous plants. Nearly all parks, however, prohibit the removal or destruction of plants, so plan on "collecting" only with a camera.

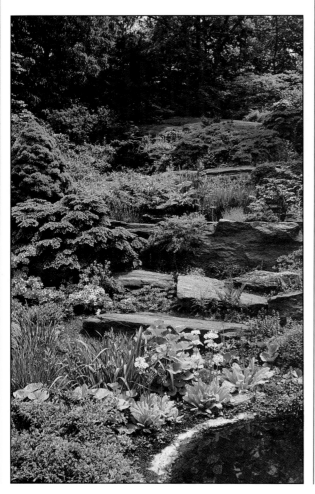

**Left** Parks frequently offer urban botanists the best opportunities to examine a large number of species. Botanical gardens, such as the New York Botanical Garden shown here, offer an added advantage, for most of their specimens are labeled, and interpretive information is presented along the trails and at the visitor's center.

**Above** To experience subtropical vegetation that is easily accessible, Bok Tower Gardens in Lake Wales, Florida is a fine place to visit.

**Right** Members of the lily family, like this day lily, are popular in municipal parks. Perennials such as these are often planted because they do not need to be replaced every year as do annuals.

# Meet-a-tree

Parks are places where people can play, and one game that is particularly fun for practical botanists is called Meet-a-tree. Originally conceived to teach children to tune in to their senses of touch, smell, hearing, and taste, it works equally well for adults. All you need is a blindfold and a partner. One partner should blindfold the other and spin him or her around several times, then lead the person on a roundabout course to a tree. Seeing partners are the eyes for blindfolded ones, and must guide them safely, alerting them to hazards and directing their steps to avoid obstacles. At the chosen tree, place his or her hands on the trunk and step back to give the person room to explore, then ask the following questions:

### Touch
● How does the bark feel? Does the texture change as you move your hands up the trunk, or out the limbs?
● How big is the trunk? Can you reach all the way around and grab your other hand? Is there more than one trunk? Can you reach the lowest branches, and if so, how high are they?
● How do the leaves feel? Is their texture on one side different from that on the other? What shape is the leaf? How big is it? What are the edges like?
● Are the roots exposed?

How many can you feel?
● If the sun is shining, which side of the tree is warmer?
● What shape and size are any buds?

### Smell
● Scratch the bark and sniff. What does it smell like? Does the bark of a twig or root smell different from that of the trunk?
● Crush a leaf and notice its smell.
● What does its fruit, if any, smell like? Crush one if necessary.

### Taste
● If the tree produces edible fruit, give your partner one to sample, but be absolutely certain of your identification.

### Sound
● Rap the trunk with your knuckles and note the sound.
● Crumple a leaf in your fingers and note the sound.
● If there is a breeze, try to distinguish the sound it makes as it moves through the tree. Some trees make peculiar creaks and groans as the wind moves them.

When the person feels well acquainted with the tree, lead him or her on another twisted course away from it, remove the blindfold, and have him or her try to find that tree again. Have them do a quick sketch of the tree first, and see how closely it resembles the real thing. Afterwards, reverse roles.

# AGRICULTURAL LANDS
## ALIEN VS. NATIVE

Plants can be placed into one or two broad categories which tell the practical botanist very much about them. "Native" plants are those which evolved in North America in the habitats in which they are largely found today. The New World has been relatively undisturbed over the millennia and these plants are accustomed to the slow pace of nature. Although our continent has long been populated by Indians, they changed little of their environment. Any alterations made were on a relatively small scale and often mimicked the forces of nature, such as using fire to open up forest and create habitats attractive to game. These minor variations were not disruptive to the native flora as a whole, so there was little pressure on plants to adapt to radical environmental changes.

Plants in the other major group are known as "alien," "introduced," or "exotic" species. These did not evolve in North America, but were imported accidentally or purposely. Most of our alien species originated in Europe or Asia where they spent thousands of years adapting to the disruptions and alterations associated with civilization. They are the survivors, the opportunists able to take advantage of the variety of new ecological niches created by human activities. Their aggressive nature makes them the scourge of gardeners and landscapers, who wage all-out war against them annually. We know them as the "weeds" of lawns, gardens, roadsides, and anywhere soil and native vegetation has been disturbed.

Native plants, by contrast, have only been exposed to civilization for two or three hundred years at the most, and the majority have only been subjected to widespread development within the past century. In the evolutionary time frame, this is an extremely short period, and native plants in general have not been able to keep up with the pressure to adapt. Consequently, many native species do not compete well in developed areas. All threatened and endangered plant species in North America are native, and habitat loss is the main threat to their existence.

Many alien plant species that have successfully established themselves in North America originated in regions of Europe and Asia where agri-culture had been practiced extensively for thousands of years, and consequently they thrive in the farmlands of this continent that mimic their "native" habitat. The conditions they require to complete their life cycles include copious direct sunlight, moderate and regular precipitation, a temperate climate, and periodic soil disturbances, such as tilling, to prepare a fresh seedbed for the next generation. Interestingly, many of these (oxeye daisy, bull thistle, common dandelion, Queen Anne's lace – to mention a few) were introduced accidentally when their seeds were harvested along with crops and sent to the New World in grain shipments. Others, like some clovers, were planted here as crops themselves but escaped cultivation and now grow wild.

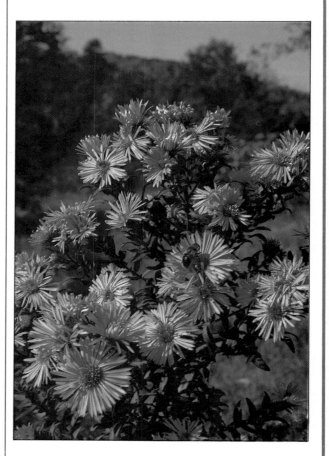

**Above** New England aster is one of the relatively few native species that thrive in such managed areas as meadows, thickets, and roadsides.

**Right** Grasses do particularly well in agricultural areas. Timothy is an import that escaped cultivation as a hay crop and now grows wild.

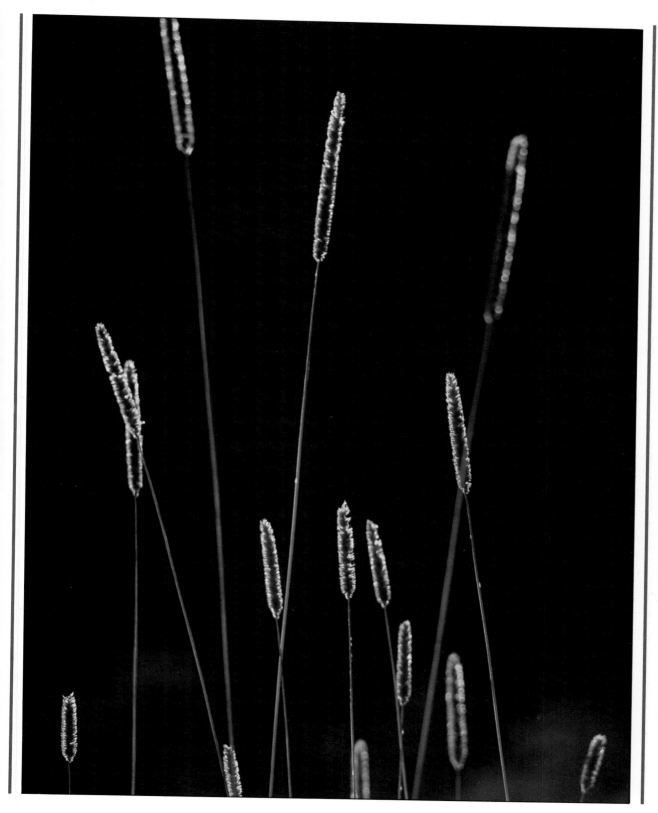

# MEADOWS AND PASTURES

Meadows and pastures are both areas cleared of brush and trees for agricultural purposes. Pastures are grassy areas where livestock are grazed, while hay meadows are artificial grasslands used to produce hay. Abandoned fields and meadows naturally exhibit a greater array of wild species than actively worked ones. These habitats should not be confused with the alpine meadows of the high country, mountaintop "balds" of the Appalachians, and other areas where meadow-like conditions are maintained semi-permanently by environmental factors such as soil type and moisture, fire, elevation, and temperature. Such natural meadows tend to support a greater diversity of species and more native varieties than agricultural meadows.

Farmers plant hay meadows with crops such as timothy, rye, clover, and alfalfa that can be harvested and fed to their animals during winter. Clover and alfalfa are legumes which, as well as supplying winter forage, enrich the soil by "fixing" atmospheric nitrogen in their root nodules. These meadows are mown annually and crops are rotated regularly, to prevent certain soil nutrients being depleted from continually supporting the same

crop. Hay meadows, therefore, are largely dominated by one species, but interlopers establish themselves on a regular basis.

Pastures are subjected to different conditions, and support a differing array of plant life. To survive in a pasture, a plant must be able to withstand or avoid grazing, and recover from trampling by heavy, hoofed animals. Grasses grow from their roots, unlike most vascular plants, which grow from their tips, so grasses suffer no permanent harm when their tips are sheared off by cows, horses or sheep. This same action would kill or seriously inhibit the growth of most other plants. (Over-grazing, when grasses are cropped to the ground and denied the chance to recover, is destructive.) Defenses against grazing include the piercing spines of thistles, common pasture inhabitants; other plants have evolved stinging hairs or extremely distasteful foliage to help them thwart livestock.

**Above** Red clover is a very common plant of meadows and pastures. A hay and forage crop native to Europe and Asia, it escaped cultivation on this continent.

**Left** Meadows like this one near Sudbury, Ontario, are excellent botanical sites, yielding native and alien species.

## Some common plants of meadows and pastures

(Check your field guide to determine which occur in your area.)

### Wildflowers

| | |
|---|---|
| curly dock | chicory |
| common dandelion | lance-leaved coreopsis |
| tall buttercup | bluets |
| oxeye daisy | bull thistle |
| black-eyed Susan | orange hawkweed |
| selfheal | pearly everlasting |
| harebell | spotted Joe-Pye weed |
| bachelor's button | yarrow |
| common sunflower | wild blue flax |
| daisy fleabane | wild geranium |
| Indian blanket | common blue-eyed grass |
| meadow goldenrod | Canada lily |
| New England aster | Turk's cap lily |
| common milkweed | catnip |
| wild mint | black mustard |
| red clover | wild blue phlox |
| California poppy | wild strawberry |
| butter-and-eggs | Indian paintbrush |
| purple coneflower | evening primrose |
| butterfly weed | Queen Anne's lace |
| mountain phlox | fivespot |
| Mexican hat | Chinese houses |
| scarlet pimpernel | tidy tips |
| sulphur flower | rocket larkspur |
| shooting star | dame's rocket |
| prairie blazing star | purple prairie clover |
| common ragweed | common mullein |

### Grasses

| | |
|---|---|
| timothy | broomsedge |
| little bluestem | wild oats |
| meadow fescue | switchgrass |
| sheep fescue | big bluestem |
| blue grama | buffalo grass |
| side oats grama | orchard grass |
| quack grass | bent grass |
| Kentucky bluegrass | |

**Below** Trees, such as eastern red cedar, will invade pastures if given the chance. Clumps of grass grow on manured soil.

# FENCEROWS, THICKETS, AND WOODLOTS

Fencerows, which often define individual fields and meadows or delineate the boundaries of neighboring farms, are an entirely separate habitat from the open spaces just a few feet away, and contain the shrubs and trees excluded from most fields. Depending on the orientation and width of the fencerow, there may be shade-tolerant wildflowers, normally associated with deciduous woodlands. At the core of many fencerows, especially in the Northeast, may be a stone wall that hosts a variety of lichens. The spaces between the stones also tend to create cool, moist microhabitats that favor the growth of mosses and ferns.

### Thickets

Thickets are patches of uncultivated land, less linear than fencerows and ranging from a few dozen square yards to acres. They generally have been cleared in their recent history, as shown by their young trees and characteristically large amount of brush. Once cleared, they may have been found too moist or too rocky for cultivation, or they may have been overlooked for other reasons. They are excellent examples of the shrub-sapling stage of succession in your area. Shrubs such as raspberry, blackberry, common barberry, multiflora rose, hawthorn, sweetbrier, and flowering dogwood may abound. Trees present are usually mature pioneer species, such as gray birch and eastern red cedar of the eastern United States, or saplings of the next seral stage. Some dense thickets contain multi-stemmed saplings of bigtooth or quaking aspen, indicating that their rootstocks remained alive under the thicket while it was in use, held in check only by grazing, mowing, or other events.

### Woodlots

Woodlots are old thickets or forest remnants surrounded by agricultural land or, more recently, by housing developments. Nearly all low-lying land in the east has been cleared at some time since the New World was colonized, but those that have been left alone for, say 75-150 years, have undergone secondary succession and reached a stage approximating the mature climax forest characteristic of the region. The distinction between

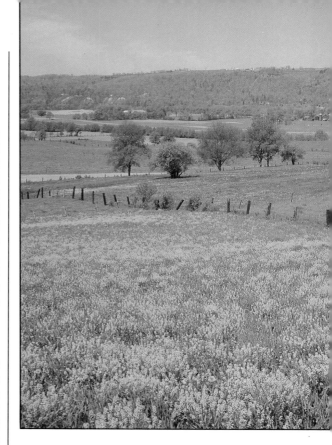

a forest and a woodlot is arbitrary, but woodlots are generally considered small, wooded areas of less than a few acres and located at least several hundred yards from other wooded areas. Larger woodlots, especially those close to other large wooded tracts, tend to develop an interior region that biologically resembles a true forest, which is covered in the chapter on woodlands.

Woodlots usually exhibit the same vegetation zones as a forest: canopy, understory, shrub layer, herb layer, and ground layer. The canopy is the uppermost vegetation and is composed of mature trees of the locally dominant species. The understory consists of smaller, shade-tolerant trees and sun-loving trees rushing to fill any holes in the canopy left by fallen trees. The next lower layer consists of shrubs, many of which were present in earlier seral stages. The shrub layer is particularly evident near the southern edge of woodlots, where more direct sunlight is likely to penetrate. Below this is the herb layer, consisting of woodland wildflowers from the woodlot's interior, and field and meadow species toward the woodlot's edges. Finally, the ground layer is home to low-growing mosses, liverworts, club mosses, and fungi.

**Left** Fields in agricultural areas are frequently bordered by fencerows, or windbreaks. These areas are havens for species that cannot withstand regular plowing or mowing.

**Below** Multiflora rose (center) and common barberry (bottom) are common plants of eastern agricultural areas, each capable of forming impenetrable thickets. In many places they are considered weeds.

## Some common plants of fencerows, thickets, and woodlots

| | |
|---|---|
| staghorn sumac | red raspberry |
| black raspberry | common barberry |
| multiflora rose | sweetbrier |
| hawthorn | flowering dogwood |
| gray birch | eastern red cedar |
| black mulberry | fox grape |
| black walnut | shagbark hickory |
| black locust | sweet gum |
| chokecherry | pin cherry |
| eastern white pine | sassafras |
| tulip tree | northern red oak |
| evening primrose | red baneberry |
| white baneberry | mayapple |
| bluets | Canada anemone |
| virgin's bower | wood anemone |
| common burdock | goldenrod |
| Jerusalem artichoke | New England aster |
| Philadelphia daisy | spotted Joe-Pye weed |
| closed gentian | wild geranium |
| cut-leaved toothwort | Canada lily |
| large-flowered trillium | smooth Solomon's seal |
| Turk's cap lily | butterfly weed |
| common milkweed | Oswego tea |
| scarlet sage | wild bergamot |
| field bindweed | bittersweet nightshade |
| nodding ladies' tresses | yellow-fringed orchid |
| fringed loosestrife | spring beauty |
| turtlehead | Asiatic dayflower |
| spotted touch-me-not | Virginia creeper |
| Japanese honeysuckle | trumpet honeysuckle |
| poison ivy | downy serviceberry |
| hedge bindweed | bracken fern |
| haircap moss | |

### Where to go

Agricultural lands with fencerows, thickets, and woodlots tend to occur in the eastern half of the continent, and especially in the Northeast. Nearly all are privately owned, but most farmers are friendly and accommodating if you introduce yourself, explain your interest, and ask permission to look around. Remember to leave everything as you found it: close gates that were closed, leave open gates open, don't disturb livestock, and walk *around* planted crops, not through them. The farmer might appreciate hearing about what you've found and receiving a personal thank-you and a photograph.

# QUADRATS AND TRANSECTS

Quadrats and transects are useful techniques for learning about composition of and relationships within plant communities. Identifying plants with field guides and keys is important but it is only the first step in studying natural history. The next step is to understand the significance of an organism's presence in a particular place. Recognizing different plant communities and analyzing them with quadrats and transects helps you predict roughly which plant species you are likely to encounter there, as well as other characteristics, including soil composition, moisture content, drainage, wildlife species and climate.

### Quadrats

A quadrat is a sample plot of a given size, usually square, but occasionally rectangular or circular. Quadrats may be single units or divided into subunits, with size depending on the characteristics of the vegetation under study. Quadrats of one-fifth of an acre are often used to study forest canopy trees, while understory trees and shrubs may be evaluated with smaller plots. Quadrats of one square yard are adequate for evaluating herbaceous plants, such as grasses and wildflowers, especially in a meadow or other habitat with dense vegetation.

The accuracy of any study depends on the number and size of quadrats used, simply because the more quadrats taken, the more it increases the chances of encountering members of the community. In a relatively uniform habitat, the increase in accuracy diminishes after about five or six samples, assuming that they are randomly chosen, so it is within the first few samples that most of the information is accumulated.

### Types of quadrats

*List Quadrat* The plants found are listed by name. A series of list quadrats provides an overview of the species present. Dividing the number of quadrats in which a particular species was found by the total number of quadrats investigated and multiplying by 100 shows the percentage of that species' occurrence within quadrats. (Example: goldenrod occurred in 25% of all quadrats in Meadow X.)

*Count Quadrat* The names and numbers of each species are recorded, showing the basic composition of the community and the abundance

The optimum size of a quadrat varies with the subjects studied: a quadrat analyzing data on large subjects, such as trees (**left**) should be larger than one analyzing meadow plants (**bottom left**). Quadrats and transects (**below**) yield different types of data; you may need to use both methods to draw accurate conclusions.

quadrat

transect

of individuals. (Example: The species composition of Meadow Y is 25% timothy, 15% little bluestem, 20% goldenrod, 15% milkweed, 10% Queen Anne's lace, 6% New England aster, 5% yarrow, and 4% tall buttercup.)

*Cover Quadrat* The percentage of ground surface shaded or covered by vegetation is recorded, either by species or for total vegetation. Estimate the area shaded or covered by each plant, total the estimates for each species, divide by the area of the quadrat, and multiply by 100 to obtain the percentage of coverage of each species.

*Chart Quadrat* Draw a scale map of the quadrat showing the locations of individual plants. This is a tedious job and is useful only to the researcher doing a long-term study of vegetation changes.

### Transects

*Line Intercept* Observations are made on a line or lines laid out randomly or systematically across the area under scrutiny. As with quadrats, accuracy increases with the number of lines surveyed.

• Stretch a tape measure between two points 50 or 100 yards (or meters) apart.

• Divide the line into intervals, such as 1 yard, 3 yards, or 5 yards.

• Move along the line, recording for each interval the species touched by the line or lying directly over or under it, as well as the distance their foliage covers along the line.

• Summarize the data by:

**a** the number of intervals in which each species occurs along the line.

**b** the frequency of occurrence for each species relative to the total number of intervals sampled.

**c** the total distance covered by each species along the transect.

**d** the total distance covered by vegetation along the line and the total uncovered distance.

**e** the total number of individuals of each species along the transect.

From this data, the following calculations can be made, their results expressed as a percentage:

• Relative Density: total individuals of species X divided by total individuals of all species, times 100.

• Dominance (cover): total intercept length of species X divided by the total transect length, times 100.

• Relative Dominance: total intercept length of species X divided by the total intercept length of all species, times 100.

• Frequency: number of intervals in which species X occurs divided by the total number of transect intervals, times 100.

• Relative Frequency: frequency value of species X divided by the frequency value of all species, times 100.

The line intercept method is easy, objective, and particularly useful for measuring changes in vegetation throughout the study area. It is less accurate for estimating frequency and abundance than the quadrat method, because the probability of an individual being sampled by line intercept is proportional to its size.

*Belt Transect* An effective combination of the quadrat and the line intercept method in which a "belt", or long, narrow unit, is laid out across the area under study and divided into segments of equal size. These segments may then be used as quadrats and surveyed. This is an accurate method for determining abundance, frequency, and distribution, especially when more than one belt is utilized. It also shows vegetation changes along a gradient, such as from dry to moist soil.

## Plant profiles

Making a plant profile (a two-dimensional representation of the plant community of a given area) is an excellent way to illustrate the changes in a plant community along an environmental gradient, such as increasing or decreasing moisture, sunlight or temperature. Lay out line intercepts in an area with a definite environmental difference from one end to another, such as a meadow with distinctly dry and wet areas. Analyze your findings according to the methods listed above, but do the calculations for only half of the transect at a time to determine whether the plants you've found exhibit a preference for one extreme over another.

If you notice a definite change in the plant profile while doing line intercepts, challenge yourself to determine the environmental factor causing it.

# ABANDONED FIELDS AND SUCCESSION

An abandoned field becomes a laboratory in which to study a classic example of secondary succession. In the spring following the last harvest, the field begins to green up on its own. Some plants are germinating from seed dropped during the last harvest, and some are grasses and dicots that were growing in the field along with the crop.

Many others, however, are invaders that began their assault during the previous several years, sending in expendable troops in order to have them in place should an opportunity for exploitation arise. The so-called weeds, with their predisposition to disturbed soils, are the vanguard of the invasion. Milkweeds, dandelions and thistles drifted from great distances. Others, such as common burdock and flax, hitch-hiked in on the fur or feathers of passing mammals and birds. In some cases, the seeds in fruits eaten by mammals and birds passed through their digestive tract before being deposited in the field. Periodically, seeds and fruits stockpiled by mice and other rodents are forgotten or abandoned, and they, too, germinate. Then there are those that spread slowly but surely by means of underground rhizomes.

During the first couple of years, opportunistic annuals and biennials tend to predominate. The exact species composition of pioneer communities is highly variable, depending on seed sources in the area, farming practices prior to abandonment, moisture content and soil condition. With each passing year, conditions improve as more organic matter is added to the soil which, along with increased shading, reduces moisture evaporation and soil temperatures, allowing plants with stricter requirements to establish themselves. Native perennials are better adapted to utilize the improved conditions, and with their shading and spirited growth, quickly crowd out the annuals. The short life cycles of annuals were advantageous at first, but once native perennials move in, annuals cannot compete with the perennials' earlier spring growth and longer life cycles.

An old field evolving into a mature climax community of the type common to that area is a marvelous opportunity for a practical botanist to witness the development of plant communities firsthand. Return several times each year throughout the growing season and make detailed notes about the appearance and disappearance of species as the field ages. Return when the plants go to seed and examine them to deduce their method of dispersal and how they found their way there. The knowledge amassed with a long-term study of secondary succession is both fascinating and invaluable.

**Left** The first plants of any stage of ecological succession to invade an area are called pioneer species. Eastern red cedar is typically among the first trees to invade abandoned fields in eastern North America.

**Above** Ecological succession will occur on nearly any new or disturbed area, but the classic example is an abandoned field like the one shown here. The so-called "weeds", well-adapted to open, disturbed soils, move in first, followed by perennial shrubs, saplings, and finally, trees.

**Left** Sumacs, such as this staghorn sumac, are also pioneers of the shrub-sapling stage. Staghorn sumac is easily identified in the fall and winter by its fuzzy, dark red seeds growing in dense, erect cones.

71

# GRASSLANDS
## GRASSLAND AS A COMMUNITY

Until quite recently, many people interested in nature saw the prairies only as a great void to be crossed to reach the mountains and coasts on either side of the continent. Its landscape, a vast sea of grass and farmland, seemed so flat and boring that its biological wealth was ignored. These grasslands, in fact, are one of the largest and most productive ecosystems in North America. They are so productive that their conversion to cropland has threatened their existence in some regions, while their vastness and seemingly monotonous nature led them to be taken for granted.

Despite their name, grasslands support much more than just grasses. They host an abundance of forbs (herbs other than grass), desert plants, shrubs, and occasional trees, the latter particularly abundant along rivers and streams. Additionally, they provide habitat for a surprising array of mammals, birds, insects, and reptiles. Grazing and burrowing animals, such as bison, pronghorns, and prairie dogs, are especially well suited for prairie life. Intact grasslands are a stable, climax ecosystem that seems to defy the principles of ecological succession, but other forces of nature are at work here.

### Types of grasslands
"Grasslands" here covers the tallgrass prairie, mixed prairie, shortgrass prairie, and intermoun- tain grasslands. One might also argue for the inclusion of alpine meadows, tidal wetlands, and desert grassland, but, while consisting largely of grass-like plants, these habitats are so radically different in composition and origin that they are covered in other chapters.

### Grassland characteristics
When grasslands are mentioned, one normally thinks of the prairie, which is indeed the largest grassland area in North America, beginning with the tallgrass prairie east of the Appalachians and blending gradually into the shortgrass prairie at the foothills of the Rockies. There are other types of grasslands in the East, Southwest, and West which are examined in other chapters.

Most grasslands share certain characteristics. With the exception of some eastern, intermountain, and California grasslands, most occur on flat or gently rolling terrain. Prairie soils, while origi- nating from different bedrock sources, are all slightly alkaline, rich in humus, deep, and very fertile. Precipitation averages between ten and thirty-nine inches per year, but is punctuated by periods of severe drought. The climate in general is marked by high rates of evaporation.

Grassland communities are stratified into three zones: roots, ground layer, and herbaceous layer. The root layer is the most pronounced of any major ecological community, with some grass species reaching six feet or more into the soil. At least half of the plant is represented underground, and virtually all of it in winter. When they finally die after supporting the plant for 20 to 50 years, the

**Left** Pawnee National Grassland, Colorado, is one of many areas set aside to preserve these botanically and ecologically fascinating habitats.

**Right** Yellow goatsbeard, a member of the sunflower family distinguished by long, pointed bracts extending beyond the yellow ray flowers, is a common grassland resident.

decomposing roots leave an intricate system of miniscule tunnels that supply air and water to the deeper layers of topsoil, a benefit to the surviving plants in the immediate vicinity. The ground layer in taller grasslands is characterized by lower temperatures, lower light levels, and higher humidity than occur in the upper herb layer exposed to drying winds and solar radiation. At ground level a layer of mulch forms, made of dead stems and leaves that decompose as they come into contact with the mineral soil. This mulch adds humus to the soil, increasing its water-retention capability. The herbaceous layer develops as the season progresses, with ground-hugging plants growing and blooming first, eventually hidden as

taller plants form a middle layer and, finally, an upper layer of very tall grasses and wildflowers that bloom in the fall.

## A word about grasses

Grasses are unique among flowering plants. The grass family, or *Poaceae*, is the third largest family of flowering plants. They are truly ubiquitous, with representatives on every continent.

Grasses are monocots, and as a group they are easy to recognize, but because of their inconspicuous flowers, they have a reputation of being difficult to identify as individual species. Their ecological and economical value is indisputable, though. Much of our food comes

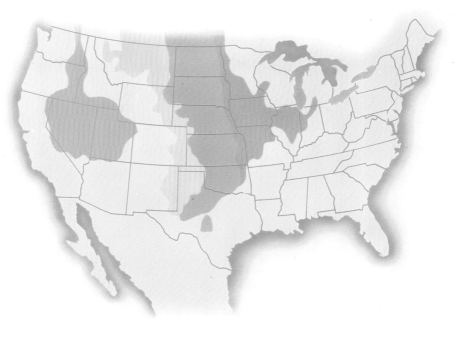

**Left** Tallgrass prairie, the most fertile of the midwestern grasslands, has succumbed to the plow throughout most of its range. Today it exists only on carefully preserved or restored tracts and on overlooked areas, such as along railroad rights-of-way.

- shortgrass prairie
- mixed grass prairie
- tallgrass prairie
- intermountain grasslands

directly or indirectly from grasses and most of our meat-producing and dairy livestock are fed grain or graze on grass which we cannot digest.

Physiologically, grasses differ from most other flowering plants in that their region of active growth is at the leaf base, near where it joins the stem, not at the tip. This enables them to survive, and even thrive, with moderate grazing, which allows sunlight to penetrate farther, sometimes making for a healthier plant. In another interesting adaptation, new blades of grass are hidden inside the hollow stems of older shoots, able to take over if the older shoot is clipped off.

To survive extreme heat, drying winds, drought, fire, heavy grazing, and long winters, grasses have developed massive root systems, which in some species are estimated to collectively equal up to three miles in length per plant. Grasses spread by underground rhizomes as well as by seed, and often these rhizomes, along with their fibrous root system, form dense tangles that lock the topsoil into a solid layer called sod, making it difficult for many would-be competitors to put down their own roots. Living blades of grass weave a tangled mat with the dead leaves of previous seasons that further retards invading plant species. Those grasses that are not sod-formers are called bunch grasses and, true to their name, grow in bunches with other plants occupying the spaces in between.

# NATURE'S FORCES AT WORK

The existence of grasslands as a stable ecosystem seems to be a direct contradiction to the normal course of ecological succession. Whether primary or secondary, one group of plants normally colonizes a given area and, in doing so, gradually alters the environment, creating conditions less favorable for their own progeny but more hospitable to the pioneer species of the next seral stage. The grass stage normally gives way to a shrub-sapling stage of sun-loving woody perennials, which is in turn succeeded by a young forest. This will ultimately be replaced by a mature climax forest.

There are many forces at work maintaining the grasslands. Because of the deep and extensive root systems which compose a large percentage of the entire plant, grasses do better in semi-arid conditions than do many trees and shrubs. Although grasslands receive moderate amounts of precipitation annually, their flat terrain poses no obstacle to drying winds, so much of their moisture gain is lost to evaporation. This is more pronounced in the warmer south, where more precipitation is needed to maintain the same type of grassland vegetation as in the north. Precipitation in grasslands is often concentrated in peak seasons interspersed with periods of drought. Finally, much more precipitation falls on the windward side of mountain ranges than on the leeward side, and thus a "rain shadow" effect occurs on the eastern slopes of the Sierra Nevada, Cascade, and Rocky Mountain ranges. The grasslands that occur here are composed of short, sparse grasses. As precipitation increases and evaporation decreases to the east, taller and lusher grasslands develop until finally the eastern forests appear.

Fire is another natural force keeping grasslands in check. Regular lightning-caused fires fanned by constant winds have always been part of grassland ecosystems, clearing organic debris that shades the soil, returning nutrients to the soil, and creating a fresh seedbed for wildflowers. Grass roots remain unscathed by the rapidly moving fire and, with the energy stored in their extensive root systems, resprout almost as soon as the ashes are cool. However, most trees and shrubs native to these regions are less tolerant of fire, and they suffer serious setbacks as a result.

One major force at work on the prairies used to be the great herds of bison and other herbivores. They roamed the prairies by the millions and their grazing stimulated renewed grass growth after they left, leaving tons of manure to fertilize the soil and sustain the vigorous new growth. Also, chunks of sod torn up by their thundering hooves left bare soil, in which annual and perennial wildflowers could establish themselves. With their population reduced to a mere shadow of its former grandeur, bison and other herbivores are no longer a significant factor in the grassland ecosystems.

**Below** The great North American grasslands lie in rain shadows, areas on the leeward side of major mountain ranges. As moist air masses move from west to east, they are forced upward as they strike the mountain ranges. As the moist air moves higher, it cools below its dew point, clouds form, and precipitation falls on the western slopes. Cresting the mountains, the air descends, warming quickly. Due to the moisture lost, the air is much drier, precipitation is scarcer, and a rain shadow is created.

cold air | warm air | moisture | dew point | cloud forming | rising wind | drizzle | rain | rain shadow

Pacific Ocean     Coast Range     Sierra Nevada and Cascades     Great Basin

**Above** Fires such as this one in the Everglades, are equally important in maintaining the prairie grasslands, especially in the tallgrass prairie where it keeps trees at bay.

**Left** These bison are a remnant of the great herds which used to exercise a regulating force on the prairies.

clouds    rain shadow    temperate deciduous forests

Rocky Mountains    grassland    Appalachian Mountains    Atlantic Ocean

77

# TALLGRASS PRAIRIE

There was a time in the not-so-distant past that the tallgrass prairie covered more than 400,000 square miles in 12 states. It was the first extensive grassland encountered by pioneers as they moved west, and it left them truly in awe. They had seen huge meadows and pastures before, but nothing like this. There are accounts of grasses so high that they could conceal a man on horseback. Where one could see over them, the monotony of the scene was overwhelming; there was seemingly nothing but a sea of grass that stretched to the horizon, an analogy that may have prompted their Conestoga wagons to be dubbed "prairie schooners."

Sadly, nothing remains of this spectacle but a few scattered nature preserves and overlooked pockets of native prairie vegetation. Ironically, pioneers first thought prairie soils were infertile because trees were absent. In fact, the area received substantial precipitation, and it was the periodic fires set by lightning or Indians that kept the forests at bay. They soon realized their misconception and set about cultivating massive areas of fertile soil, aided by a product of the Industrial Revolution, the Prairie Queen. This tempered steel plow, produced by John Deere, was sturdy enough to rip through the dense black sod with the aid of strong beasts of burden.

Tallgrass prairie is not always tall. Winter snows and wind beat the lofty vegetation nearly to ground level, and the new grass shoots do not reach their maximum height until mid-July. In the meantime, the low-growing forbs of the area bloom first in the spring, followed by progressively taller wildflowers, and finally the taller grasses produce their plumes of less-conspicuous flowers in the late summer.

Tall grasses, including big bluestem, switchgrass, Indian grass, and, in wetter areas, slough grass dominate this system. Despite the preponderance of grasses, some trees also grow along riverbanks and in upland areas. Cottonwoods, green ash, box elder, and American elm follow the watercourses, while bur oak is common in drier upland areas, developing a four-foot taproot in its first year in order to compete with the deep-rooted grasses.

**Below** Tallgrass prairie, displaced throughout most of its range by agricultural fields, receives enough precipitation to support a forest. Regular fires maintained it as a grassland for hundreds of thousands of years.

Prairie blazing star (**above**) is a common wildflower of the tallgrass prairie, which is defined by a predominance of big bluestem grass, (**left**).

## Some common plants of the tallgrass prairie

### Grasses

| | |
|---|---|
| big bluestem | switchgrass |
| Indian grass | slough grass |
| prairie cordgrass | foxtail barley |
| needlegrass | grama grass |
| little bluestem | prairie dropseed |
| bluejoint | timothy |
| redtop | Kentucky bluegrass |

### Wildflowers

| | |
|---|---|
| compass plant | marsh pea |
| goldenrod | white snakeroot |
| bluets | pale lobelia |
| two-flowered Cynthia | rattlesnake master |
| alumroot | goat's rue |
| prairie false indigo | black-eyed Susan |
| yarrow | swamp saxifrage |
| boneset | prairie coreopsis |
| prairie blazing star | rough blazing star |
| white sweet clover | pineapple weed |
| ragweed | smooth aster |
| horse nettle | common milkweed |
| sundrops | prairie phlox |
| shooting star | downy painted cup |
| long-headed thimbleweed | Canada anemone |
| star-flowered Solomon's | blue flag |
| seal | smaller redroot |

| | |
|---|---|
| northern bedstraw | spiderwort |
| hoary puccoon | marsh marigold |
| wild geranium | bird-foot violet |
| spreading dogbane | common sunflower |
| butterfly weed | death camas |
| Indian blanket | Jerusalem artichoke |
| Indian paintbrush | pasqueflower |
| New England aster | smooth aster |
| purple prairie clover | evening primrose |
| spotted Joe-Pye weed | plains larkspur |
| showy evening primrose | giant sunflower |
| Maximilian's sunflower | crazyweed |
| New York ironweed | prickly pear |

### Trees and shrubs

| | |
|---|---|
| pasture rose | shrubby cinquefoil |
| black oak | common chokecherry |
| eastern cottonwood | bur oak |
| quaking aspen | common barberry |
| leadplant | eastern red cedar |
| American plum | paper birch |
| prairie crabapple | smooth sumac |
| bigtooth aspen | post oak |
| green ash | hackberry |
| Siberian elm | common prickly-ash |

# MIXED GRASS PRAIRIE

As one proceeds west, the mixed grass prairie marks the beginning of the Great Plains. It also divides the tallgrass prairie, where trees grow if not precluded by fire, from the shortgrass prairie, where they will not. Most trees found in the mixed grass prairie are riparian species (willows, cottonwoods, elms, hackberry, and green ash) common along watercourses. The few trees that grow elsewhere in the mixed grass prairie are found in the eastern part of this grassland.

Unlike tallgrass prairies to the east which are maintained primarily by fire, the grassland habitat in mixed grass prairies is largely determined by its low annual precipitation, ranging between fourteen and twenty-three inches per year. Wind speed and the rate of evaporation are also higher than on tallgrass prairies, which increases the region's aridity.

Mixed grass prairie is dominated by little bluestem, needlegrass, Junegrass, and, in the northern reaches, western wheatgrass. Also common are buffalo grass and blue grama, the two

dominant species of the shortgrass prairie, which, in this region, occur more frequently at higher (and therefore drier) elevations. Big bluestem is also present, mostly along river terraces and other moist areas. Due to the shorter height of the vegetation, sunlight is better able to reach lower plants in mixed grass prairie than in tallgrass prairie. Thus, mixed grass prairie exhibits a more layered plant community in mid-summer when the grasses are fully grown than does the tallgrass prairie.

**Left** As the name implies, mixed grass prairies exhibit a mixture of both shortgrasses and midgrasses. Though this grassland is usually at least partially green through the summer, severe droughts result in parched scenes like this in Badlands National Park, South Dakota.

In combination with others, little bluestem (**below**) is one of the indicator species of the mixed grass prairie. Purple prairie clover (**bottom**) is just one of the common wildflowers of this region.

**Left** Leadplant, so named for the dense gray hairs covering its foliage, is one of the most common shrubs of the mixed grass prairie.

## Some common plants of the mixed grass prairie

### Grasses

| | |
|---|---|
| little bluestem | needlegrass |
| Junegrass | western wheatgrass |
| blue grama | buffalo grass |
| switchgrass | prairie cordgrass |
| big bluestem | foxtail barley |
| Kentucky bluegrass | needle-and-thread |
| Indian grass | timothy |
| redtop | |

### Wildflowers

| | |
|---|---|
| Indian paintbrush | pasqueflower |
| tall goldenrod | butterfly weed |
| birdfoot violet | wild blue flax |
| sego lily | black-eyed Susan |
| spreading dogbane | horse nettle |
| prairie rose | mouse-ear chickweed |
| plains larkspur | Carolina anemone |
| evening primrose | prairie false indigo |
| bladder campion | common sunflower |
| death camas | snow-on-the-mountain |
| silverleaf scurf pea | Indian blanket |
| giant sunflower | locoweed |
| compass plant | purple prairie clover |
| blue salvia | prairie smoke |
| rough blazing star | prickly pear |
| prairie blazing star | stiff goldenrod |
| many-spined opuntia | prairie gentian |
| spotted Joe-Pye weed | common milkweed |
| Jerusalem artichoke | prairie mimosa |
| pale agoseris | Maximilian's sunflower |
| crazyweed | Mexican hat |
| hairy golden aster | |

### Trees and shrubs

| | |
|---|---|
| leadplant | prairie acacia |
| shrubby cinquefoil | smooth sumac |
| eastern cottonwood | eastern red cedar |
| bur oak | American plum |
| osage orange | green ash |
| hackberry | Siberian elm |
| Russian olive | common chokecherry |
| common prickly-ash | |

# SHORTGRASS PRAIRIE

Proceeding west from the mixed grass prairie one comes to the shortgrass prairie, an area of light, infrequent precipitation, low humidity, and high winds. These factors combine to produce an extremely high rate of evaporation, second only to that of a true desert. Due to these arid conditions, a permanent dry zone exists deep in the subsoil, into which plant roots do not penetrate.

The two dominant grasses on the shortgrass prairie, buffalo grass and blue grama, have adapted well to such a demanding environment. Although their roots are shorter than most other prairie grasses, they account for more than 90% of each plant! Both are sod formers by nature, but can also grow in isolated clumps in drier areas. Buffalo grass is easily recognized by the above-ground stolons, or runners, it sends out to put down roots and colonize new areas, and blue grama is characterized by its arched, one-sided flower stalks. They concentrate their growth in the cooler, moister weather of spring and fall, becoming dormant during the heat of midsummer, once they use all available moisture in the soil. (This characteristic distinguishes shortgrass prairie from mixed grass and tallgrass prairies, where moisture is generally retained in the soil year-round.) When this happens, the grasses lose their brief greenery and take on a parched, yellowish-brown appearance, emphasizing the dryness of the area.

Due to their severe climate and reduced humus, shortgrass prairies have been largely unaltered by agriculture. They are, however, susceptible to overgrazing by livestock. Unlike their wild counterparts, the bison and pronghorn, which are constantly on the move and give grasses and forbs a chance to recover between grazings, livestock is liable to be confined to one area for long periods. Their close cropping weakens plants' root systems, so that other grasses better adapted to constant grazing, such as Kentucky bluegrass and cheatgrass brome, are able to invade, changing the character of the shortgrass prairie. Severe overgrazing, along with the removal of cattle for slaughter, may permanently destroy the prairie by breaking the nutrient cycle of growth and decomposition. And without the protection of the moist, shady mulch created by decomposing grass, the soil bakes in the sun, becoming susceptible to the wind erosion that occurred in the Dust Bowl of the 1930s.

As one travels west across the prairies and into the rainshadow of the Rockies, plants begin to exhibit more and more desert adaptations protecting stems and leaves, the plant's main water storage organs from desiccation. Among the more common are light-colored leaves that reflect heat and light; dense, hairy or wooly stems and leaves that insulate them from temperature extremes and reduce the flow of moisture-robbing winds over the surface, and a waxy or resinous coating on the foliage that reduces transpiration.

**Right** Many people associate cacti only with deserts, and are quite surprised to find them in grasslands as well. In reality, grasslands often receive only slightly more precipitation than do deserts. Plains pricklypear is one of several species common to the prairies.

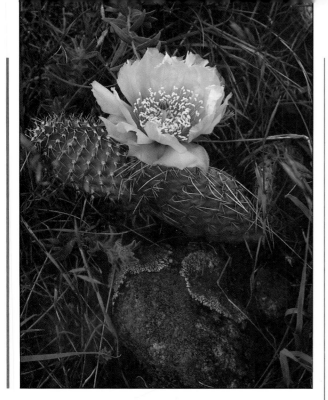

## Some common plants of the shortgrass prairie

### Grasses

buffalo grass
needle-and-thread
little bluestem
Junegrass
foxtail barley

blue grama
Kentucky bluegrass
western wheatgrass
red three-awn

### Wildflowers

yellow bell
purple prairie clover
cowpen daisy
western wallflower
common sunflower
arrowleaf balsam root
Hooker's evening primrose
sego lily
wild blue flax
Rocky Mountain bee plant
western pink vervain
locoweed
crazyweed
vase flower
scarlet globemallow
plains yucca
hairy golden aster
camphorweed
plains pricklypear
Mexican hat

white prairie clover
blackfoot daisy
Tahoka daisy
mule's ear
Indian blanket
curlycup gumweed
pasqueflower
silverleaf scurf pea
plains wallflower
prairie gentian
many-spined opuntia
wooly locoweed
death camas
plains larkspur
buffalo gourd
desert plume
field milkvetch
dotted blazing star
candelabra cactus

### Trees and shrubs

fringed sage
Rocky Mountain juniper
Siberian elm
four-wing saltbush
common chokecherry
quaking aspen
winter fat

snakeweed
prairie sage
rabbit brush
eastern cottonwood
osage orange
Russian olive

**Left** The shortgrass prairie extends eastward from the foothills of the Rocky Mountains and grades into the mixed grass prairie. Grassland boundaries are neither distinct nor permanent, but shift back and forth with changes in climate and precipitation patterns.

# INTERMOUNTAIN GRASSLANDS

Flanked by the Cascade and Sierra Nevada ranges to the west and the Rockies to the east, the intermountain grasslands cover the majority of Utah and Nevada, the eastern third of Oregon and Washington, and a small portion of southern Idaho. They encompass the Great Basin, a huge area with no drainage to the sea, in which most streams and rivers drain into the Great Salt Lake.

Although considered a grassland, one of the dominant plants is not a grass, but sagebrush. The grasses found here are bunchgrasses that space themselves widely by putting out horizontal as well as vertical roots to obtain moisture. A shortage of summer rainfall favors cool-season species, such as bluebunch wheatgrass and Idaho fescue, which are dormant during summer. Unfortunately, in many areas bluebunch wheatgrass has been displaced by cheatgrass brome, an exotic invader that capitalized on the cultivation of wheat in the northern part of the intermountain region and spread from there. The overgrazing that accompanied the cattle boom of the 1880s weakened the bluebunch wheatgrass, hastening its replacement with cheatgrass brome, which had evolved

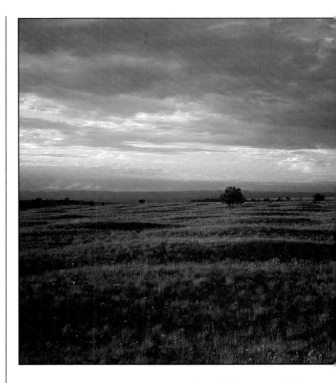

**Below** One of the dominant forms of vegetation in the intermountain grasslands is big sagebrush. Grasses and herbs reign in the spaces between the sagebrush plants.

**Left** The intermountain grasslands are not always vast expanses of grass, as shown in this view near Long Creek, Oregon. Depending upon the topography, they may occupy only narrow bands on mountain slopes between the dry, desert areas at lower elevations and the pinyon/juniper woodland or lodgepole pine forest at higher, moister elevations.

**Left** Bluebunch wheat grass is an indicator species of the intermountain grasslands. Unfortunately, in some areas this native has been largely displaced by cheatgrass brome, an alien species accidentally imported from Asia with wheat shipments.

## Some common plants of the intermountain grasslands

### Grasses

| | |
|---|---|
| Idaho fescue | bluebunch wheatgrass |
| Kentucky bluegrass | cheatgrass brome |
| foxtail barley | bottlebrush squirreltail |

### Wildflowers

| | |
|---|---|
| scarlet globemallow | fragile pricklypear |
| hood phlox | longleaf phlox |
| prairie star | arrowleaf balsam root |
| threadleaf groundsel | cream cup |
| desert paintbrush | scarlet gilia |
| locoweed | hoary cress |
| yellow bee plant | field milkvetch |
| vase flower | spreading dogbane |
| mule's ears | pale agoseris |
| sego lily | many-spined opuntia |
| yellow bell | broom snakeweed |
| elegant camas | prairie smoke |
| pale wallflower | western wallflower |
| hawk's beard | sweet fennel |
| fiddleneck | desert plume |
| flatpod | crazyweed |

### Trees and shrubs

| | |
|---|---|
| big sagebrush | winter fat |
| desert sage | greasewood |
| shadscale | rabbitbrush |
| snakeweed | little horsebrush |
| four-wing saltbush | Mormon tea |
| Utah juniper | Russian olive |
| singleleaf pinyon | curlleaf cerocarpus |
| Siberian elm | threadleaf phacelia |
| iodine bush | |

to withstand the year-round grazing of camels and wild horses on the steppes of Asia, whence the contaminated shipments of wheat originated. Overgrazing also led to an increase in sagebrush, which in many places grows more densely now than it did in past centuries.

The vegetation of this region varies with changes in elevation and latitude. Only ten to fifteen inches of precipitation falls annually, with higher elevations receiving more than the basins. Consequently, plants less tolerant of drought are found higher on the mountain slopes. South-facing slopes, which receive the most direct sunlight, are warmer and therefore drier than northern slopes, so the orientation of the mountainsides also affects the types of vegetation. In the northern intermountain zone, sagebrush grassland occupies the basins and lower mountain slopes, but to the south it remains only on the lower mountain slopes, giving way to true desert plants in the southern basins, the hottest and driest parts of this region. Forbs occur in the intermountain grasslands, but not in the abundance in which they are found throughout the prairies.

# WOODLANDS
## THE FOREST AS A COMMUNITY

At first glance, forests, with their myriad species, may seem indecipherably complex. Complex they are, but all forests follow orderly patterns that govern their structure and function. Just as an ornithologist must be able to recognize birds of prey before learning to distinguish broad-winged hawks from goshawks, the practical botanist should concentrate on recognizing general ecosystems before trying to unravel the intricacies of any particular one.

Forests, like all ecosystems, are primarily composed of a given set of species that are consistently present wherever that particular habitat is encountered. Of course, there are always exceptions, variations, and overlap between various habitats, but generally speaking, the combined presence of a few key *indicator species* tells you which type of habitat you are observing. By first narrowing possibilities, you reduce your task to a manageable level. By knowing what other species you might expect to encounter, you increase the likelihood of actually finding them. For instance, if you are in a forest dominated by American beech and sugar maple, you may correctly surmise that you are in the northern hardwood forest, the northern tier of the eastern deciduous woodlands, and can expect such companions as yellow birch, striped maple, hobblebush and eastern hemlock. More importantly, it eliminates a host of other plants that you should not expect to find here, such as sweetgum or magnolia.

An ecosystem functions like one giant organism, and like any organism, it has a definite structure and orderly functions. Forests have a structure that is particularly easy to discern. Typical forests are stratified vertically, having five distinct vegetation zones, although one or more of these may be reduced or absent in certain forest types. From the top down they are the canopy, understory, shrub layer, herb layer, and ground layer. The canopy, of course, consists of the tallest trees, while shade-tolerant trees make up the understory and shade-tolerant shrubs, the shrub layer. Ferns and ephemeral spring wildflowers are the primary constituents of the herb layer, and the ground layer, which may be considered part of the herb layer, hosts low-growing plants like mosses, liverworts, fungi, and club mosses.

In a temperate deciduous forest, winter is the dormant period when most trees shed their leaves and enter a resting state. In spring, the plants do not come into leaf all at once. Instead, in a very orderly

Decomposers, like this fungi (**left**) known as chicken-of-the-woods, play a crucial role recycling nutrients in a forest. Interactions among different species such as this are what makes a forest an orderly community and not just a disjointed assemblage of organisms. Showy lady's slippers (**right**) are important as well as beautiful members of the forest community; deducing their significance is part of the fun of botany.

alpine
subalpine
boreal forest
altitude
low
tropical rain forest
temperate deciduous forests
oak-hickory forest
beech-maple forest
boreal forest
tundra
ice and snow
south
north
latitude

procession, the herb layer develops and flowers first, followed by the shrub layer, the understory, and finally the canopy. This is no accident. As a matter of survival, herbaceous plants of deciduous forests evolved early season growth as their means of securing enough solar energy to reproduce and develop food reserves to carry them through another year. Shrubs also need an early start for the same reason, but the selective pressure on them is not as great as that affecting herb-layer plants, so shrubs can wait until a bit later in spring to produce leaves. Thus, the zone with the greatest biological productivity is the one that came into leaf most recently. Once the canopy's leaves are fully formed, it becomes the forest's primary zone of photosynthesis for the rest of the season. It has been estimated that once the canopy of a typical eastern deciduous forest is in full leaf, as little as 1% of the available direct sunlight reaches the

**Above** Plant communities change with elevation as well as with latitude. Climbing a few thousand feet in elevation from the base of a North Carolina mountain will take you through the same plant communities as would walking 1,000 miles or so due north.

ground, the other 99% being absorbed or reflected by the canopy leaves.

There are exceptions to this model of forest stratification. Both xeric (very dry) and hydric (very wet) deciduous forests tend to have more open canopies, so stratification is less evident and the orderly pattern of coming into leaf from bottom to top is not so critical. Dark, dense coniferous forests dominated by evergreen needleleaf trees often have reduced or absent zones underneath the canopy because there is little opportunity for those plants to garner the sunlight they need.

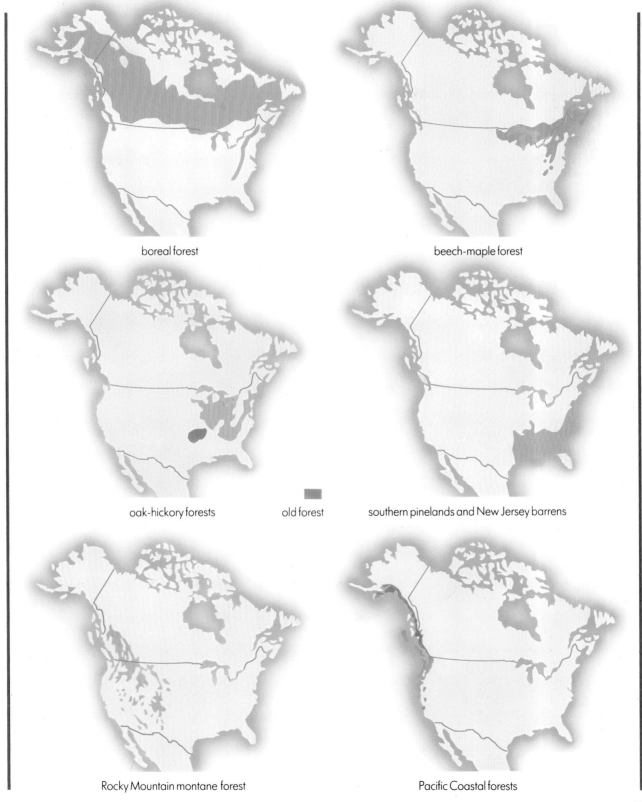

boreal forest

beech-maple forest

oak-hickory forests     old forest

southern pinelands and New Jersey barrens

Rocky Mountain montane forest

Pacific Coastal forests

# FIRE AND FOREST ECOSYSTEMS

Many people have grown up with the image of Smokey the Bear depicting the catastrophic effects of forest fires and warning that only *we* could prevent them. Countless scenes on television and in the movies also portrayed fire as a major destructive force in nature that robbed us of our natural resources.

As it turns out, Smokey the Bear and his message may have been the forests' own worst enemy. Fire, in fact, is an integral part of many temperate forest and grassland ecosystems. In a forest, plants grow, die, and decompose as they are recycled to build the soil and to provide nutrients to future generations of plants. Often, there is a lag period between the time a tree dies and when it actually hits the ground, where active decomposition takes place. It may stand for years as a dead snag, providing valuable nesting sites and food sources for wildlife. When it finally does fall, it may get caught on other trees, so it is still suspended in the air. Branches usually fall or get knocked off separately, and their irregular shape often keeps them off the ground. As long as dead wood is kept from contact with the moist soil, circulating air continues to dry it.

Since the accumulation of this debris occurs faster than the decomposition of the material under it, a mechanism is needed to periodically clean out the forest floor without cheating the soil of the nutrients due it. Periodically, perhaps every 10 to 25 years, droughts desiccate the debris even further, fires are sparked by lightning, and a "cool" ground fire sweeps through the forest, devouring the downed "fuel" and depositing a nutrient-rich ash on the forest floor, which provides a fresh seed bed for new growth. Fanned by a breeze, this type of fire usually moves fast, barely lingering long enough to scorch the bark of mature trees, which many times suffer no harm at all. Moving slowly against the wind, the fire may indeed kill some trees, creating a natural meadow and providing the edge habitat critical to so many wildlife species before

In many cases, forest fires actually improve the health of the forest, clearing debris and returning nutrients to the soil. Even areas in Yellowstone National Park that were devastated by the wildfires of 1988 (**top**) have begun their recovery (**bottom**).

**Above** Many plants thrive in the wake of fire. Here, quaking aspens sprout prolifically from their rootstocks after a fire, and lodgepole pines produce many seed cones sealed with resin that require the heat of a fire to release their seeds.

succession guides it back to a mature forest. Eventually the fire reaches a firebreak, such as a stream, road, or a recently burned area, and is extinguished for lack of fuel. All is well.

Once it was decided that fires were evil, everyone set about snuffing them out with a vengeance. Fire towers kept watch across our nation's forests, and at the first wisp of smoke an army of firefighters would descend upon the flames and extinguish them before they could properly be called a forest fire. Meanwhile, the forest continued producing new wood, trees continued to die at their normal rate, and the fuel piled up. Firefighters found it harder and harder to contain the blazes. The accumulating flammable material, combined with periodic droughts, created a tinderbox that, when ignited, led to a crown fire that raced through the canopy, killing trees, leaping firebreaks and outpacing the efforts of firefighters. Such uncontrolled fires are commonly called wildfires and, under the most extreme circumstances, a fire storm results where desiccated trees burst into flame from the intense heat before the blaze even reaches them. These truly destructive fires are the direct result of human interference. This expensive lesson was graphically demonstrated during the incineration of Yellowstone National Park in the summer of 1988, during which nearly 1,000,000 acres in and around the park were blackened by an inferno fueled by 80+ years' worth of debris and winds that topped 70 miles per hour.

Fire is now accepted as a natural part of most natural ecosystems in North America, and as essential to the health and vigor of many habitats. Areas like the Everglades and California's sequoia forests are actually preserved by regular fires. Some plants, such as the jack pine, whose cones only open in intense heat, require fire to reproduce. Hopefully, the overwhelming scientific evidence will convince us to see fire as a part of nature's process of renewal. Fire management should be left to the proper authorities; arson is both dangerous and criminal.

# BOREAL FORESTS

Up north, where winters are long and people are scarce, stretches the largest tract of forest in North America, the boreal forest. It covers much of Canada and Alaska, from the U.S. border to the arctic treeline and from the Atlantic coast of New-foundland to the Bering Sea. It is primarily a coniferous forest, composed largely of needle-leafed, cone-bearing trees, and can roughly be divided into three east-west belts of vegetation. The southernmost pine/hemlock band is overshadowed by the middle spruce/fir zone, followed by the northernmost taiga zone, in which the firs and spruces become increasingly dwarfed until they finally give way to arctic tundra.

Because of the harsh climate, the diversity of life in the boreal forest is rather low compared to other North American ecosystems; only the arctic tundra supports fewer species. What it lacks in diversity, however, the boreal forest makes up in sheer numbers. At first glance, the forest seems totally dominated by black spruce, white spruce, and balsam fir, but closer scrutiny reveals other trees. Red, white, and jack pines are common in the southernmost regions. Jack pines thrive in poorer, dry soil, colonizing such areas first and eventually yielding to red pine. Quaking aspen, balsam poplar, bigtooth aspen, and paper birch, the primary deciduous species, inhabit clearings opened by fire or other disturbances.

In much of the boreal forest, interlaced ever-green branches block the sunlight so effec-tively that the understory, shrub, and herb lay-ers are greatly reduced or missing entirely. Other barriers to undergrowth are the thick, spongy carpet of discarded needles, and the nutrient-poor soil made acidic by decomposing needles. Sphagnum moss often carpets the ground in wetter areas, and lichens and mushrooms abound. Wildflowers include starflower, bluebead lily, bunchberry, bearberry, twinflower, and northern white violet. Other wildflowers and shrubs are largely restricted to clearings and the edges of lakes and streams where sunlight is available. Among the more common shrubs are blueberry, elderberry, sheep laurel, and thimbleberry.

Bogs and meadows, the remnants of filled-in bogs, dot the landscape. These are products of glacial activity that scoured out depressions in the

ground and then deposited huge chunks of ice as they retreated, which melted and filled the hollows. Though surrounded by the boreal forest, these bogs are unique communities, covered in the Wetlands chapter (see pp113-15).

An extension of the boreal forest reaches south to Georgia along the highest peaks and ridges of the Appalachian Mountains. Here, white spruce and balsam fir are replaced by red spruce and Fraser fir, but otherwise it bears many of the hallmarks of a boreal forest.

## Some common plants of the boreal forest

### Trees and shrubs

| | |
|---|---|
| black spruce | white spruce |
| balsam fir | jack pine |
| red pine | quaking aspen |
| bigtooth aspen | paper birch |
| balsam poplar | tamarack |
| red maple | mountain ash |
| sheep laurel | blueberry |
| thimbleberry | elderberry |
| mountain maple | green alder |
| white pine | |

### Ferns and mosses

| | |
|---|---|
| sphagnum moss | bracken fern |
| oak fern | |

### Wildflowers

| | |
|---|---|
| bluebead lily | one-sided pyrola |
| bunchberry | starflower |
| twinflower | bloodroot |
| nodding trillium | pink lady's slipper |
| northern white violet | shinleaf |
| harebell | pinesap |
| yellow lad's slipper | partridgeberry |
| common wood sorrel | fireweed |
| purple-fringed orchid | bearberry |
| calypso | |
| orange hawkweed | |
| goldthread | |
| Canada mayflower | |
| red baneberry | |

The boreal forest (**above**) is the largest forest community in North America. Composed largely of coniferous trees, its dense canopy admits little light, thus the dark, moist forest floor supports a relatively low diversity of plant species. Two of the most common trees of the boreal forest are white spruce (**far left**) and balsam fir (**left**).

Two species that thrive in the dimly lit herb layer of the boreal forest are starflower (**above**) and bunchberry, a member of the dogweed family (**left**).

93

# NORTHERN HARDWOOD FOREST

Also known as the transition forest because it shares many species with the cool, dark, moist boreal forest, and continues to the warmer, drier oak-hickory forests to the south, the northern hardwood forest is the northern tier of the eastern deciduous woodlands. It also lies between the boreal forests of the higher Appalachian Mountain peaks and the oak-hickory forests at their bases. The winters here are shorter and milder and the growing season longer than in the boreal forest, and since its canopy is more open than the boreal forest, the northern hardwood forest also supports richer understory, shrub, and herb layers.

Much of the canopy is dominated by American beech or sugar maple. Interestingly, researchers have found that beech seedlings grow better under maples than they do under other beeches, and vice versa. Consequently, American beeches may usurp

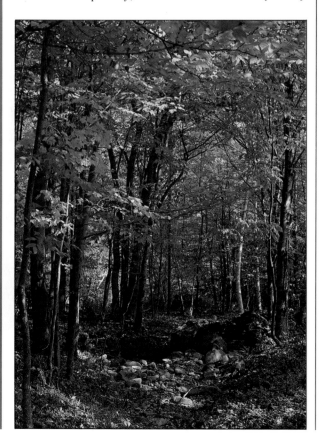

**Left** The predominance of American beech and sugar maple indicate that this New Hampshire scene is part of the northern hardwood forest.

**Above** Paper birch, with its white bark, and sugar maples are common members of the northern hardwood forest.

the canopy while the sugar maples inhabit the understory and bide their time until the current generation of beeches dies off. They then grow to fill the canopy while a new crop of beech seedlings grows underneath them, and so on. The third most common hardwood species in this region is yellow birch. In the moist lowlands, northern red oak, American basswood, and American elm are prominent.

Two needle-leaved species, eastern hemlock and eastern white pine, grow abundantly here. Eastern hemlocks are particularly plentiful in cool, moist, shady ravines and north-facing mountainsides, while white pine thrives in open or disturbed areas, together with gray birch and pin cherry. Striped maple, downy serviceberry, and nannyberry are common understory species, and the shrub layer often sports hobblebush. Compared to the rather barren floor of the boreal forest, the herb layer is a botanist's delight. Many members of the lily family grace the floor of the northern hardwood forest, including painted trillium, purple trillium, large-flowered trillium, trout lily, Canada mayflower, false Solomon's seal, bluebead lily, and others. Red baneberry, white baneberry, pink lady's slipper, bunchberry, starflower, fringed polygala, and Jack-in-the-pulpit are also present.

Species composition of the northern hardwood forest, largely dependent upon local factors such as soil type, moisture, and temperature, varies from one community to the other. For instance, in the midwestern regions eastern hemlock and yellow birch diminish while white, red and bur oaks become prominent, and American basswood replaces American beech as a dominant canopy species. The best way to familiarize yourself with local variations is to write or visit state and national parks and forests and ask for their interpretive brochures and booklets on the local flora.

## Some common plants of the northern hardwood forest

### Trees and shrubs

| | |
|---|---|
| American beech | sugar maple |
| yellow birch | eastern hemlock |
| white pine | northern red oak |
| gray birch | American mountain ash |
| paper birch | mountain maple |
| nannyberry | hobblebush |
| striped maple | mountain laurel |
| American basswood | downy serviceberry |
| tamarack | witch hazel |
| balsam poplar | red spruce |
| quaking aspen | great laurel |
| highbush blueberry | red maple |
| black cherry | |
| pin cherry | |

### Wildflowers

| | |
|---|---|
| painted trillium | purple trillium |
| pink lady's slipper | goldthread |
| common wood sorrel | bluebead lily |
| trout lily | large-flowered trillium |
| partridgeberry | red baneberry |
| white baneberry | spring beauty |
| starflower | Canada mayflower |
| foamflower | harebell |
| Indian pipe | purple-fringed orchid |
| false Solomon's seal | common blue violet |
| sweet white violet | wild bergamot |
| wild columbine | fringed polygala |
| wild sarsparilla | bloodroot |
| Jack-in-the-pulpit | sessile bellwort |
| downy yellow violet | bunchberry |

### Ferns and fern allies

| | |
|---|---|
| ground pine | |
| bracken fern | ground cedar |
| shining club moss | stiff club moss |
| interrupted fern | maidenhair fern |

**Left** Frequently encountered in the herb layer of the northern hardwood forest are (clockwise from top): large-flowered trilliums, trout lilies, and bluebead lilies, all members of the lily family. Each spring, members of the herb layer race to grow and flower before the forest canopy leafs out and restricts their light.

# OAK-HICKORY FOREST

This is by far the largest of the eastern deciduous forests. It is sometimes known as mixed deciduous forest, for while oaks and hickories are the most plentiful trees, up to three dozen species may vie for a place in the canopy. The term refers to two forests that were formerly considered separate: the true oak-hickory forest of Arkansas, southern Missouri, and eastern Oklahoma, and the former oak-chestnut forest of southern New England, the Middle Atlantic states, and the southern Appalachian mountains. However, with the mass demise of the American chestnut after the chestnut blight fungus was accidentally imported to this country in 1906, hickories and more oaks assumed their places in the canopy. Interestingly, the American chestnut roots are blight resistant and continue to sprout and grow as an understory species before being struck down by the infection. They seem to grow larger with each effort before succumbing, which may indicate that they are developing a resistance to the blight. Perhaps some

day they shall regain their rightful place as monarchs of the eastern forests.

An abundance of both oaks *and* hickories defines this forest. White oak, scarlet oak, black oak, chestnut oak, northern and southern red oaks, mockernut hickory, pignut hickory, and bitternut hickory are all good indicator species. Wetter sites often host sweetgum, shagbark hickory, red maple, and sourwood. Pioneering trees in disturbed areas include gray birch, eastern red cedar, quaking aspen, bigtooth aspen, black locust, white pine and pitch pine in the north, and slash pine in the south. The understory of the oak-hickory forest, much more highly defined than in the northern hardwood forest or the boreal forest, includes American chestnut, flowering dogwood, downy serviceberry, sassafras, hackberry, hophornbeam, witch hazel and redbud.

The shrub layer in this forest can be quite dense. Entanglements of great laurel and mountain laurel, which at times seem almost impenetrable, paint the forest pink with their spring flowers. The elegant pinxter flower and flame azalea are also noteworthy. Highbush blueberry, lowbush blueberry, and deerberry are plentiful. The herb layer shares many species with the northern hardwood forest: violet wood sorrel, Dutchman's breeches, cut-leaved toothwort, teaberry, mayapple, common cinquefoil, sweet white violet, birdfoot violet, Jack-in-the-pulpit, spring beauty, round-lobed hepatica, rue anemone, bloodroot, yellow lady's slipper, large-flowered trillium, trout lily, wild bergamot, wood betony, and wild columbine are just a few. Ferns are richly represented, with hay-scented fern, marginal woodfern, interrupted fern, Christmas fern, and lady fern being particularly common in the uplands. Royal fern and cinnamon fern are two species often encountered in the moist lowlands. Clubmosses, including ground cedar, shining clubmoss, and tree clubmoss, are common.

**Above** Flowering dogwood is a major understory species in these woods. Large white | bracts surround clusters of flowers before its leaves emerge in spring.

**Above** Among the many wildflowers common to the herb layer of the oak-hickory forest is wild columbine, which is frequently found on sunny, well-drained mountain slopes.

**Left** The oak-hickory is the largest North American deciduous forest, although most of it was once oak-chestnut forest prior to the onslaught of chestnut blight.

## Some common plants of the oak- hickory forest

### Trees, shrubs and vines

| | |
|---|---|
| white oak | scarlet oak |
| black oak | northern red oak |
| southern red oak | chestnut oak |
| shumard oak | bear oak |
| bur oak | northern pin oak |
| shingle oak | blackjack oak |
| post oak | pignut hickory |
| mockernut hickory | bitternut hickory |
| shagbark hickory | sweetgum |
| red maple | sourwood |
| black cherry | black walnut |
| white ash | green ash |
| blackgum | gray birch |
| eastern white pine | pitch pine |
| black locust | quaking aspen |
| slash pine | shortleaf pine |
| Virginia pine | American chestnut |
| flowering dogwood | downy serviceberry |
| sassafras | hackberry |
| hophornbeam | witchhazel |
| redbud | great laurel |
| mountain laurel | pinxter flower |
| flame azalea | highbush blueberry |
| lowbush blueberry | deerberry |
| spicebush | mapleleaf viburnum |
| poison ivy | Virginia creeper |
| fox grape | |

### Wildflowers

| | |
|---|---|
| Dutchman's breeches | mayapple |
| cut-leaved toothwort | bloodroot |
| violet wood sorrel | Jack-in-the-pulpit |
| round-lobed hepatica | rue anemone |
| large-flowered trillium | purple trillium |
| trout lily | wild sarsparilla |
| wild columbine | wood betony |
| yellow lady's slipper | teaberry |
| birdfoot violet | bunchberry |
| common blue violet | fringed polygala |
| harebell | pinesap |
| Indian pipe | starflower |
| sweet white violet | twinflower |
| spring beauty | yellow-fringed orchid |
| pink lady's slipper | smooth Solomon's seal |
| false Solomon's seal | |

### Ferns and fern allies

| | |
|---|---|
| hay-scented fern | Christmas fern |
| marginal woodfern | interrupted fern |
| lady fern | royal fern |
| cinnamon fern | haircap moss |
| ground cedar | shining clubmoss |
| tree clubmoss | pincushion moss |

# SOUTHERN PINELANDS

Southern pinelands is a catch-all phrase describing the broad crescent of coastal plains in the southeastern United States, stretching from the pine barrens of New Jersey to eastern Texas. While the unifying feature of this area is a preponderance of pines, many other tree species occur, and while pines remain dominant, the species composition can vary radically from one region to another.

One reason for this is that pinelands are not a climax community, the endpoint of ecological succession, but a "fire climax," an arrested state of succession held in check by periodic forest fires. Without fire, these areas would eventually succeed to a forest dominated by oaks, beech, hickories, and magnolia. Pinelands are constantly trying to evolve, but are regularly being returned to a state favorable to the growth of pines. Historically, fires in the southern pinelands occurred naturally from lightning strikes, but more recently, pulp and paper companies, which own huge tracts of these timberlands, have adopted the policy of regular burning, to reduce excess fuel which could lead to a wildfire and threaten their investments. In turn, fire clears the ground and prepares a fresh seedbed necessary for the germination of pine seeds. Fire also prevents the broadleafed understory taking over as the pines age, and shading the sun-loving pine seedlings.

Differences in precipitation, soil character, and drainage further alter the specific composition of different plant communities. Obviously, some plants are better adapted to wet (hydric) soil, some to dry (xeric) soil, and some prefer a happy medium (mesic soil). Pineland soils are typically nutrient-poor. Since pine needles are resistant to decay, the species richness in old pine stands is fairly low because most available nutrients are tied up in standing trees and in the carpet of pine needles on the forest floor. By contrast, the species diversity in a recently burned area is much higher because the nutrients previously locked up in forest debris have been returned to the soil and made available to other plants.

The pinelands, then, are not one type of forest, but dozens. They are defined more geographically than botanically, but some species do present themselves repeatedly. Longleaf pine is the most widespread and the leader in economic importance. It is often mixed with slash pine and saw palmetto. In the northern part of this range, loblolly pine and shortleaf pine commonly occur together. Turkey oak, another fire-adapted species, often forms solid stands on the higher elevations of the coastal plains. Live oak, the quintessential symbol of the Deep South, with its massive trunk

Spanish moss (**left**) draped profusely from branches is a common sight in the southern pinelands. An indicator species of this community is the longleaf pine (**above**).

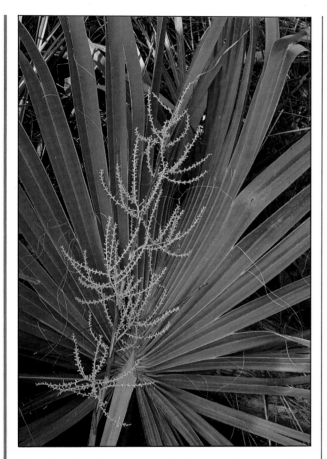

**Above** Another indicator species of southern pinelands | is the saw palmetto, a member of the rather limited shrub layer.

## Some common plants of the southern pinelands

### Trees, shrubs and vines

| | |
|---|---|
| longleaf pine | slash pine |
| loblolly pine | shortleaf pine |
| Virginia pine | live oak |
| turkey oak | post oak |
| myrtle oak | laurel oak |
| southern red oak | shumard oak |
| black oak | blackjack oak |
| water oak | willow oak |
| overcup oak | southern magnolia |
| mockernut hickory | pignut hickory |
| water hickory | bitternut hickory |
| American beech | blackgum |
| sweetgum | sweetbay |
| southern catalpa | common persimmon |
| Carolina holly | southern bayberry |
| saw palmetto | shining sumac |
| spicebush | one-flowered hawthorn |
| pinxter flower | Virginia creeper |
| poison ivy | American sycamore |
| yaupon | |

### Wildflowers

| | |
|---|---|
| Spanish moss | pinesap |
| Indian pipe | downy false foxglove |
| mayapple | round-lobed hepatica |
| bird-foot violet | common blue violet |
| bloodroot | Jack-in-the-pulpit |
| partridgeberry | pink lady's slipper |
| wood betony | scarlet sage |
| passionflower | mistletoe |
| crested dwarf iris | grassleaf golden aster |

### Grasses

| | |
|---|---|
| wiregrass | little bluestem |
| yellow stargrass | |

and wide, spreading crown draped in Spanish moss, is intolerant of fire but thrives in wetter soils and along the coast. Post oak, myrtle oak, laurel oak, southern red oak, southern catalpa, common persimmon, and Carolina holly are also indicator trees of this area. Common shrubs include saw palmetto, shining sumac, spicebush, southern bayberry, one-flowered hawthorn, and pinxter flower. Grasses such as wiregrass, little bluestem, and yellow stargrass dominate the herb layer. Spanish moss, an epiphyte or "airplant," cascades prolifically from tree branches throughout the southern pinelands. It is not parasitic, but photosynthesizes its own food, obtains minerals leached naturally from the foliage of the host tree, and collects rainwater by means of scales covering its stems. Another epiphyte, greenfly orchid, is also endemic.

# FLOODPLAIN FORESTS

Floodplain forests of low river valleys may be considered subtypes of the larger forests that surround them, but in many respects they are different enough to merit separate consideration. Often, the species composition changes drastically in the uppermost reaches of floodwaters.

Flooding is a sort of safety valve that protects communities downstream. When receiving excess drainage from a storm or the spring melt, a river confined to a deep, narrow channel would have no choice but to increase its velocity and, therefore, its power and destructive potential. The forceful waters would tear at the sides of the channel, removing everything from soil to rocks; severe currents can move boulders. The torrent would turn into a brown soup as its load of sand, silt, and clay increased. Eventually, the river would widen, the current slow and lose power, and its cargo of sediment would settle. Were this to happen at the mouth of the river where it meets the ocean, the estuary located there would be devastated. Estuaries, the nurseries of our oceans, are biologically the most productive areas on earth. Subjected to unchecked floodwaters, they would be smothered under countless tons of sediment.

Fortunately, a mechanism exists that controls the destructive potential of rivers and has indirectly resulted in the evolution of floodplain forests. As the waters rise and their velocity increases, they crest the bank of their normal channel, spreading out across a flat plain and promptly slowing down and depositing their load along the length of the river, instead of just at the end. With each flood, alluvium, a rich layer of silt full of nutrients and organic matter, is deposited on the already fertile soil of the floodplain.

The plants that grow in floodplains generally require moister and/or more fertile soil than those of the surrounding region. Of course, floodplain forest plants have had to adapt to take advantage of this bonanza; they must be able to survive periodic flooding or repopulate in the face of it.

Many trees will drown in soil that is saturated for any length of time. Green ash and willow species, all common residents along stream and river banks, are stimulated to form new, air-filled roots to replace those that die due to flooding. Lenticels, tiny openings in their bark, expand to allow more

**Above** Black willows are residents of riverbanks, lakeshores, and low, wet places in the east. They often grow right by the water's edge.

air into the trees. Under extreme conditions, these species can switch to anaerobic respiration, which does not require oxygen. Many riparian (river) species depend on the very waters that may kill the parents to distribute the seeds of the next generation. The seeds of some willows and cottonwoods, for example, actually need to be submerged in order to germinate.

Farther back from the river bank, cottonwoods colonize levees, low ridges or mounds parallel to the river that are composed of coarse sediments deposited by the higher floodwaters. The larger size of the sediment particles means more space between them and better drainage, so that even in close proximity to the water this soil may be quite dry, and cottonwoods must put down deep taproots to protect themselves from drought.

Beyond the levees, the species composition, which varies geographically, grades into those progressively less tolerant of prolonged flooding. In the Northeast, a community of sycamore, black ash, boxelder, American and slippery elms, and red, silver, or black maples occurs after the cottonwoods, with American beech and tulip poplar just above the normal high water mark. In the Southeast, levees are often followed by overcup oak, water hickory, waterlocust, and red maple, which in turn may be replaced by sycamore, sweetgum, water oak, willow oak, and Nuttall oak.

In this region, the highest floodwaters may see shagbark hickory, post oak, and swamp chestnut oak. In the arid West, floodplain forests may represent a distinctly different community from the surrounding area. Willows and cottonwoods still abound along the river banks. Floodplains in the Rockies accommodate quaking aspen, balsam poplar, and blue spruce, while in the Southwest they host tamarisk, Russian olive, and screwbean mesquite. Redwoods, white alder, box elder, Oregon ash, and California white oak commonly inhabit the various California floodplains, and in the Pacific Northwest, red alders dominate the floodplain, gradually deferring to bigleaf maple, western hemlock, and sitka spruce.

Moisture-loving vines proliferate in the floodplains, as do ferns, which require a damp environment for reproduction. Other herbaceous plants also thrive, but may be reduced in areas of frequent flooding.

Seldom found far from water, turtlehead (**left**) and the brilliant cardinal flower (**below**) are regular eastern floodplain residents. Both are late summer bloomers.

## Some common plants of floodplain forests

(Consult your field guides to determine geographic distribution.)

### Trees

| | |
|---|---|
| green ash | eastern cottonwood |
| Fremont cottonwood | black cottonwood |
| eastern sycamore | black willow |
| sandbar willow | peachleaf willow |
| American elm | slippery elm |
| black ash | boxelder |
| red maple | silver maple |
| black maple | American beech |
| tulip poplar | overcup oak |
| blackgum | pecan |
| water elm | swamp white oak |
| water oak | willow oak |
| Nuttall oak | post oak |
| swamp chestnut oak | water hickory |
| waterlocust | sweetgum |
| quaking aspen | balsam poplar |
| blue spruce | French tamarisk |
| redwood | Russian olive |
| screwbean mesquite | white alder |
| Oregon ash | California white oak |
| red alder | bigleaf maple |
| western hemlock | sitka spruce |

### Wildflowers and vines

| | |
|---|---|
| poison ivy | river grape |
| trumpet creeper | peppervine |
| bur cucumber | Virginia creeper |
| American black currant | wax currant |
| spotted jewelweed | pale jewelweed |
| turtlehead | cardinal flower |
| trout lily | sweetflag |
| mayapple | stinging nettle |
| Dutchman's breeches | virgin's bower |
| Spanish moss | |

101

# ROCKY MOUNTAIN FORESTS

The forests of the Rockies actually consist of four major forest types characterized by the dominant tree species. Unlike eastern forests, the boundaries of the mountainous western forests are defined more by elevation than by latitude. And while species diversity in the Appalachian Mountains decreases with temperature from the base of a mountain to the summit, in the Rockies it increases with precipitation from the lower slopes to the treeline, which is largely determined by temperature.

### Ponderosa pine forest

When traveling into the Rocky Mountains, whether from the eastern shortgrass prairies or the sagebrush grasslands of the Great Basin, often the first tall woodlands encountered in the foothills are dominated by ponderosa pine. (Ponderosa pine forests are also prominent in the Black Hills of South Dakota and in the Bighorn Mountains of northeastern Wyoming.) It inhabits the warmer, drier lower slopes of this range, abutting not only grassland, but also sagebrush, pinyon-juniper woodland, and dense, evergreen oak thickets called chaparral.

Trees in the ponderosa pine forest are generally well spaced to avoid competition for moisture and nutrients, conveying an open, airy feeling compared to the thick, lush eastern forests. The understory is frequently reduced or absent, but areas with some moisture support understories and

**Above** Western serviceberry is a familiar deciduous | understory tree in ponderosa pine forests.

---

## Some common plants of ponderosa pine forests

(Check your field guides to determine geographic distribution.)

### Trees and shrubs

| | |
|---|---|
| ponderosa pine | Douglas fir |
| blue spruce | lodgepole pine |
| birchleaf spirea | western serviceberry |
| western chokecherry | mountain snowberry |
| common juniper | bearberry |
| black hawthorn | creambush |
| Pacific ninebark | antelope brush |
| common snowberry | Colorado pinyon |
| Rocky Mountain juniper | rubber rabbitbrush |
| big sagebrush | wax currant |
| western larch | |

### Grasses

| | |
|---|---|
| Arizona fescue | bluebunch wheatgrass |
| blue grama | Idaho fescue |
| cheatgrass brome | needle and thread |
| western needlegrass | western wheatgrass |

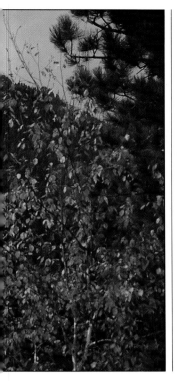

**Left** Quaking aspens mingle with ponderosa pines in Custer State Park, South Dakota. Ponderosa pine forests are found in the Black Hills of South Dakota and lower, drier elevations in the Rockies.

**Right** This view of Moraine Park in Rocky Mountain National Park, Colorado shows widely spaced ponderosa pines on the sunny, dry, south-facing hillside. The cooler, damper north-facing ridge in the middle hosts a Douglas fir woodland, and subalpine forest is visible in the background.

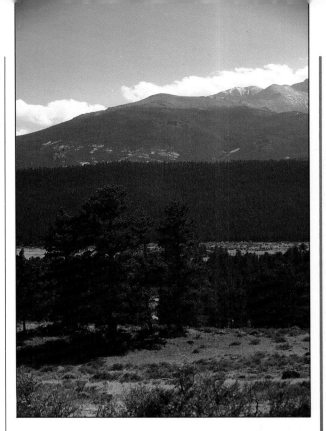

shrub layers that may include western serviceberry, western chokecherry, mountain snowberry, common juniper, bearberry, black hawthorn, creambush, Pacific ninebark and birchleaf spirea. In drier areas, sparse grasses and wildflowers may be the ponderosa pines' only companions.

## Douglas fir forest

Higher into the Rockies, the open ponderosa pine merges with the denser Douglas fir forests of midslope. Douglas fir is particularly prominent in the northern Rockies west of the Continental Divide. East of the Divide, cooler temperatures and diminished rainfall conspire against the Douglas fir, and in the southern Rockies, precipitation is also its limiting factor. Douglas fir can form open forests, as the ponderosa pine does, or dense stands.

Douglas fir is a climax species in the Rocky Mountains, wresting dominance from pioneering predecessors such as lodgepole pine or quaking aspen. Often, the dark-green Douglas firs of moist, north-facing slopes and sheltered valleys contrast starkly with yellowish-green, widely-spaced ponderosa pines inhabiting sunnier slopes a short distance away. With water in short supply in many

### Some common plants of the Rocky Mountain Douglas fir forest

(Check your field guides to determine geographic distribution.)

**Trees and shrubs**

| | |
|---|---|
| Douglas fir | ponderosa pine |
| grand fir | western larch |
| white spruce | black spruce |
| western white pine | lodgepole pine |
| quaking aspen | Engelmann spruce |
| subalpine fir | narrowleaf cottonwood |
| thin-leaf alder | willows |
| blue spruce | water birch |
| mountain alder | white fir |
| Chihuahua pine | Arizona pine |
| western serviceberry | New Mexican locust |
| Gambel oak | mountain snowberry |
| birchleaf spirea | Wood's rose |
| bearberry | creeping barberry |
| Nootka rose | |

Rocky Mountain regions, it is not surprising that linear micro-forests of water-loving species spring up along streams within the drier coniferous forests. Lining the stream banks are deciduous hardwoods such as Rocky Mountain maple, water birch, western serviceberry, mountain alder, quaking aspen, and narrowleaf cottonwood, as well as the coniferous Rocky Mountain juniper and blue spruce. Bearberry and creeping barberry, two low-growing shrubs, create patches of ground cover throughout.

### Lodgepole pine forests

Known to early explorers as Big Piney Woods, large expanses of forest populated by lodgepole pine, a pioneer and fire-climax species, are common in the central and northern Rocky Mountains. At times, they may form climax stands when other conifers are inhibited by local soil composition, temperature, or precipitation. On mountain slopes, lodgepole pine forests are typically located between the Douglas fir forest below and the subalpine forest above.

Lodgepole pines are quite flammable. Fire eliminates the older trees while clearing an area for the next generation of lodgepole pines, which are highly intolerant of shade. Some cones remain on the tree, tightly sealed with resin and ready to open in the intense heat of a forest fire, spreading vast numbers of seeds over the newly prepared seed bed. Lodgepole pines grow straight and tall, hence their common name, and often are so close together that the shaded lower branches die and fall off, creating a "bottle-brush" appearance.

The understory, shrub, and herb layers are quite varied due to the extensive geographic range of this forest. Often the understory contains young Engelmann spruce, Douglas fir, or subalpine fir, shade-tolerant species that eventually assume dominance over the lodgepole pines in the absence of another fire.

### Aspen forests

Aspens love nothing better than a good fire. While the blaze kills most vegetation in the area, the extensive root systems of sun-loving aspens remain alive and vigorously send up new shoots, or suckers, which are genetic clones of the parent plant. For this reason, aspens are sometimes called the phoenix tree, seeming to rise immediately from the ashes of destruction, like their mythical namesake. The hearty root system already in place gives these trees a significant competitive advantage over other species that must start over as seedlings and put down their own meager roots.

Like lodgepole pines, quaking aspens are indicative of disturbed areas, and are very good at colonizing them, but are quite intolerant of shade, and quickly give way to the shade-tolerant species that eventually grow up among them. Even so, they often manage to hold their own along mountain streams, subsisting on the sunlight that reaches through the gap in the coniferous canopy.

**Below** Aspen forests may be found nearly anywhere in the Rocky Mountains below the subalpine zone, and even there individual quaking aspens may mingle with various conifers. They are especially common along streams and rivers.

| **Some common plants of lodgepole pine forests** | |
| --- | --- |
| **Trees and shrubs** | |
| lodgepole pine | Douglas fir |
| ponderosa pine | subalpine fir |
| red fir | western larch |
| white spruce | quaking aspen |
| western white pine | thimbleberry |
| western serviceberry | creambush |
| bearberry | balsam poplar |
| creeping barberry | |

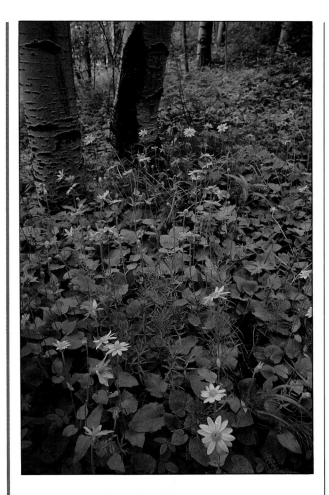

**Above** Many members of the herb layer in Rocky Mountain forests are found in a variety of forest types. Heartleaf arnica, for example, is more likely to be found among aspens, ponderosa pines, or lodgepole pines than with Douglas firs.

Their vast range, the largest of any tree in North America, means that their understories are nearly impossible to characterize because of the geographic overlap with so many other species. Invariably, however, they are more diverse than their counterparts in the shady coniferous forests. In the Rocky Mountains, companion species include western serviceberry, mountain snowberry, bearberry, common chokecherry, common snowberry, assorted willows and alders, black cottonwood, narrowleaf cottonwood, ponderosa pine, spreading snowberry, Douglas fir, lodgepole pine, red fir, Jeffrey pine, white fir, Engelmann spruce, upright snowberry, and subalpine fir.

## Some common plants of the aspen forest

### Trees and shrubs

| | |
|---|---|
| mountain alder | mooseberry |
| limber honeysuckle | creeping barberry |
| bearberry | narrowleaf cottonwood |
| black cottonwood | Scouler willow |
| peachleaf willow | antelope bitterbrush |
| Bebb willow | paper birch |
| curlleaf mountain | Rocky Mountain maple |
| mahogany | Nootka rose |
| red-osier dogwood | western serviceberry |
| Wood's rose | common chokecherry |
| quaking aspen | ponderosa pine |
| mountain snowberry | lodgepole pine |
| common snowberry | Engelmann spruce |
| Douglas fir | white fir |
| Jeffrey pine | spreading snowberry |
| red fir | upright snowberry |
| Sitka alder | subalpine fir |

## Some common wildflowers of Rocky Mountain forests

| | |
|---|---|
| blue columbine | beargrass |
| Nuttall's larkspur | common monkeyflower |
| queen's cup | mission bells |
| sego lily | western starflower |
| arrowleaf balsam boot | pinedrops |
| Fendler's meadowrue | pipsissewa |
| mule's ears | heartleaf arnica |
| blue-eyed grass | fireweed |
| yellow bell | spotted coral root |
| Engelmann aster | golden columbine |
| red columbine | orange agoseris |
| mountain bluebell | bunchberry |
| Canada violet | elegant camas |
| pussy paws | Rocky Mountain lily |
| amber lily | golden lily |
| wood nymph | yarrow |
| western monkshood | western wallflower |
| arrowhead groundsel | giant red paintbrush |
| fringe cups | false Solomon's seal |
| vase flower | silky phacelia |
| twinflower | mountain globemallow |
| Hooker's evening primrose | towering lousewort |

105

# PACIFIC NORTHWEST COASTAL FORESTS

The lushness of the coastal forests stretching from northern California to the Kenai Peninsula contrasts boldly with arid landscapes that, in some instances, are located less than two hundred miles inland. Moderate year-round temperatures and high annual precipitation, both the result of the Pacific Ocean's close proximity, encourage forests of massive trees and thick, luxuriant undergrowth. Because they are isolated by the Pacific Ocean to the west, dry mountains and sagebrush desert to the east, and cold arctic tundra to the north, many of the botanical inhabitants of these woodlands are found nowhere else in the world.

The heavy rainfall is the result of two co-incidental environmental factors. Relatively warm westerly winds pick up moisture as they flow over the Pacific's great expanse. Upon reaching land, they are abruptly forced upward by towering coastal mountain ranges. One of the basic principles of meteorology is that warm air can hold more moisture, expressed as relative humidity, than can cold air. The warm air cools as it is forced up the coastal mountains, decreasing its moisture-holding capacity and increasing its relative humidity, and clouds of water vapor begin to form. When the relative humidity reaches 100%, or dew point, precipitation occurs. As the air continues to be forced higher and cooled further, more and more moisture is wrung from the clouds until they crest the highest peaks and begin to flow back downhill. At this point, the process reverses; the air warms as it moves downhill, and precipitation ceases as the relative humidity rapidly drops below 100%, causing a rain shadow, or greatly diminished precipitation, on the leeward side. Desert-like conditions therefore result from the persistent, drying winds flowing down the eastern mountain slopes, only a short distance from temperate rainforests on the western side.

### Sitka spruce-western hemlock forests
The Pacific Northwest coastal forests are fragmented into several subtypes, depending upon their locations. From southern Alaska to southern Oregon, western hemlock and Sitka spruce are the dominant trees along the immediate coast and

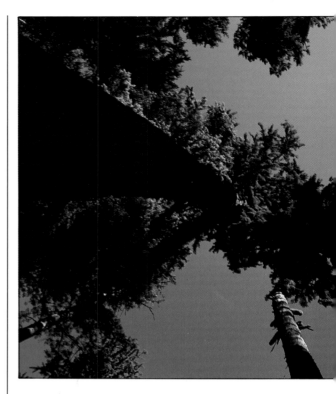

inland along rivers, and create the lushest understory of any North American forest. Because of the stifling mat of vegetation covering the ground, the conifers depend heavily upon "nurse logs," fallen, decaying timber rich in nutrients, for the germination of their seeds.

### Douglas fir forests
Unlike their counterparts in the Rocky Mountains, the Douglas fir forests of the Pacific Northwest are generally not climax communities. They colonize burned areas, but are eventually succeeded by western hemlock in all but the drier areas. Even so, they are associated with the so-called "old-growth" forests of this region, stands of which may exceed 600 years in age. Common understory species in these forests are Pacific madrone, bigleaf maple, and Pacific yew. Other locally common trees are sugar pine, incense cedar, tanoak, canyon live oak, Port Orford cedar, coast live oak, California laurel, and giant chinkapin.

### True fir forests
True fir forests, although located at higher elevations and/or more northerly latitudes than either of the first two Pacific Northwest coastal

**Left** Sitka spruces and western hemlocks dominate the magnificent Cathedral Grove on Vancouver Island, British Columbia. The towering giants of Pacific coastal forests result from moderate temperatures and heavy rainfall, both due to the close proximity of the Pacific Ocean.

**Below** Old-growth Douglas fir forests have shrunk to a fraction of their former range due to timber companies' continuing harvest of these ancient monarchs.

## Some common plants of Pacific Northwest coastal forests

### Trees and shrubs

| | |
|---|---|
| Douglas fir | western hemlock |
| Sitka spruce | noble fir |
| Pacific silver fir | western red cedar |
| western white pine | Pacific madrone |
| bigleaf maple | Pacific yew |
| subalpine fir | grand fir |
| Engelmann spruce | western larch |
| lodgepole pine | Alaska cedar |
| mountain hemlock | sugar pine |
| incense cedar | tanoak |
| canyon live oak | Port Orford cedar |
| red alder | black cottonwood |
| evergreen huckleberry | crowberry |
| alpine laurel | wild cranberry |
| red huckleberry | fool's huckleberry |
| devil's club | coastal red elderberry |
| coast live oak | California laurel |
| giant chinkapin | thinleaf huckleberry |
| delicious huckleberry | snow bush |
| Pacific blackberry | Cascade Oregon grape |
| Pacific rhododendron | salal |
| creambush | vine maple |

### Wildflowers and ferns

| | |
|---|---|
| starry Solomon's plume | sword fern |
| queen's cup beadlily | rosy twisted stalk |
| vanilla leaf | foamflower |
| fireweed | pearly everlasting |
| white-flowered hawkweed | snow queen |
| evergreen violet | rattlesnake orchid |
| Oregon goldthread | yellow skunk cabbage |
| western starflower | western monkshood |
| beargrass | northern inside-out flower |
| common monkeyflower | towering lousewort |
| calypso | Hooker's evening primrose |
| orange agoseris | spotted coral root |
| Washington lily | tiger lily |
| pinedrops | blue anemone |
| Canada violet | bunchberry |
| queen's cup | fringe cups |
| Indian pipe | phantom orchid |
| glacier lily | twinflower |
| pipsissewa | oak fern |

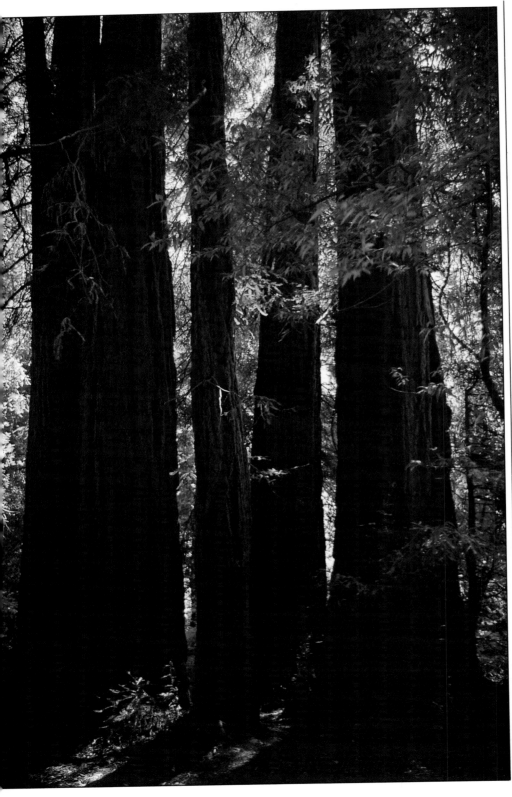

**Left** Redwood forests exist only in California and extreme southwestern Oregon, just inland from the coast, but they are worthy of mention because of their uniqueness. They require the deep, well-drained soils of floodplains and river deltas; they also need humid conditions, hence their location in what is known as the fog belt, where dense fogs sweep in regularly from the sea.

**Right** Relatively few wildflowers thrive in the dim, humid interiors of redwood forests. One of those species that fares very well here is redwood sorrel.

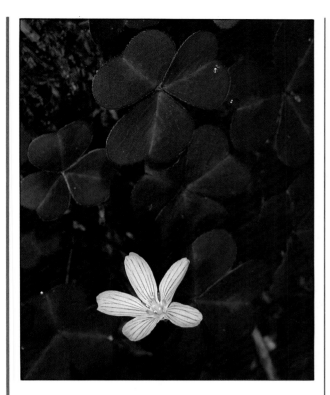

forests discussed, have many species in common with them. The major difference is that here, noble fir and Pacific silver fir dominate in place of the less common western hemlock and Douglas fir. Western red cedar and western white pine are also notable companions of the dominant species. Locally common are subalpine fir, grand fir, Engelmann spruce, western larch, lodgepole pine, Alaska cedar, and mountain hemlock. Thinleaf huckleberry is the characteristic shrub of true fir forests.

### Redwood forests

The southernmost of these forests are the redwoods of northern California. They are true giants among trees, and their immensity is mind-boggling, for their trunks may exceed 15 feet in diameter and 300 feet in height. The more ancient specimens are over 2,000 years old, a testament to their extremely thick fireproof and insectproof bark, flood tolerance, and regenerative powers in case of injury.

Only the most shade-tolerant plants grow under the sun-blocking canopy of these mammoths: moisture-loving ferns, mosses, bryophytes, and lichens create a thick green cushion. The high humidity and warm temperatures encourage decomposition, and myriad fungi take advantage of

this. Wood fern, sword fern, and chain fern are among the more common species that thrive. The shrub layer, dominated mostly by members of the heath family and quite dense at times, may include Pacific rhododendron, western azalea, evergreen huckleberry, California huckleberry, California hazelnut, vine maple, upright snowberry, and Pacific bayberry. Full-grown conifers of other species may mingle with the redwoods, forming a tall understory; among these may be Douglas fir, western hemlock, Sitka spruce, or grand fir. Tanoak and Pacific madrone, the two most common broadleaf trees in the redwood forest, are occasionally joined by Pacific dogwood, California laurel, Oregon ash, bigleaf maple, red alder, Oregon white oak and white alder.

## Some common plants of the redwood forests

### Trees and shrubs

| | |
|---|---|
| redwood | Douglas fir |
| western hemlock | Sitka spruce |
| grand fir | tanoak |
| Pacific madrone | Pacific dogwood |
| California laurel | Oregon ash |
| bigleaf maple | red alder |
| white alder | Oregon white oak |
| Pacific rhododendron | western azalea |
| evergreen huckleberry | California huckleberry |
| California hazelnut | vine maple |
| upright snowberry | Pacific bayberry |
| thimbleberry | Pacific ninebark |
| creambush | coyote bush |
| salal | salmonberry |
| western red cedar | Tracy willow |
| Goodding willow | Pacific willow |
| heart-leaved willow | red willow |

### Wildflowers and ferns

| | |
|---|---|
| redwood sorrel | checkermallow |
| miners lettuce | Pacific houndstongue |
| fringecup | milkmaids |
| yerba de selva | true forget-me-not |
| northern inside-out flower | fireweed |
| fringed loosestrife | western trillium |
| red clintonia | evergreen violet |
| wood fern | sword fern |
| chain fern | deer fern |

# WETLANDS
## WHAT ARE WETLANDS?

Habitats in which water saturation is the major environmental influence on soil formation and the accompanying plant and animal life are called wetlands. They are transition zones between aquatic and upland habitats. A high water table occurs at or slightly below ground level, so that the soil is saturated, or the soil is covered with shallow water (up to six feet deep, as defined by the United States Fish and Wildlife Service). Wetlands are characterized by emergent vegetation, plants that protrude above the water's surface, and often, their boundaries are indistinct. In gently rolling terrain, there may be a subtle moisture gradient in which the soil's water content gradually increases as you approach an aquatic habitat such as a lake or pond, and the plant species present are increasingly adapted to wet conditions. In steeper topography, the transition zone may be abrupt, perhaps only a matter of feet, and may not even be properly called a wetland at all. And wetlands in flat terrain can occupy hundreds of thousands of acres and be populated by huge numbers of certain species.

With few exceptions, freshwater wetlands are biologically among the most productive areas on earth, surpassed only by estuaries (the meeting of freshwater and salt-water environments) in the amount of organic material produced per acre. This is not surprising, since water is the solvent in which all of life's processes occur, and a surplus of water should equate to increased productivity. Oceans, however, the ultimate aquatic ecosystems, are actually relatively barren compared to wetlands, because organisms also need the favorable temperatures and light, nutrients, and atmospheric gases that characterize so many wetland areas.

**Wetland plant adaptations**
Plants and animals depend upon respiration to liberate their stored energy and carry out life's functions. Aerobic respiration (respiration in the presence of oxygen), is most common, but in the absence of oxygen, anaerobic respiration takes place.

A major problem to wetland plants is a dearth of oxygen. While we tend to think of soil as a solid substance, it is actually quite porous, and those pores conduct oxygen and other atmospheric gases to plant roots and soil organisms. Many of us have accidentally killed a houseplant with kindness by overwatering it, flooding the pores of the soil and displacing the needed oxygen. If this did not kill the plant directly, it may have created a favorable environment for soil micro-organisms that attacked the weakened plant.

Lack of oxygen in the soil is a major environmental obstacle in wetlands. Plants that flourish here have had to evolve means to acquire the needed oxygen or do without it. Water lilies, representative of deeper wetland water, are submerged except for their flowers and the upper surface of their leaves. Stomata, the pores generally

**Left** Once viewed as undesirable places to be drained or filled for development, wetlands are now recognized as crucial to the health of our environment. Wetlands cleanse pollutants from water, recharge groundwater supplies, regulate flooding, and protect shorelines from erosion. Lacustrine wetlands (**right**) occur around lake and pond perimeters and are characterized by emergent vegetation such as water lilies.

located on the undersides of leaves and responsible for gas exchange with the atmosphere, are located on the *tops* of water lily leaves. As well as stomata on their leaves, many wetland trees and shrubs have lenticels, openings on their bark that expand to admit oxygen as needed. Many wetland plants (water lilies, cattails, pickerelweed and arrowhead) have evolved air-filled conduits in their stems which transport oxgyen to their submerged parts. Some wetland plants (black willows and green ash) have adopted anaerobic respiration, converting the potentially toxic by-products into more benign compounds to be used for growth.

A few wetland plants have turned their watery environment to their advantage in reproduction and seed dispersal. While many are conventionally pollinated by wind or insects, some, such as hornwort and water celery, have developed specialized flowers and water-borne pollen. Quite a few (sedges, green ash, pecan, cranberries) produce buoyant seeds that float some distance from the parent plant before germinating.

**Top** Wetlands exhibit vegetation gradients determined by water depth or soil saturation. The two dominant plants shown here are pickerelweed and purple loosestrife.

**Above** Black willows are common trees of wet sites in the eastern U.S., often growing closer to the water's edge than any other tree species.

# BOGS

Bogs are unique in their origin and in the vegetation they support. A bog is a relatively stagnant body of water collected in a depression, often partially or completely covered by a floating mat of vegetation that, in many places, is strong enough to support the weight of large mammals. Jumping up and down on the firmer portions of this mat produces the quaking sensation associated with bogs.

Most northern bogs resulted from the last great Ice Age. The mile-high sheet of ice that covered Canada and northern United States gouged depressions in the earth, and debris carried on the ice like a great conveyor belt was deposited in huge piles, called moraine, which sometimes dammed valleys that had been widened and deepened by the glacier. About 10,000 years ago, as the climate warmed, the southern terminus of the glacier began to melt faster than the ice could advance, and it retreated. In its wake, the depressions and blocked valleys filled with water, some from high water tables, others from precipitation or runoff from the melting glaciers, and lakes formed. Sometimes huge chunks of ice broke off as the glacier withdrew. Partly buried in glacial debris, the ice eventually melted, forming a cold, stagnant pool, the perfect prelude to bog formation. Southern boggy areas in the Piedmont and coastal plain originated after the Atlantic Ocean receded and freshwater lakes formed.

Over time, sediments from erosion and organic material began to fill these depressions as the lakes aged. Sedges growing on the banks wove themselves into floating mats that advanced over the perimeter of the lakes, and shortly thereafter, moisture-loving sphagnum moss found these conditions to their liking and thickly colonized the top of the sedge mats. Soon the mats grew thick enough to support shrubs such as Labrador tea and

**Below** Bogs are unique habitats. Plants that grow here are adapted to very harsh and specific conditions.

**Above** There are several types of bogs, the most familiar of which are the quaking bogs. These form as vegetation encroaches over the water's surface from the edge of a lake. These plants become interwoven to form a floating mat of vegetation, which "quakes" when walked upon and eventually may cover the entire lake. As it fills with poorly decomposed organic matter, it becomes known as a peat bog. Because of the underlying wet, acidic conditions it may never succeed completely to the surrounding climax forest.

leatherleaf, whose roots help to bind the mats tightly together.

The water of northern bogs is cold because of its depth, its stagnant nature (no influx of water from a warmer source), the floating mat of vegetation that blocks the sun's warming rays, and the fact that bogs are often located in a depression where pockets of cold air collect. Its temperature, acidic nature imparted by the abundance of sphagnum moss, and low oxygen content, result in decomposition that is incredibly slow, sometimes almost non-existent. The organic material building up the bottom and the vegetation mat sinking under its own increasing weight contain large amounts of poorly decomposed, spongy organic matter, called peat. Where the sinking mat meets the rising bottom and becomes "grounded," black spruce and tamarack trees find enough support to grow. Eventually, the entire bog may fill with compacted peat and become a bog forest, but a bog rarely succeeds to the upland forest of its surroundings. Bog plants are specially adapted to grow in an acidic, nutrient-poor environment, conditions which persist long after the bog has filled in, and which many upland plants cannot tolerate. Also, the water level of even peat-filled bogs remains high, because of the impermeable depression underlying them, resulting in a wet, spongy floor with no true soil.

Surprisingly, plants of these northern wetlands have many characteristics in common with desert plants, since they have to overcome many of the same problems. Many have thick, leathery leaves with a waxy covering to prevent water loss. Some, such as Labrador tea, bog rosemary, and bog laurel, have leaves that curl inward, or a dense wooly covering on their undersides to reduce the flow of dry air over the stomata. Why do wetland plants growing literally on top of the water still need to conserve it? The answer lies with one of the factors responsible for bog formation, the extremely cold water. It is not unusual for the roots of bog plants to be partially frozen in the mat, and therefore non-functioning, as late as July, while the portion of the plant above the mat bakes in the summer sun!

The high productivity of other wetlands, such as marshes, is due to their warmer climates, the efficient nutrient cycling that accompanies rapid decomposition, and their constant recharging with mineral-laden ground water. The lack of such conditions greatly reduces the productivity of bogs. Their cold, acidic nature makes for poor nutrient cycling, and their water level is maintained primarily by mineral-poor precipitation. Two types of carnivorous plants, sundews and pitcher plants, have evolved to cope with these conditions. Sundews secrete jewel-like drops of sticky fluid on the tips of hair-like structures on their leaves. When an insect alights and gets stuck, the hairs draw it down to the leaf surface where enzymes are secreted and digestion takes place. Pitcher plants produce elegantly-veined, vessel-shaped leaves that collect rainwater. Recurved hair-like projections allow insects to crawl into the "pitcher," but pose an obstacle to retreat. Eventually, the insects falter, fall into the accumulated water, and drown. Enzymes secreted by the plant help to digest the food, but most of the breakdown is due to the activity of bacteria.

Bogs are very nutrient-poor environments. Plants like sundews (**above**), and pitcher plants (**below**) have adapted to capture and digest small invertebrates in order to obtain nutrients.

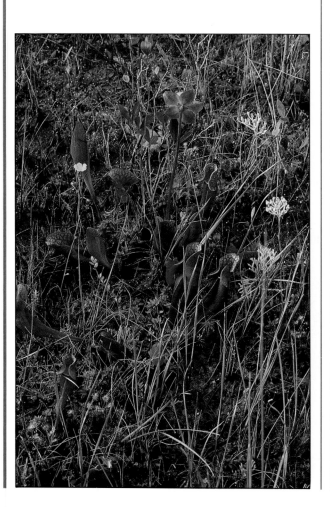

## Some common plants of bogs

### Trees and shrubs

| | |
|---|---|
| leatherleaf | Labrador tea |
| large cranberry | sheep laurel |
| bog rosemary | bog laurel |
| water willow | sweet gale |
| rhodora | creeping snowberry |
| mountain cranberry | white swamp azalea |
| highbush blueberry | tamarack |
| black spruce | northern white cedar |
| Atlantic white cedar | poison sumac |
| red maple | balsam willow |
| eastern hemlock | balsam fir |

### Wildflowers

| | |
|---|---|
| grass pink | rose pogonia |
| bog rein orchid | white fringed orchid |
| pitcher plants | sundews |
| pink lady's slipper | showy lady's slipper |
| false Solomon's seal | goldthread |
| marsh blue violet | swamp loosestrife |
| swamp pink | |

### Other herbaceous plants

| | |
|---|---|
| cotton grasses | sensitive fern |
| sphagnum mosses | bulrushes |
| bladderworts | |

# MARSHES AND WET MEADOWS

Marshes are among the wetland systems classified as *palustrine*, a category which includes bogs, swamps, and wet meadows, and accounts for more than 94% of all freshwater wetlands in the lower 48 states. The remaining wetland systems are *lacustrine*, found around lake perimeters; and *riverine*, which occur along rivers and streams.

Most marshes are a mid-stage in the ecological succession of a deeper aquatic habitat. Their longevity as marshes depends on a variety of factors, including size, drainage, and general climate. Some exist in the shallower perimeter of a lake or pond, or in poorly drained depressions along streams and rivers. Others may represent an entire lake in an advanced state of eutrophication, or aging, as sediments and organic matter gradually fill it in. Eventually, this marsh is likely to succeed to a wet meadow, which is commonly found on the upland side of a marsh. As the marsh dries, life becomes impossible for water-loving plants, which give way to those less tolerant of submersion. The wet meadow may ultimately become a dry upland meadow and evolve into the climax community of the area, unless an outside force, such as man, fire, glaciation, or geological activity, intervenes. Or, if periodic flooding continues, it may remain wetland, perhaps succeeding to a shrub or forested swamp in a warmer, drier climate, or to a bog in a cooler, wetter climate.

**Above** Wild rice, a wetland plant common from Kansas and Virginia north.

**Above** Sedges, grass-like plants of wetlands, have stems that are triangular in cross-section.

Continuously flooded shallow marshes, where water levels range from six to twelve inches during the growing season, are characterized by herbaceous, emergent plants such as cattails, golden club, arrow arum, arrowhead, pickerel-weed, bulrushes, spikesedges, smartweeds, bur reeds, and others. Water hyacinth, an exotic South American species, is prolific in southern marshes. Deeper marshes also host reeds and wild rice, as well as submerged species such as water lilies, water celery, bladderworts, and

**Left** Cattails spread by branching, horizontal rootstocks, often forming dense colonies that dominate marshes. The flowers of this monocot grow in dense spikes, with the male flowers on top. By early summer the stamens are shed, leaving only the club-like mass of female flowers below.

## Some common plants of marshes

### Grasses, rushes, and sedges

| | |
|---|---|
| bulrush (a sedge) | spike rush |
| wild rice | tussock sedge |
| wool grass | soft rush |
| giant reed | reed canary grass |
| rice cut grass | millet |
| slough grass | foxtail grass |
| manna grass | white top |
| maiden cane | blue joint grass |
| spike grass | giant reed |
| tule | leafy three-square |

### Marsh wildflowers

| | |
|---|---|
| cattails | bur reed |
| arrowhead | pickerelweed |
| purple loosestrife | sweet flag |
| blue flag | yellow iris |
| Joe-Pye weeds | boneset |
| yellow pond lily | fragrant water lily |
| marsh pink | water plantain |
| arrow arum | golden club |
| swamp milkweed | fringed loosestrife |

### Free-floating plants

| | |
|---|---|
| duckweed | water meal |
| water hyacinth | |

### Wet meadow plants

| | |
|---|---|
| ironweed | Turk's cap lily |
| yellow-eyed grass | grass pink |
| spotted jewelweed | marsh marigold |
| Canada anemone | marsh bellflower |
| marsh St. Johnswort | swamp candles |
| arethusa | rose pogonia |
| fringed gentian | common ladies' tresses |
| Canada lily | purple-fringed orchid |
| yellow-fringed orchid | cardinal flower |
| three-leaved sundew | venus flytrap |
| three-awn grass | beak rush |
| marsh fern | sensitive fern |
| steeplebush | buttonbush |
| red maple | black ash |

**Above** Arrowhead, obviously named for the shape of its leaves, produces male and female flowers in separate whorls of three. In wetlands, it is usually located between cattails of shallow water and pickerelweed of slightly deeper water.

pondweeds. Free-floating duckweed, the smallest flowering plant, with leaves no bigger than a matchhead, often coats the surface of open water, and microscopic algae, the base of many marsh food chains, abounds.

Some marshes, particularly those in the prairie pothole region of the upper Midwest, dry out completely during seasonal droughts, resulting in an ongoing struggle between upland and wetland plants. In the arid Great Basin region, excessive evaporation leaves behind high concentrations of salts, creating saline marshes that are fed by freshwater sources. The tule marshes of northern California and southern Oregon, renowned for their tremendous congregations of waterfowl during migration, are examples of saline marshes.

Wet meadows either flood seasonally or merely remain saturated. In wet meadows on the upland side of marshes, truly aquatic species yield to moisture-loving grasses, sedges, rushes, and such wetland wildflowers as jewelweed, marsh marigold, grass pink, yellow-eyed grass, ironweed, and Turk's cap lily. The grass-like plants may seem difficult to tell apart. Three-sided sedges are the easiest to distinguish; remember the saying, "Sedges have edges." Round-stemmed grasses and rushes look similar, but rushes are solid stemmed and grasses are hollow stemmed.

Marshes are common throughout North America, especially east of the Rockies. They reach their greatest density in the prairie pothole region of North Dakota, South Dakota, Minnesota, Manitoba, and Saskatchewan; tragically, these are disappearing rapidly due to farmers filling them in and converting them to agricultural usage. Wetlands in general have long been undervalued by most people, who saw them only as wasted space, as barriers to development, to be drained and filled to become "productive." Only recently have people become aware of the vital role that wetlands play in maintaining the health of the world. They soak up flood waters like megasponges and slowly release them again, preventing widespread damage and erosion. They filter pollutants from the water and recharge the underground aquifers that supply much of our drinking water. They are the nurseries for a large portion of the world's food supply. They are undeniably indispensable.

# EVERGLADES

Though technically a marsh, the Everglades are so large and its plant population so exotic that it deserves special consideration. It also encompasses numerous "hammocks", raised, forested islands in a sea of grass. These hammocks actually consist of subtropical forests unknown in the United States outside of southern Florida.

The Everglades are fed by a wide, shallow river originating from Lake Okeechobee and flowing in sheets forty miles wide and less than one foot deep.

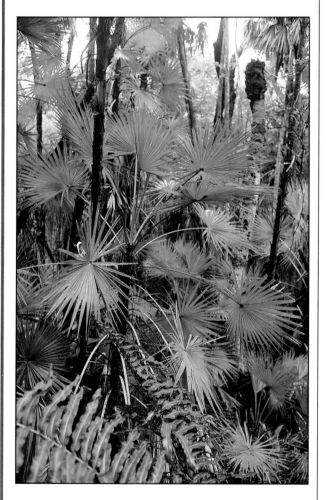

**Above** Though more akin to subtropical forests than to wetlands, the hammocks that dot the Everglades are an integral part of this vast wetland. Plants like the gumbo-limbo tree, epiphytes, and the bizarre strangler fig make these a welcome botanical diversion from the sea of sawgrass.

A vast sawgrass "prairie" hides the river from view in many places. Sawgrass, a type of sedge sometimes reaching ten feet in height, spreads by underground rhizomes and, in many places, forms pure stands that tend to exclude other species. Still, many herbaceous plants do make their home among the sawgrass, including white-topped sedge, water pimpernel, salt-and-pepper, blue-eyed grass, bluehearts, wild petunias, yellowtop, horrid thistle, and marsh pinks. Waxmyrtle, a shrub, also makes periodic appearances.

The real wealth of plant life in the Everglades resides in the hardwood hammocks, raised areas one to three feet above their surroundings that are high enough to keep most of the tree roots above the water-soaked soil of the sawgrass prairies. Most of these tropical hardwoods originated in the West Indies and are not found anywhere else in the United States.

A common species and the largest of these trees is the gumbo-limbo, easily recognized by its flaking, coppery bark. Poisonwood is perhaps the most abundant tree. Related to poison ivy and producing similar effects, it is easily identified by the bright yellow margin and midrib of its shiny green leaves. The West Indies mahogany was once abundant but has been extensively harvested. Royal palm, winged soapberry, snowberry, pigeon plum, Jamaica dogwood, and wild coffee are among the tropical species that grow here. More temperate-climate species, such as live oak, red mulberry, and sugarberry, are interspersed with these and other tropical trees.

One of the more unusual inhabitants of tropical hammocks is the strangler fig. After being excreted by a bird onto a tree limb, the undigested seed of the strangler fig germinates and sends aerial roots downward around the trunk of the tree and into the ground, and grows upward into a leafy crown. Upon reaching the ground, the roots expand and fuse, killing the host while the strangler fig remains.

Numerous vines, notably moon flower, inhabit hammock forests, climbing the trees to ensure their own place in the sun above the dense shade of the canopy. On their way up, they pass through a virtual hanging garden of orchids and other epiphytes, the so-called "air plants." Epiphytes are not parasitic; their roots serve as anchors and they utilize various mechanisms to collect precipitation or dew and nutrients naturally leached from the surrounding foliage. Resurrection fern, sword fern, long strap

## Some common plants of the Everglades

**Trees and shrubs**
coastal plain willow
baldcypress
redbay
gumbo-limbo
West Indies mahogany
winged soapberry
pigeon plum
wild coffee
sugarberry
strangler fig
buttonbush
waxmyrtle
pondcypress
sweetbay
poisonwood
royal palm
snowberry
Jamaica dogwood
live oak
red mulberry
southern bayberry
marlberry

**Epiphytes**
Florida butterfly orchid
clamshell orchid
Spanish moss
wild pine

**Wildflowers**
water pennywort
arrowhead
common butterwort
water lettuce
grass pink
spider lily
fragrant water lily
duckweed
arrow arum
yellow butterwort
water hyacinth
common cattail
rose pogonia
fire flags
swamp lily
floating hearts

**Ferns**
wild Boston fern
fan maidenhair
maiden fern
resurrection fern
long strap fern
sword fern

**Sedges**
sawgrass
white-topped sedge

fern, and Florida butterfly orchid are but a few epiphytic species to be found here.

Islands of woody species not yet developed into hammocks are referred to as heads. They begin as willow heads when coastal plain willows colonize wet depressions during a dry period. The ensuing buildup of organic matter raises the soil to a slightly elevated, less saturated mound that can support various bay species, such as redbay, bull bay, and sweetbay. Cypress domes, so named because of the domed shape of their canopies, develop when baldcypress or pondcypress become established in some shallow ponds.

**Left** An introduced tropical plant, water hyacinth has been clogging the waterways of southern states, including the Everglades.

**Above** Water lettuce, a small, floating aquatic plant, often grows so densely as to give the illusion of solid ground.

119

# SWAMPS

The presence of woody trees, shrubs, or both, differentiate swamps from marshes. Northern forested swamps are most prevalent in the Great Lakes states of Minnesota, Wisconsin, and Michigan, while shrub swamps are common both here and in the Piedmont region and coastal plains. Both types of swamps are also present in New England and in isolated regions west of the Mississippi River. Cypress swamps and southern hardwood swamps are the forested wetlands of the Southeast, and are located in lowland areas along rivers and in the coastal plain.

Since swamps often occur in river floodplains, it can be difficult to distinguish them from floodplain forests, especially because there is a great deal of species overlap. The general distinction between the two lies in the proportion of time they are submerged. If the area is inundated from time to time for short periods when the river rises above flood stage, but drains completely when flood waters recede, it is a floodplain forest. If drainage is poor and the soil is covered with water for longer periods, it is a swamp. Obviously, there is a large gray area between the two extremes, and some regions could be classified as either.

### Shrub swamps

Shrub swamps may be characterized according to species. Pussy-willow swamps and alder swamps are common across much of the continent. Pussy willows are well known for their fuzzy gray catkins that appear as one of the first sure signs of spring. As these catkins expand and flower, it becomes evident that female and male flowers are produced on separate plants, the bright yellow male flowers easily distinguished from the dull green female flowers. Pussy willows commonly grow in thickets and may reach nine feet in height. They may also include silky dogwood and red-osier dogwood. Beneath their low canopy, many wildflowers, such as bedstraws, tall asters, bluebells, and goldenrods may grow. Alders, close relatives of birch, also produce dense thickets in wetland areas. Buttonbush, an emergent shrub, can thrive in wetter areas than either alders or pussy willows.

A unique type of shrub swamp, called the pocosin (an Algonquin Indian name that literally means "swamp on a hill"), develops in southern boggy areas. This is the home of small evergreen trees such as redbay, sweetbay, loblolly-bay, and pond pine, as well as shrubs such as waxmyrtle, zenobia, titi, and fetterbush. High water levels and fire help to maintain pocosins and prevent their succession to a higher seral stage.

### Northern swamps

Boreal swamps are populated mostly by the same trees that characterize the boreal forest. Farther south, red maple swamps are common, as are those populated by black gum, swamp white oak, American elm, yellow birch, white ash, black ash, and sweetgum. Spicebush is common in the understory of northern hardwood swamps. Cinnamon fern, sensitive fern, marsh marigold, and skunk cabbage are just some of the herb layer.

Skunk cabbage is particularly interesting for its ability to generate heat. One of the earliest signs of spring in the swamp, skunk cabbage flowers consist of a sheath-like spathe that nearly encloses a ball-like cluster of flowers, the spadix. Using the food reserves in its huge roots, skunk cabbage begins to generate heat inside the spathe in late winter, enough to maintain a temperature of 68 degrees Fahrenheit around the spadix even when external temperatures are sub-freezing. This adaptation not only allows skunk cabbage to flower early, but the warmth it produces helps to disseminate the fetid odor that attracts its primary pollinators, carrion flies.

**Left** Cypress swamps have gained a reputation as dark, brooding places, but they are botanically fascinating.

**Below** Terrestrial plants have had to make many adaptations to thrive in swamps, such as the aerial "knees" of baldcypress that allow the roots to breathe.

## Some common plants of cypress swamps and southern hardwood swamps

### Trees and shrubs

| | |
|---|---|
| baldcypress | black ash |
| Carolina ash | water tupelo |
| water elm | buttonbush |
| redbay | sweetbay |
| loblolly-bay | black tupelo |
| Dahoon holly | black willow |
| honeylocust | overcup oak |
| swamp chestnut oak | water hickory |
| Atlantic white cedar | nutmeg hickory |
| titi | yaupon |
| waxmyrtle | strangler fig |
| water oak | black willow |
| willow oak | sugarberry |
| sweetgum | water locust |
| swamp tupelo | ironwood |
| sweet pepperbush | red buckeye |
| swamp azalea | flowering dogwood |
| swamp dogwood | possum haw holly |

### Ferns

| | |
|---|---|
| leather fern | resurrection fern |
| sword fern | strap fern |
| cinnamon fern | royal fern |

### Vines

| | |
|---|---|
| climbing hydrangea | supplejack |
| American wisteria | Kentucky wisteria |
| wild grape | peppervine |
| Virginia creeper | trumpet creeper |
| crossvine | |

### Wildflowers

| | |
|---|---|
| butterfly orchid | clamshell orchid |
| wild pine | Spanish moss |
| water lettuce | pickerelweed |
| arrowhead | fire flags |
| swamp lily | golden club |
| crimson pitcher plant | red iris |
| swamp honeysuckle | spotted touch-me-not |
| water hyacinth | spider lily |
| green-fly orchid | switch cane |
| cardinal flower | butterweed |
| ladies tresses | rose pogonia |
| grass pink | water-spider orchid |

## Southern swamps

Cypress swamps are dark, brooding places in the southeast, characterized by baldcypress trees often enshrouded in Spanish moss. Baldcypress, which is actually not a cypress at all but a member of the redwood family, is a deciduous conifer that produces conspicuous aerial roots, called "knees", to absorb oxygen otherwise unavailable to their submerged roots. They develop swollen, buttressed trunks to help support themselves in the unstable, waterlogged sediments. Air plants such as Spanish moss, bromeliads, and numerous orchids perch on the branches of baldcypress and other trees, obtaining moisture from the rainwater they collect, and nutrients and minerals from dust in the air and from those naturally leached from their host's foliage and bark.

Southern hardwood swamps are regions flooded for less than four months a year. They also contain baldcypress, but are dominated by hardwoods and have a richer herb and fern layer.

**Above** Skunk cabbage's high rate of respiration in late winter allows it to metabolize energy in the roots, keeping the air surrounding its flowers at about 70°F.

# SEASHORES
## PLANT ADAPTATIONS TO SALT

The plants of saltwater environments face rigors unknown to those of terrestrial and freshwater habitats. During osmosis, water molecules tend to flow from regions of higher water molecule concentration (fewer dissolved substances such as salts) to areas of lower concentration (more dissolved substances) in an attempt to equalize the osmotic imbalance. In this manner, vascular plants of terrestrial and freshwater habitats are able to absorb water through their roots because the osmotic concentration (of dissolved substances) of cell fluids is naturally higher than that of the water they absorb.

This situation is reversed in saltwater habitats, where the salinity, or saltiness, of seawater is equal to or greater than that of the fluids in the plant cells. Though surrounded by water, saltwater plants actually live in a very "dry" environment. Without special adaptations, not only could plants not absorb the water vital to photosynthesis, but they might actually lose water to the surrounding seawater and would quickly die.

To overcome this challenge, shoreline plants, known as halophytes ("salt-lovers") have evolved numerous adaptations. Those with the most exposure to saltwater maintain an osmotic pressure in their cells many times that of terrestrial and freshwater plants; in other words, their cytoplasm is saltier. Vascular plants have the special ability to selectively concentrate salt in their roots as necessary to ensure a higher salinity than that of the salt water; therefore, the water they absorb is "fresh," since it is primarily the water molecules only which move toward the higher salt concentration.

Any excess salts the plants do absorb must be secreted, lest the plant absorb too much water, rupturing the cells under the tremendous osmotic pressure. To accomplish this, many of these plants have special salt-secreting glands on their foliage. Often, salt crystals or droplets of extremely salty water may be observed on the undersides of leaves; these will be washed away by the next high tide or rainfall. Other plants excrete salt through their roots, and still others accumulate salt in their leaves, which are then shed.

Like desert plants, shoreline plants must also protect themselves against "drought," when saltwater does not reach them, rainfall is lacking, air temperatures and evaporation rates are high, and the sun is beating down. To combat this, they produce a thick, waxy covering on their leaves to minimize water loss through evaporation, just like their desert counterparts. Many are also succulents, storing large amounts of water in their tissues for just such situations.

### Shoreline zonation

Just as plants around freshwater habitats grow in distinct zones according to their tolerance for water-saturated soil, plants at the meeting of saltwater and terrestrial or freshwater habitats also grow in distinct vegetation zones. In this case, however, the limiting factors are not only moisture but also salinity. Those with the greatest tolerance for salt will grow closest its source. As the concentration of salt or the chance of encountering salt from high tides or spray decreases, those less tolerant of salt are able to establish themselves. This is particularly evident in the salt marshes associated with estuaries, the areas where saltwater mixes with the freshwater of streams and rivers. In the flat salt marshes of the Atlantic and Gulf coasts, a difference of as little as two inches in elevation can determine two distinct plant communities with differing salt tolerances. The borders of such zones are often quite well defined, but are not always obvious from ground level.

The meeting of land and sea is an extremely demanding environment for plants. Plants of rocky shores (**above**) arrange themselves in distinct zones, while the vegetation of sandy shores (**right**) is concentrated behind dunes well back from the water's edge.

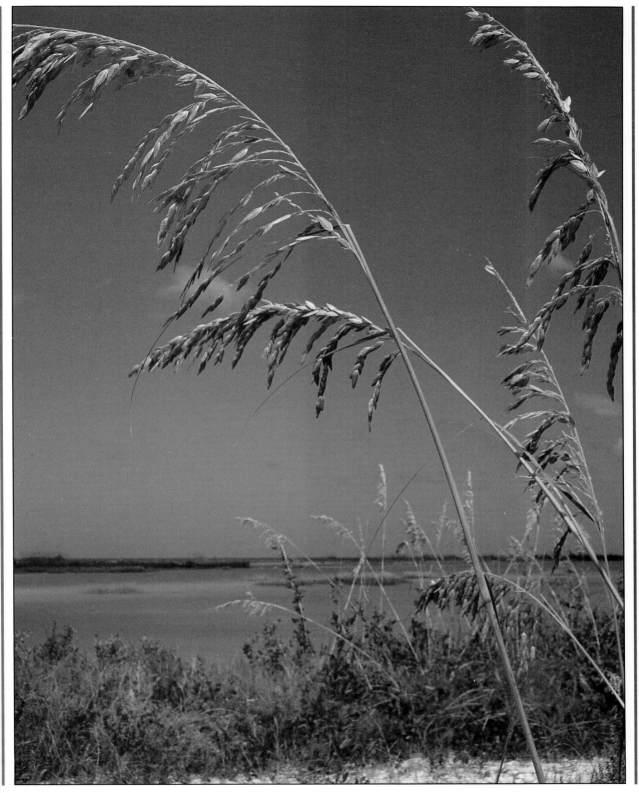

# BEACHES AND DUNES

Beaches are a restless and unstable environment, constantly at the mercy of shifting winds and unpredictable wave action. Because of this, the salty conditions, and the searing temperatures as the sand bakes in the sun, little grows on them. It is not until you examine the higher dunes above the reach of the tides that plants grow with any frequency.

Dune formation begins with any irregularity, such as a piece of debris, on the beach that disrupts the onshore winds and causes them to slow and drop grains of sand behind the obstruction. As the mound grows, it causes more disturbances as the wind flows over it, and eventually forms a dune perpendicular to the beach. It is in the shelter of the dune that plants establish themselves. Seeds of American beach grass (sea oats in the Southeast and European beach grass on the Pacific coast) are also deposited with the sand grains. As the plant grows and sends out rhizomes, which in turn sprout new plants, the spreading root systems anchor the sand while the plants further disrupt the air currents and more sand is deposited on the fledgling dunes.

Eventually, these small perpendicular dunes are joined as more sand is deposited between them, forming a secondary dune parallel to the beach. Beach grass advances down the face of the secondary dune, causing new disruptions in the wind flow until a primary dune develops in front of the secondary dune. As the two dunes grow, the hollow between them widens.

Sea oats and short dune grass are also dune colonizers, particularly in the Southeast. Lavender-flowered sea rocket is able to exist on the ocean side of primary dunes by storing water in its succulent leaves and stem. Sea elder, a succulent shrub, and low-profiled seaside spurge also fare well here, as do beach pea, a nitrogen-fixer that

fertilizes the soil, and dusty miller. On the back side of primary dunes and on secondary dunes in the East, one may also find glades morning glory, seaside goldenrod, buttonweed, and camphor-weed. Marsh hay cordgrass is frequently the dominant grass here, accompanied by sandspur.

In the shelter of the primary dune, vegetation grows more densely, further stabilizing the sand and adding humus, a fundamental component of soil, setting the stage for other plant species to invade. Beach plum, rugosa rose, and bayberry may

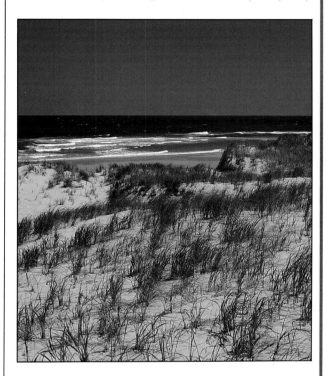

**Above** Sand dunes form a sheltered niche, protected from tides and salt spray, where plants can grow. Plants, in turn, stabilize the dunes to create a fairly long-term habitat.

**Below** Despite its name, the secondary dune is actually the first of the two to form, beginning with small irregularities disrupting the sand-laden winds.

grasses or shrubs     taller shrubs     taller shrubs and trees

ocean     beach     primary dune     trough     secondary dune     back dune     bay establish themselves in the shelter of the primary dune, providing shade for other plants less tolerant of the blazing sun. Beach heather, poison ivy, and bearberry may help to cover the dunes. Were it not for periodic violent storms, the dune succession would inevitably continue until a climax community was achieved. Indeed, dunes that form farther inland do eventually develop into a climax pine or oak forest, but because moisture drains so quickly in the sandy soil and because these species are such poor nutrient recyclers, they are rarely accompanied by more demanding species.

Pioneering plants on Pacific coast sand dunes include European sea rocket, yellow sand verbena, beach morning glory, silky beach pea, silver beach weed, and American dune grass. A stable plant cover is established by large-headed sedge and seashore bluegrass. Their enhancement of the soil leads to their replacement by such species as seashore lupine, camphor dune tansy, and red fescue. Where protected from the wind, a climax forest characteristic of the area is able to develop.

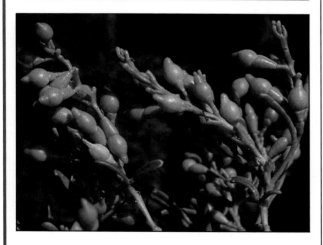

Yellow sand verbena (**top**), adorned with yellow, trumpet-shaped flowers, is a familiar dune inhabitant of the Pacific coast. Its trailing stem helps keep it ahead of shifting sands. The succulent stems and leaves of sea rocket (**bottom**), a prostrate plant of the Atlantic coast, enable it to retain water under salty conditions, allowing it to colonize unprotected beaches.

## Some common plants of sand dunes

### Atlantic and Gulf coasts

| | |
|---|---|
| American beach grass | sea rocket |
| sea oats | short dune grass |
| beach pea | dusty miller |
| seaside goldenrod | sea elder |
| seaside spurge | glades morning glory |
| buttonweed | camphorweed |
| marsh hay cordgrass | sandspur |
| beach plum | rugosa rose |
| bayberry | beach heather |
| poison ivy | bearberry |
| golden aster | prickly pear cactus |
| greenbrier | large cranberry |
| highbush blueberry | sphagnum moss |
| sheep laurel | pitch pine |
| red maple | black cherry |
| eastern red cedar | Japanese honeysuckle |
| sassafras | American holly |

### Pacific coast

| | |
|---|---|
| European beach grass | American dune grass |
| European sea rocket | yellow sand verbena |
| beach morning glory | silky beach pea |
| silver beach weed | large-headed sedge |
| seashore bluegrass | red fescue |
| camphor dune tansy | seashore lupine |
| salal | evergreen huckleberry |
| ground cone | common ice plant |
| beach strawberry | beach silvertop |
| narrow goldenrod | seaside daisy |
| sea fig | Menzies' wallflower |
| giant coreopsis | showy Scotch broom |
| spiny gorse | Douglas fir |
| Sitka spruce | lodgepole pine |
| western red cedar | western hemlock |

# ROCKY SHORES

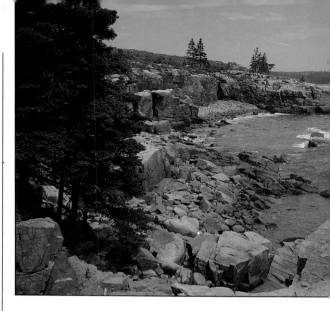

As difficult as it may seem for plants to survive on coastal sand dunes, it is even tougher for them along the rocky shores of North America, for here there is no protective dune to shelter them and little soil in which to sink roots. Where hardy terrestrial individuals are able to gain a toehold, they must still deal with salt spray and the occasional nor'easter.

Marine organisms inhabiting the intertidal zone constitute the majority of plant life on rocky shores. These must cope with the battering action of waves, desiccation when the tide recedes, salinity, and extreme temperature changes, particularly in the summer when they may spend hours in intense solar radiation, then plunge into frigid waters at the next high tide. Because of their differing tolerances for these variables, plants and animals of the rocky shore distribute themselves in horizontal bands on the rocks.

A variety of lichens colonize the rocks above the highest high tides. *Xanthoria parientina*, a crustose lichen growing within range of wind-driven salt spray, frequently paints the rocks with splashes of bright orange and yellow. Proceeding downward, the first marine-life zone is the black zone, composed of a thick growth of lichens (*Verrucaria* spp.) and blue-green algae of the genus *Calothrix*. To prevent desiccation, these algae are encased in gelatinous capsules; when wet, they are extremely slippery. This zone is often soaked by spray but

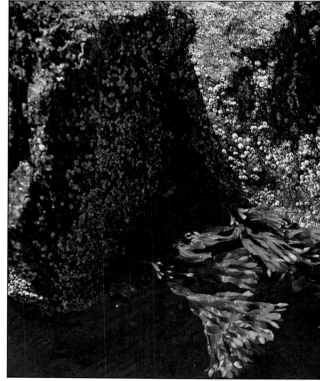

**Above** Irish moss, a leathery alga of variable color and form, is a frequent inhabitant of eastern tidal pools. It is an ingredient in many commercial food products.

**Right** Few plants can grow in the thick encrustation of barnacles and mussels on rocky shores, but immediately below them lies an extensive zone of rockweeds.

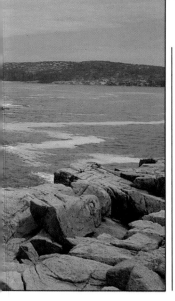

**Left** Rocky coasts pose special challenges to plants, which grow in specific zones according to their ability to meet those challenges.

found two red algae: laver (*Porphyra* spp.), growing in wavy sheets or ribbons, and the self-descriptive thread algae (*Bangia* spp.).

Next is the barnacle zone, where the rocks are often completely encrusted with barnacles and mussels. Below that lies the middle littoral zone, consisting of seaweeds. Seaweeds do not have true roots, but secure themselves against the crashing surf by means of rootlike, grasping structures at their base called holdfasts. The species occupying the uppermost part of this zone is spiral rockweed. Immediately below spiral rockweed, on rocks not directly facing the surf, is knotted rockweed, followed by the tough bladder rockweed. Lower still than the rockweeds are Irish moss, dulse, coralline algae, sea lettuce, and an encrusting red algae (*Hildenbrandia* spp.) reaching past the low tide mark. Below the lowest low tides are the kelps.

The upper reaches of high tide on the Pacific coast's rocky shores are also denoted by a black band, and barnacles inhabit the upper littoral zone here as well. Seaward from the barnacles are various species of rockweed plus sea lettuce and sea sack, followed by a red algae, called Turkish towel, and sea palm.

rarely inundated except during spring tides, the two highest tides of each month.

Below the black zone lies the upper littoral zone, where conditions are perhaps the most extreme; temperature and salinity may fluctuate drastically in the tide pools of this region. On the Atlantic coast, slender, tubular green algae (*Enteromorpha* spp.) grow in the highest pools. In lower pools are

**Above** Lacking true roots like those of vascular plants, kelps and other colonial algae anchor themselves by means of specialized structures called holdfasts.

## Some common plants of rocky shores

### Atlantic coast

| | |
|---|---|
| lichens | blue-green algae |
| enteromorpha green algae | purple laver |
| thread algae | spiral rockweed |
| knotted rockweed | bladder rockweed |
| Irish moss | dulse |
| coralline algae | sea lettuce |
| kelps | encrusting stony red algae |

### Pacific coast

| | |
|---|---|
| lichens | blue-green algae |
| rockweed | little rockweed |
| sea lettuce | sea sack |
| Turkish towel | sea palm |
| winged kelp | sugar wrack |
| bull kelp | black pine |
| enteromorpha green algae | coralline algae |
| nail brush | giant perennial kelp |
| feather boa | fir needle |
| encrusting coral | tar spot |
| surf grass | sea staghorn |

# SALT MARSHES

Salt marshes form along the coast in areas where the water calms enough to drop its load of suspended sediments. On the low, gently sloping Atlantic and Gulf coasts this can occur behind barrier islands, where wave action is minimal, or along estuaries, where the mouths of rivers fan out, allowing water to slow down while mixing with the salt water of the ocean. On the steeper Pacific coast, salt marshes are limited to narrow strips bordering estuaries. They typically begin as mud flats colonized by algae and eelgrass.

The pioneer species of salt marshes is cordgrass, a very salt-tolerant plant that colonizes the zone between high and low tides. Saltmarsh cordgrass, an eastern species, occurs in two forms. Tall saltmarsh cordgrass, green and up to seven feet tall, inhabits the intertidal zone, while the short, yellow variety establishes itself just above mean high tide. Unlike areas of tall cordgrass, where plant debris is flushed out twice a day at high tide, a mulch is formed by this debris in the short cordgrass, keeping the mud moister and cooler by shading it from the sun. With short cordgrass grow fleshy, translucent-stemmed glassworts, which turn bright red in autumn, and sea lavender, spear scale, and sea blite.

Slightly higher in the marsh is a zone of marsh hay cordgrass, a fine, dense grass that forms tight swirling mats called cowlicks. Spike grass often grows in this same zone. A few more inches in elevation triggers a transformation to black grass, a dark-green plant that turns nearly black in fall. Black grass is covered only by the highest tides of spring and fall, and occasional storm tides. Behind black grass is a shrubby zone of marsh elder and groundsel tree, their further invasion of the marsh inhibited by storm tides. Beyond the reach of tides, the shrub zone may contain bayberry, sea hollyhock, swamp rose mallow, seashore mallow, saltmarsh pink, marsh thistle, glades morning glory, and sea oxeye. The first trees encountered upon leaving eastern salt marshes are usually pitch pines, black oaks, northern red oaks, scrub oaks, and possibly beach plum.

Typical salt marshes are laced with tidal creeks and rivers, drainage channels that flush the marsh with saltwater at high tide and carry it back to the sea at low tide. The exposed banks of tidal creeks

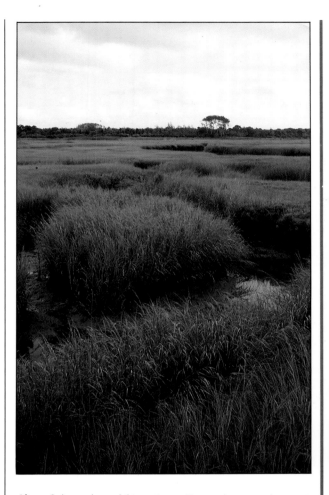

**Above** Salt marshes exhibit very definite zones of vegetation determined largely by an area's frequency of inundation at high tide. Exposure to salt water is a very rigid limiting factor, and a difference of as little as two inches in elevation can result in two entirely different plant communities.

contain dense populations of mud algae which are swept seaward with each receding tide. This algae and the tremendous amount of saltmarsh detritus (decomposing organic material), contribute to the enormous productivity of estuaries and intercoastal waterways.

Pacific cordgrass forms the front line in western salt marshes. Immediately behind it, just above mean high tide, pickleweed reigns, with jaumea and seaside arrowgrass growing in patches among it. Dodder, a bright yellow or orange parasitic plant, often grows in web-like masses among pickleweed.

**Right** Spike grass is a short, wiry grass which grows at higher elevations in a salt marsh. It often forms dense colonies, especially around the edge of evaporation pools.

**Far right** Despite the misleading name, saltmarsh bulrush is not a rush, but a sedge with a typical three-sided stem and numerous sharp, pointed leaves. It grows in the intertidal regions of salt marshes.

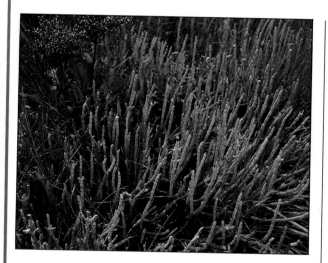

**Above** Glassworts, also known as pickleweeds, form mats of prostrate woody stems from which erect, translucent green stems grow. Their succulent stems store large quantities of water necessary for their survival.

Spike grass and marsh gum-plant form the zone behind pickleweed, with Pacific silverweed and various grasses and sedges that cannot stand prolonged inundation with saltwater. Marsh rosemary typically delineates the upland boundary of the marsh. Alkali heath, saltbush, saltmarsh sand spurry, and brass buttons will colonize disturbed sites, as when ocean debris washes up and smothers a patch of pickleweed.

## Some common plants of salt marshes

### Atlantic and Gulf coasts

| | |
|---|---|
| saltmarsh cordgrass | glassworts |
| sea lavender | spearscale |
| sea blite | marsh hay cordgrass |
| saltmarsh bulrush | spike grass |
| black grass | marsh elder |
| groundsel tree | bayberry |
| sea hollyhock | swamp rose mallow |
| seashore mallow | saltmarsh pink |
| marsh thistle | glades morning glory |
| sea oxeye | seaside plantain |
| seaside goldenrod | saltmarsh aster |
| wigeongrass | |

### Pacific coast

| | |
|---|---|
| Pacific cordgrass | pickleweed |
| jaumea | seaside arrowgrass |
| spike grass | marsh gum-plant |
| alkali heath | saltbush |
| saltmarsh sand spurry | brass buttons |
| marsh rosemary | Pacific silverweed |
| saltmarsh bulrush | tufted hairgrass |
| dodder | creeping alkali grass |
| bear sedge (Alaska) | (Alaska) |
| curlycup gumweed | eelgrass |
| three-square bulrush | redtop |
| sea milkwort | tule |
| seaside plantain | |

# MANGROVE SHORES

Some stretches of the southern Florida coast fit none of the shorelines previously described. These are the mangrove shores, a sort of saltwater swamp. The leggy prop roots of red mangroves allow them to advance into the salt water and to withstand the tides and the abusive waves accompanying tropical storms.

Mangroves are land-builders that extend shorelines and form islands in much the same way that beach grass builds sand dunes. The tangled mangrove roots slow circulating water enough for suspended sediments to settle out and accumulate around the roots. Red mangroves produce the most extensive prop roots and form the outermost zone of advancing mangroves. Its seeds sprout and grow while on the tree, then drop off and float away. They float on their side at first, exposing themselves to the sun so they can photosynthesize their food. As they continue to grow, their center of gravity shifts and the seeds tip vertically in the water, thus increasing their chances of lodging in a suitable location, at which time they undergo phenomenal root growth to quickly stabilize themselves in their new home.

Black mangroves grow nearer to shore in the mud of shallow water previously deposited around the roots of red mangroves. They send up aerial roots similar to baldcypress "knees", to obtain oxygen for their roots buried in the oxygen-poor mud. Black mangroves continue with the process of land-building, and are followed by white mangroves, buttonwood, and finally, a tropical hardwood forest.

Mangroves can be identified by the roots they produce. Red mangroves develop arching prop

**Below** Because the leggy roots of red mangroves trap suspended sediment, advancing the shoreline as it accumulates, the trees move seaward and are succeeded, in turn, by black mangroves, white mangroves, buttonwood, and tropical hardwoods.

**Above** Mangrove swamps in North America are found only along the southwestern coast of Florida and in the keys. These red mangroves establish

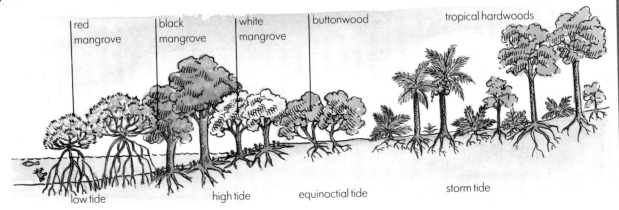

red mangrove | black mangrove | white mangrove | buttonwood | tropical hardwoods

low tide | high tide | equinoctial tide | storm tide

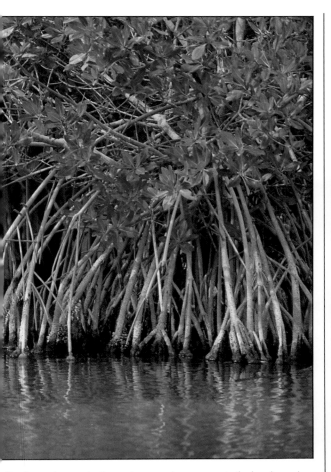

roots for support that are also capable of taking in oxygen through lenticels in their bark and shuttling it to the roots buried in anaerobic mud. Black mangroves produce aerial roots, while white mangroves growing on fairly solid ground exhibit neither of these two types. Because mangroves are so well adapted and their environment so demanding, few other species grow with them until the tropical hardwoods or sawgrass take over.

themselves in shallow salt water with virtually no competition from other vascular plants.

**Right** Among the tropical hardwoods that succeed mangroves you find species

common to the hardwood hammocks of the Everglades, such as sweetbay (bottom). Still farther from the shoreline on higher ground, you will find saw palmetto (top).

## Some common plants of mangrove shores and accompanying tropical forests

| | | | |
|---|---|---|---|
| red mangrove | paradise tree | slash pine | willow bustic |
| white mangrove | Bahama lysiloma | saw grass | inkwood |
| cabbage palmetto | false mastic | glassworts | |
| saw palmetto | milkbark | sweetbay | |
| sea grape | Florida nectanra | West Indies mahogany | |
| sedges | black mangrove | wingleaf soapberry | |
| strangler fig | buttonwood | gumbo-limbo | |

131

# DESERTS
## DESERT PLANT ADAPTATIONS

The three most important goals of desert plant adaptations are to conserve water, conserve water, and conserve water! A variation on an old joke, this summation is essentially correct. Instead of not knowing where their next meal is coming from, most desert plants do not know when they will get their next drink. In areas of sparse rainfall, low humidity, and searing heat, plants must be adept at collecting and hoarding every possible molecule of water to survive.

**Succulents**
The best-known desert plants are the succulents, which include cacti, yuccas, and agaves. Of all the members of the plant kingdom, succulents are the most able to store water. Their leaf or stem cells contain many vacuoles, or storage organelles, which can swell enormously with water when moisture is available to the plant's roots. The stems of many cacti are corrugated, allowing them to expand to accommodate greater volume when more water is being stored. Then, when drought sets in, succulents have a ready supply of water to carry on photosynthesis and maintain turgor, or internal cell pressure, which prevents wilting.

Cacti possess one of the most radical adaptations for preventing moisture loss. Their leaves are reduced to mere spines or bristles because water loss through transpiration is largely proportional to the leaf surface area. The spines are also an effective deterrent to most animals which would otherwise eat the succulent tissue of cacti to obtain moisture and food. Photosynthesis, the major function of leaves, occurs in the outer region of swollen cacti stems.

The stems of cacti and the leaves of other succulents are covered by a leathery or waxy cuticle, an effective barrier to moisture loss. Cacti also have evolved stomata which open only at night, when the air is cooler, to collect and store carbon dioxide in the form of organic acids for the next day's photosynthesis, in contrast with most vascular plants' stomata, which open only during daylight photosynthetic activity. In this way, cacti avoid gaseous exchanges during the heat of the day, which would result in greater moisture loss through transpiration.

One of the more notable features of desert vegetation is that all perennials are rather widely spaced. Succulents have extensive, shallow root systems that quickly gather the sparse precipitation before most of it has a chance to percolate deeper into the ground. Roots of the giant saguaro cactus may cover an area up to 90 feet in diameter. The shallow, spreading roots prevent overcrowding and thus regulate competition for precious resources. The roots of some species actually secrete natural herbicides to keep competing species at bay. "Bare" soil between larger perennials is not necessarily devoid of plant life. Lower plants, such as mosses, lichens, fungi, and algae, may inhabit the sandy

**Left** Monument Valley, which straddles the eastern border between Utah and Arizona, is a good example of a sagebrush habitat.

**Right** Desert paintbrush is one of the annuals that splash color beneath the drab greenish gray sagebrush after winter rains.

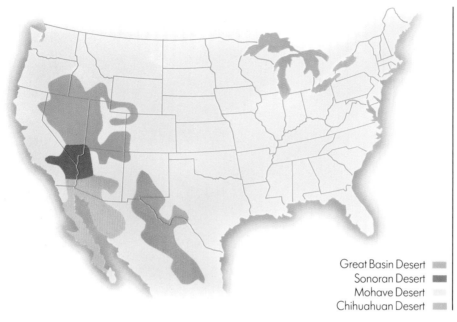

Great Basin Desert ▬
Sonoran Desert ▬
Mohave Desert ▬
Chihuahuan Desert ▬

**Below** Desert plants have had to make some remarkable evolutionary adaptations. Annuals like bladderpods (**below**) have adapted by concentrating their entire life cycle into one brief burst of growth following seasonal rains. In contrast, the stately saguaro (**bottom**), there for the long haul, has combined an extensive shallow root system with a massive water storage capacity.

soil, sometimes forming a stabilizing crust that retards erosion. These plants are able to garner moisture from dew that forms during the night, and can withstand the drying of their tissues until moisture again becomes available.

### Desert annuals

Conserving water may also mean becoming dormant during extended droughts. Many deserts do have one or more "rainy" seasons, when they receive a relatively large percentage of their annual rainfall. Desert annuals have adjusted their life cycles to take advantage of the wetter season. Their seeds contain a germination inhibitor that is washed away by a certain minimum rainfall. After these rains, the desert landscape nearly explodes in greenery and flowers as desert annuals rush to complete their entire life cycle within the short period of abundant moisture, for most have no other adaptations to cope with drought.

Desert annuals are divided into two groups: the summer annuals, adapted for life in the intense summer sunlight, and winter annuals hardy enough to cope with cooler temperatures and reduced sunlight. Annuals have protective mechanisms that regulate germination according to temperature and day length as well as precipitation, so that a winter annual is not fooled into germinating during summer rains, only to be faced with searing

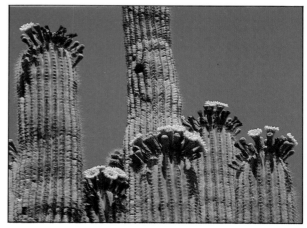

summer temperatures for which it is unprepared, and vice versa.

In some desert areas, there is not always a wet season every year, and in such places the seeds of desert annuals have been known to remain dormant for ten years and still sprout with vigor when rain finally falls. In other areas, particularly in the Sonoran Desert, rainy seasons may occur twice a year, in summer and winter. Some annuals sprout during one seasonal rain and enter another dormant period as low-profiled rosettes covered with dense, woolly gray or white hair that drastically cuts the flow of dry air over the leaf surfaces. Their low-rosette stage keeps them out of the moisture-robbing winds until the following rainy season, when they burst into bloom.

## Desert shrubs

Desert shrubs grow as low, densely-branched, dome-shaped clumps, reducing their exposure to dry winds. Their leaves are small and often coated with a waxy or resinous substance to retard moisture loss, or with dense, light-colored hair that reduces airflow across the leaf surface and reflects most of the intense solar radiation. Big sagebrush, brittlebush, and some saltbushes can produce two different types of leaves, one for moist periods and another better suited to droughts. In some species, the leaves droop and curl up in response to drought, reducing their exposed surface area. Under more extreme conditions, the deciduous leaves are shed and the shrub enters a dormant period until moisture becomes more abundant.

Creosote bush is a widespread shrub of the hot, southwestern deserts. In the cool desert of the Great Basin, however, shrubs such as sagebrush and saltbushes (which include shadscale, greasewood, hop sage, and winterfat) are dominant, while cacti and other succulents are less prevalent.

## Trees

Very few trees can endure the rigors of desert life, but two groups that do are the pinyon pines and junipers. They have found their niche in the upper desert elevations, above the grasslands and sagebrush and below the ponderosa pine forests. These are low trees, usually less than 30 feet tall, with wide, spreading crowns that effectively distribute them to avoid overcrowding, creating an open, grassy savannah. The needles of pinyon pines and scalelike leaves of junipers both reduce

**Above** One of the few common desert trees, junipers, like this Utah juniper, grow at higher elevations where rainfall is greater.

the surface area they present to drying winds.

The large seeds of pinyon pines, primarily distributed by birds and mammals who either drop them accidentally or store them in caches and forget them, pack enough stored energy to help the new rootlets grow quickly to reach needed water deep in the soil. Other desert plants are also adapted to secure their water from deep in the earth. Certain mesquites, for example, have been found to have roots reaching as deep as 175 feet!

## Riparian vegetation

The term "riparian" commonly refers to life associated with river banks, and indeed there are occasional rivers and streams flowing across desert areas. In the desert, however, "riparian" also refers to washes and other drainage areas that may be dry at some times and host intermittent streams at others. The runoff from paved roads may simulate wash conditions at the roadside, creating an artificial riparian habitat. Even shallow drainages less than two inches deep can conduct enough water during rains to make a difference to plants living there; burrobush and smoke tree are common in these temporary drainage channels. Riparian vegetation has adapted to desert life by growing in these areas of relatively abundant moisture. They are often quite different from the plants of the surrounding desert.

Along the permanent desert waterways there are typically two terraces. The lower terrace is covered by ordinary flood waters, while the upper terrace is inundated only during the more extreme floods. The lower terrace is therefore wetter and conducive to the growth of different species than the upper

**Left** Riparian vegetation grows along desert streams and washes where soils are moister. Cottonwoods grow where there is the greatest amount of moisture, while other riparian species that require somewhat less moisture grow farther from the drainage's center.

terrace. Various willows and cottonwoods grow closest to the water. Farther back on the first terrace arrow weed can often be found, followed by quail bush and screwbean mesquite. Other mesquites inhabit the upper terrace along with tamarisk, a European import, desert broom, seep willow, desert willow, Apache plume, acacias, and others.

### Great Basin Desert

Of the four great North American deserts, the Great Basin Desert is the only one classified as a "cold" desert, meaning that it receives most of its precipitation during winter in the form of snow. It is the most northerly of the four deserts, and also has the highest average elevation. Geographically, it overlaps the intermountain grasslands, which occur at slightly higher elevations than does the true desert of this region.

Shrubs dominate the landscape here, and cacti, while present, consist of fewer species and play a less significant role than they do in the hot deserts. Absent is the multitude of annual species that cause the hot deserts to periodically erupt in color. Also absent are the riparian species that line the drainages of hot deserts; having evolved in a warm moist climate, they require both the moisture of the waterways and the warmer temperatures found in the lower elevations of southern deserts.

Sagebrushes, led by big sagebrush, and salt-bushes are the dominant shrubs. Grasses commonly accompany sagebrush, particularly at higher elevations. Mormon tea is another shrub often associated with sagebrush, and the region's primary cactus species, plains pricklypear, also mingles with these two species. Common herbaceous species found among sagebrush

## Some common plants of the Great Basin Desert

### Trees and shrubs

| | |
|---|---|
| big sagebrush | sand sagebrush |
| black sagebrush | shadscale |
| green rabbitbrush | winter fat |
| greasewood | littleleaf horsebrush |
| Mormon tea | spiny hopsage |
| iodinebush | rubber rabbitbrush |
| snakeweed | blackbrush |
| turpentine broom | desert peach |
| antelope bitterbrush | four-wing saltbush |
| Wood's rose | curlleaf cerocarpus |
| tamarisk | singleleaf pinyon |
| Colorado pinyon | Utah juniper |
| cherrystone juniper | cliff rose |
| hop sage | |

### Wildflowers

| | |
|---|---|
| alkali sacaton | rushes |
| pickleweed | sego lily |
| Indian paintbrush | desert paintbrush |
| lupines | scarlet globemallow |
| hood phlox | longleaf phlox |
| tumbleweed | halogeton |
| bur buttercup | tansy mustard |
| clasping pepperweed | arrowleaf balsamroot |
| blanket flower | desert dandelion |
| hairy golden aster | locoweeds |
| scarlet gilia | mule's ears |
| Gunnison mariposa | meadow death camas |
| goldenrods | yarrow |
| plains pricklypear | Simpson's hedgehog cactus |
| claret cup cactus | yellow bee plant |
| Nuttall's larkspur | golden prince's plume |
| desert four o'clock | desert candle |
| sulphur flower | threadleaf groundsel |
| cushion cactus | tahoka daisy |
| desert trumpet | |

### Grasses

| | |
|---|---|
| bluebunch wheatgrass | cheatgrass brome |
| bottlebrush squirreltail | Indian ricegrass |
| giant wildrye | needlegrass |
| needle-and-thread | foxtail barley |
| western wheatgrass | secunda bluegrass |
| red three-awn | prairie junegrass |
| Idaho fescue | Nevada bluegrass |

**Above** The Great Basin is characterized by an abundance of shrubs. Mormon tea (**top**) is very common, along with sagebrush, Fewer species of annuals grow here than in other North American deserts, but two typical residents are sego lily (**left**) and Nuttall's larkspur (**right**)

than before, which has led to the decline of big sagebrush in some areas.

To the south, where the Great Basin Desert merges with the Mohave Desert, blackbrush predominates, often forming pure stands. This community may also contain turpentine broom, desert peach, Mormon tea, sagebrushes, and saltbushes.

### Mohave Desert

The smallest of the North American deserts, the Mohave Desert is slightly higher in average elevation than the neighboring Sonoran Desert, even though it includes Death Valley at 282 feet below sea level. It lies within the basin and range province that constitutes the Great Basin, and some argue that it is really part of the Great Basin Desert, but botanically it is separate.

This desert is dominated by widely spaced, low shrubs. Creosote bush is easily the most prominent plant in the hot deserts of North America, reaching its northernmost limits in the Mohave Desert. Readily recognized by its yellowish-green leaves with their resinous coating and strong resinous odor, and its numerous yellow flowers, creosote bush is extremely efficient at obtaining water from the soil; so much so, in fact, that its own seedlings cannot grow nearby. It frequently reproduces by sending out runners that sprout upon reaching a suitable location. Other shrubs likely to be encountered are Parry saltbush, woolly bur sage, Mohave sage, white bur sage, desert holly, cattle spinach, brittlebush, spiny mendora, goldenhead, blackbrush, and others. In dry washes one is likely

include lupines, globemallows, paintbrushes, locoweeds, phloxes, and sego lily. Saltbushes, like shadscale, winterfat, greasewood, and hop sage, are common in alkaline soils at lower elevations, with shadscale dominating. Iodinebush, saltgrass, rushes, alkali sacaton, and pickleweeds occur on the more saline sites.

In areas disturbed by fire, big sagebrush may be temporarily displaced by snakeweeds, rabbitbrushes, and horsebrushes. Also found on disturbed sites are tumble weed, halogeton, bur buttercup, tansy mustard, and clasping pepperweed. An exotic grass introduced from Asia in the 1870s, cheatgrass brome has displaced much of the native grasses, such as bluebunch wheatgrass. Since cheatgrass brome produces much more fuel (leaves and stems) than the native species, fires that occur are hotter and more frequent

**Above** The presence of creosote bush defines the hot deserts of North America. The resinous coating of its pungent leaves serves to retard the loss of water vapor.

137

## Some common plants of the Mohave Desert

### Trees and shrubs

| | |
|---|---|
| creosote bush | Parry saltbush |
| woolly bur sage | white bur sage |
| Mohave sage | desert holly |
| cattle spinach | brittlebush |
| spiny mendora | goldenhead |
| blackbrush | bladderpod |
| honey mesquite | screwbean mesquite |
| Fremont cottonwood | tamarisk |
| arrow weed | four-wing saltbush |
| desert willow | seep willow |
| smoke tree | Anderson lycium |
| burrobush | catclaw |

### Wildflowers

| | |
|---|---|
| California poppy | filaree |
| fiddleneck | tidy tips |
| desert dandelion | pincushion flower |
| owl clover | notch-leaved phacelia |
| pygmy lupine | birdcage evening primrose |
| yellow bee plant | Mohave aster |
| Mohave desert star | Death Valley sage |
| desert candle | desert chicory |
| desert trumpet | desert sand verbena |
| desert four o'clock | desert globemallow |
| rattlesnake weed | golden prince's plume |
| western jimsonweed | Canterbury bells |
| Arizona lupine | spreading fleabane |
| desert five-spot | desert marigold |
| desert gold | scalloped phacelia |
| diamond cholla | barrel cactus |
| beavertail cactus | claret cup cactus |
| plains pricklypear | Joshua tree |
| blue yucca | Mohave yucca |

### Grasses

| | |
|---|---|
| big galleta | bush muhly |
| fluffgrass | Indian ricegrass |
| gramas | |

Among the more than 250 species of annuals lending their colors to the seasonal displays are tidy tips, desert dandelion, pin-cushion flowers, owl clover, notch-leaved phacelia, and many others. Eighty percent of annuals found in the Mohave Desert do not exist anywhere else.

Succulents, symbolized by Joshua tree, the largest of the yuccas, come into their own in the Mohave Desert. Blue yucca and Mohave yucca are

**Below** Joshua tree is indigenous to the Mohave Desert. Not really a tree but a species of yucca, it may grow densely, sometimes forming "forests" within its range.

to find burrobush, catclaw, and honey mesquite.

The Mohave Desert is the site of some of the most awesome displays of desert annuals following favorable winter rains. California poppy, fiddle-neck, and filaree may cover acres with uniform color as a single species forms pure stands.

The Mohave Desert primarily hosts winter annuals; one of the most prolific is California poppy (**left**), the state flower of its namesake, which blooms so profusely that it often turns entire hillsides orange. Desert plume (**above**) produces tall, slender wands of yellow flowers.

also common here. Needless to say, cacti are abundant, though many are low-growing.

## Sonoran Desert

No other plant better symbolizes the Sonoran Desert than the stately saguaro. Towering as much as 50 feet above the desert, it is the state flower of Arizona where it and all other cacti are protected by law. The saguaro usually occurs on upper desert slopes together with barrel cactus, ocotillo, golden cholla, teddybear cholla, hedgehog cactus, desert agave, and small trees, such as blue palo verde and desert ironwood. Where the Sonoran Desert merges with the grasslands fringing its upper elevations, desert spoon, with its five- to eight-foot spikes of yellow flowers, thrives.

The valley floors are often dominated by creosote bush and white bur sage or bur sage, as are those in the Mohave Desert. In areas with sandier soil, creosote bush is replaced by Mormon tea and indigo bush. Representative of the cacti at lower elevations are various chollas as well as beavertail cactus. The valley floors and lower slopes are criss-crossed by drainages which harbor just enough moisture to support such riparian species as burrobush, graythorn, and lycium.

In the United States, the eastern portion of the Sonoran Desert, known as the Arizona uplands, is the most scenic and botanically diverse. All species of cacti native to the Sonoran Desert are plentiful. In addition to cacti, foothills palo verde grows everywhere except on the valley floors. Desert ironwood, a small tree, is also characteristic of the Arizona uplands. Noticeable shrubs of this area include whitethorn acacia, creosote bush, bur sage, desert buckwheat, ratany, paperflower, brittlebush, jojoba, fairy duster, and limber bush, with flexible, reddish branches carrying attractive bright green, heart-shaped leaves. Along washes and roadsides, desert willow, desert broom, and burrobush do quite well.

The Sonoran Desert receives the most precipitation of the four North American deserts, and it also receives both late summer and winter rains, so that it supports summer and winter annuals. Colorful spring wildflowers following winter rains include Parry's penstemon, gold poppies, purple mat, Coulter's lupine, chia, owl clover, and pincushion flowers.

Nothing symbolizes the Sonoran Desert better than the towering saguaro cactus (**right**) which may reach 50 feet in height and 200 years in age. Its pleated stems expand in girth to store great quantities of water when precipitation is available. The ocotillo (**left**) is a resident cactus of both the Sonoran and Chihuahuan Deserts.

## Some common plants of the Sonoran Desert

### Trees and shrubs

| | |
|---|---|
| bur sage | white bur sage |
| indigo bush | Mormon tea |
| graythorn | Anderson lycium |
| blue palo verde | foothills palo verde |
| desert ironwood | desert hackberry |
| whitethorn acacia | creosote bush |
| desert buckwheat | ratany |
| paperflower | brittlebush |
| jojoba | fairy duster |
| limber bush | burrobush |
| desert broom | desert willow |
| arrow weed | desert holly |
| elephant tree | Gregg catclaw |
| honey mesquite | screwbean mesquite |
| smoke tree | shadscale |
| snakeweed | tamarisk |
| triangle-leaf bursage | chuparosa |
| California fan palm | Fremont cottonwood |
| velvet mesquite | desert spoon |

### Succulents

| | |
|---|---|
| beavertail cactus | saguaro |
| barrel cactus | ocotillo |
| golden cholla | teddybear cholla |
| jumping cholla | cane cholla |

| | |
|---|---|
| buckthorn cholla | hedgehog cactus |
| organpipe cactus | fishhook barrel cactus |
| prickly pear cactus | desert Christmas cactus |
| fishhook cactus | pincushion cactus |
| night-blooming cereus | Mohave yucca |
| soaptree yucca | dudleya |
| Parry's century plant | rainbow cactus |

### Wildflowers

| | |
|---|---|
| gold poppy | Parry's penstemon |
| purple mat | Coulter's lupine |
| Mohave desert star | fiddleneck |
| desert dandelion | owl clover |
| wild heliotrope | chia |
| pincushion flower | yellow twining snapdragon |
| birdcage evening primrose | Arizona jewel-flower |
| desert four o'clock | desert five-spot |
| desert globemallow | desert marigold |
| desert sand verbena | western peppergrass |
| yellow bee plant | Indian blanket |
| desert candle | desert chicory |
| desert trumpet | desert velvet |
| spectacle pod | Mohave aster |
| desert sunflower | yellow cryptantha |
| common ice plant | Coulter's globemallow |

**Above** With both summer and winter rains, the Sonoran Desert hosts the most species of annuals and cacti of the four deserts. One common Sonoran cactus is beavertail.

## Chihuahuan Desert

As in the other hot deserts of North America, creosote bush dominates the lower elevations of the Chihuahuan Desert. Tarbush is often codominant with creosote bush, and mariola, with its pungent foliage, is a frequent companion of both. In some areas, creosote bush is accompanied by whitethorn acacia and sandpaper bush. Crucifixion thorn, buffalo gourd, and Mormon tea likewise frequent the Chihuahuan lowlands, along with herbaceous species such as desert marigold, little golden zinnia, desert zinnia, white horse-nettle, and fluffgrass.

Precipitation occurs mostly during the summer, resulting in a preponderance of summer annuals in the valleys, but sufficient winter precipitation occurs in some areas to support winter annuals as well. At slightly higher elevations, the increased annual precipitation brings a corresponding increase in succulents, particularly yuccas and

**Above** Among the many summer annuals of the Chihuahuan Desert is the little golden zinnia, a member of the sunflower family that grows in low, round clumps.

agaves. Soaptree yucca, banana yucca with its stiff blue-gray leaves, false agave, and lechuguilla, an agave sometimes mistaken for a yucca, are a few that increase in frequency on the lower slopes. Somewhat higher, ocotillo and the shrubs Texas silverleaf and ratany become more common.

Higher still, the desert begins to merge with grassland. Yuccas and agaves, such as Harvard agave and Parry's century plant, so named for the many years that elapse before the mature plant flowers, mingle with two grass-like members of the lily family, beargrass (in New Mexico) and sacahuista (in Texas), with their creamy, club-shaped flowers. Desert spoon, another member of the lily family, produces an elongated spike with thousands of yellow flowers, and is also found in this zone.

Cacti abound throughout the Chihuahuan Desert. Along with such colorfully descriptive names as horse crippler and Turk's head, they may include prickly pear, Texas prickly pear, claret cup cactus, cushion cactus, night-blooming cereus, rainbow cactus, tree cholla, desert Christmas cactus, and clavellina, a low cactus that may form mats up to 10 feet in diameter.

Washes in the Chihuahuan Desert host such riparian species as graythorn, Apache plume, catclaw, and little leaf desert sumac. The lowest depressions are home to four-wing saltbush, burrograss, and tobosa, a coarse grass. Disturbed ground supports snakeweed, tumbleweed, and Russian thistle.

## Some common plants of the Chihuahuan Desert

### Trees and shrubs

| | |
|---|---|
| creosote bush | tarbush |
| mariola | whitethorn acacia |
| sandpaper bush | crucifixion thorn |
| buffalo gourd | Mormon tea |
| Texas silverleaf | ratany |
| graythorn | catclaw |
| little leaf desert sumac | honey mesquite |
| desert spoon | four-wing saltbush |
| Mexican palo verde | rabbit brush |
| screwbean mesquite | snakeweed |
| tamarisk | arrow weed |

### Succulents

| | |
|---|---|
| Torrey yucca | soaptree yucca |
| ocotillo | lechuguilla |
| false agave | banana yucca |
| Harvard agave | Parry's century plant |
| horse crippler | Turk's head |
| prickly pear cactus | Texas prickly pear |
| plains prickly pear | claret cup cactus |
| cushion cactus | night-blooming cereus |
| rainbow cactus | tree cholla |
| desert Christmas cactus | clavellina |

### Wildflowers

| | |
|---|---|
| bear grass | sacahuista |
| Apache plume | white horsenettle |
| desert marigold | desert zinnia |
| desert four o'clock | desert gold |
| desert poppy | pale trumpets |
| spectacle pod | trailing four o'clock |
| filaree | Fendler's bladderpod |
| little golden zinnia | Arizona jewel flower |
| tahoka daisy | Coulter's lupine |
| Chihuahua flax | spreading fleabane |
| Indian blanket | golden prince's plume |
| jackass clover | western peppergrass |
| devil's claw | desert tobacco |

### Grasses

| | |
|---|---|
| Indian ricegrass | fluffgrass |
| burrograss | tobosa |

# HIGH COUNTRY
## WHAT IS TUNDRA?

Tundra is the term for the colder terrestrial regions where temperature is the limiting factor suppressing tree growth. In North America there are two types of tundra that are different botanically as well as geographically. Arctic tundra is that great treeless expanse north of the boreal forest. Here, the active photosynthetic period of plants is only about three months a year, but due to the long days, the plants photosynthesize food around the clock, so they can reproduce and store enough to last through the long arctic winter. Several feet below the soil's surface, permafrost, permanently frozen subsoil, prohibits the development of tree roots. Permafrost, the severe climate, and the very slow nutrient recycling due to the effect of cold on decomposers, combine to make tree growth impossible.

Alpine tundra, found on mountain summits, is the result of elevation instead of latitude. Though the winters here are shorter, the climate is in some ways more severe than that of the arctic tundra. High winds constantly buffet the landscape, and the thin atmosphere at higher elevations screens out less of the damaging ultraviolet radiation from the sun. Primary succession, the development of soil and plant communities from bare rock, is remarkably slow due to retarded plant activity, and the little soil that does form is subjected to erosion by the strong winds and large volumes of precipitation that accompany high elevations. Therefore, bare rock is a common component of the alpine tundra landscape, colonized only by lichens. In the most exposed locations, even lichens may not grow. Other plants of the alpine tundra are largely restricted to the spaces between rocks where a small amount of soil has accumulated.

### Alpine plant adaptations

Despite its heavy annual precipitation, alpine areas are, in effect, a type of desert. Because there is little soil to absorb moisture, much of the water from rainfall and melting snow is unavailable to plants, lost as runoff to mountain streams. In addition, the constant winds, while frequently bearing moisture as they sweep up the mountain slopes and cool past their dew point, nevertheless can rob moisture from exposed plants faster than they can absorb it, so alpine plant adaptations are quite similar to those of desert plants.

Aside from rock-colonizing lichens, most alpine tundra plants grow as dense mats or dome-shaped cushions. In summer, these shapes keep the plants low and out of drying winds while allowing them to present a respectable surface area to the sun for photosynthesis. Their compact shapes also keep them warmer by restricting the access of cold air to the plant's interior, sometimes resulting in temperatures 20 degrees warmer than the surrounding air. Many species grow primarily on the leeward side of rocks or other obstructions, which also helps to keep them warm and moist. In

One most accessible alpine tundra areas is located along Trail Ridge Road in Rocky Mountain National Park, Colorado (**left**). Alpine tundra plants exhibit many of the same adaptations as desert plants; both habitats experience high evaporation rates, and alpine areas have little water-retaining soil. Also adapted to survive low temperatures, many, like moss pink (**right**) grow in low, dense clumps that conserve warmth.

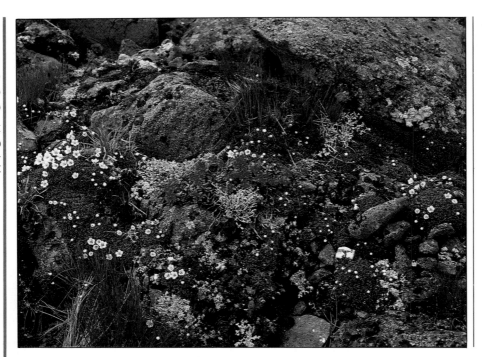

the winter, these same shapes allow the plants to remain under a protective blanket of snow, quite warm when compared to the air temperature and wind chill, and out of destructive winds. Those areas that are windswept and barren in winter are also likely to support the fewest plants, and those that do survive are stunted.

Other adaptations common to desert and alpine plants help conserve water and/or reduce exposure to solar radiation. Narrow leaves, dense foliage, and thick cuticles (surface tissue) are common characteristics that reduce evaporation. Some alpine plants store water in waxy, succulent leaves and stems. Leaves of many species also have a dense, woolly covering of light-colored hairs that restrict the flow of desiccating air over their surface, insulate the leaves, and reflect some of the harmful solar radiation bombarding them.

The small size of alpine plants is itself an adaptation to the harsh environment, for the plants use their energy to survive, rather than expending it on large, showy growth. All alpine plants are perennials, another energy-conservation measure which allows them to spend winter in a state of readiness for the unpredictable start of their short growing season. They flower immediately after the snows melt, allowing time for their seeds to be dispersed,

germinate, and establish themselves before the next winter starts. One seeming extravagance is the production of large, showy blossoms that often dwarf the rest of the plant, but this is crucial to reproduction, for in such a barren landscape, small flowers could easily be overlooked by bees and other pollinating insects.

### Alpine tundra

While we commonly think of alpine tundra as a habitat of the high Rocky Mountain, Sierra-Nevada, and Cascade peaks, there are many isolated examples in the Appalachian Mountains of the northeastern United States as well. Perhaps the best and most accessible alpine tundra flora in the east is via the Auto Road up Mt. Washington in the White Mountain National Forest, New Hampshire. The Alpine Garden Trail, beginning about one mile from the summit, goes through alpine habitat hosting more than one hundred plant species, many of which are relatively rare in the east. Heath shrubs, abundant due to the cold climate, include bog bilberry, mountain cranberry, alpine bearberry, Lapland rosebay, and alpine azalea, moss plant, and mountain heath. Other species likely to be encountered are diapensia, alpine goldenrod, dwarf yellow cinquefoil, alpine bluet, Mt. Washington avens, Greenland sandwort, and wine-leaved cinquefoil. Lichens occur regularly on rock surfaces.

Timberline (the imaginary line beyond which trees do not grow because of cold) in the west is directly related to latitude. In the southern Rockies, tundra does not occur below 12,500 feet, while in south-central Alaska timberline may occur as low as 1,500 feet. One of the more accessible regions of alpine tundra in the west occurs along Trail Ridge Road in Rocky Mountain National Park, Estes Park, Colorado. Following an ancient trail used by the Ute and Arapaho Indians of the area, this road winds its way up to an elevation of 12,183 feet while transversing the major mountain range of the park. Numerous pull-offs and several paved trails, which restrict

Alpine wallflower (**top**) grows as a low tuft of basal leaves, keeping out of the bitter, drying winds of alpine tundra. The succulent stems and leaves of king's crown (**above**) store water as a hedge against desiccation.

## Some common plants of alpine tundra and meadows

### West

| | |
|---|---|
| mountain sorrel | alpine avens |
| tufted phlox | greenleaf chiming bells |
| moss campion | alpine wallflower |
| fairy primrose | snowball saxifrage |
| dwarf clover | alpine sunflower |
| king's crown | arctic gentian |
| yellow monkeyflower | elephant heads |
| little elephant heads | dwarf lewisia |
| eriogonums | sandworts |
| alpine everlasting | spreading phlox |
| alpine lupine | alpine columbine |
| Drummond's cinquefoil | penstemons |
| club-moss ivesia | primrose monkeyflower |
| alpine buttercup | sibbaldia |
| alpine paintbrush | dwarf knotweed |
| American bistort | granite gilia |
| goldenbush | whitesquaw |
| red mountain heather | white mountain heather |
| shrubby cinquefoil | alpine laurel |
| alpine willow | pussypaws |
| glacier lily | beargrass |
| alpine prickly currant | ballhead sandwort |

### East

| | |
|---|---|
| bog bilberry | mountain cranberry |
| alpine bearberry | Lapland rosebay |
| alpine azalea | moss plant |
| mountain heath | diapensia |
| alpine goldenrod | dwarf yellow cinquefoil |
| alpine bluet | Mt. Washington avens |
| Greenland sandwort | wine-leaved cinquefoil |

foot traffic and protect the fragile tundra environment, allow easy access to the alpine ecosystem.

The similarity of their environments means that alpine tundra plants often have a large geographical range; alpine tundra in New Mexico is, after all, much the same as alpine tundra in Alberta. Plant communities within a small area may differ markedly, however, depending upon their exact microhabitats. For instance, plants found on gravel flats and scree slopes are fully exposed to the elements. Those not buried by winter snow tend to be very compact; examples

145

include sandworts, phloxes, eriogonums, spring locoweed, dense-leaved draba, and alpine fescue, a bunchgrass. A similar habitat that does receive snow cover may contain alpine paintbrush, alpine lupine, or club-moss ivesia. By contrast, the relative shelter of boulder fields, talus slopes (piles of rock fragments at the foot of a cliff), and rock crevices is ideal for shrubs such as granite gilia, whitestem goldenbush, and whitesquaw, plus herbaceous species too large to survive elsewhere on the tundra.

Western alpine areas differ from eastern ones in sheer size, and contain more sheltered areas where soil accumulates to form alpine meadows. Such meadows are usually dominated by sod-forming grasses and sedges, particularly hairgrass. Herbaceous wildflowers common to well drained meadows include Lyall's lupine, alpine everlasting, club-moss ivesia, dwarf lewisia, Drummond's cinquefoil, alpine goldenrod, and Sierra daisy. Shrubs are not abundant in alpine meadows, but miniature thickets of various dwarf willow species may be found together with alpine laurel, dwarf huckleberry, white mountain heather, and red mountain heather. Wetter meadows below melting snowbanks or near alpine lakes and streams will host species such as sibbaldia, alpine shooting star, elephant's head, little elephant's head, primrose monkeyflower, alpine buttercup, dwarf knotweed, Anderson's alpine aster, alpine goldenrod, alpine paintbrush and rosy stonecrop. Alpine meadows are fairly sheltered relative to the rocky plant communities found at the summits, and many species found in alpine meadows are also common to subalpine meadows below timberline.

## Subalpine forests

These are transition zones between alpine tundra and montane forests. They are defined by one or two dominant tree species, starting where they compose the majority of the canopy and ending at the treeline. As in any transition zone, they share some species with each adjacent habitat.

The subalpine forest of the Pacific Northwest coastal forests is dominated by mountain hemlock. Engelmann spruce and subalpine fir are the indicator species for subalpine forests in the Rocky Mountains, and those of the Sierra Nevada, Klamanth, and some western Great

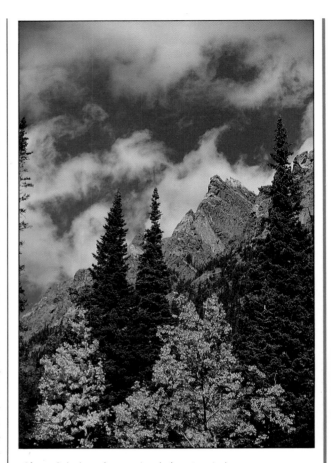

**Above** Subalpine forests, the transition zones between alpine tundra and montane forests, vary in their species composition with geographic location. Indicator tree species in the Rocky Mountains are Engelmann spruce, shown here along with quaking aspen, and subalpine fir.

Basin ranges contain a mixture of whitebark pine, lodgepole pine, mountain hemlock, and foxtail pine. On the higher Great Basin ranges, limber pine and bristlecone pine (some of which are considered to be the oldest living organisms on earth) characterize the subalpine zone. In the East, subalpine forests contain white spruce, black spruce, balsam fir, and paper birch; they are, in fact, nothing more than a southerly extension of the boreal forest along the spine of the Appalachian Mountains.

One feature common to many subalpine forests is the stunted, misshapen conifer trees at the treeline. Known as krummholz (German for "crooked wood"), they have been shaped by the relentless wind, into a natural version of a giant bonsai tree. Some, called "banner trees," exhibit flagging, in which all branches grow on the leeward side of the prevailing winds. Other trees are so severely beaten by the wind that they form tangled, shrubby mats rather than a main trunk. The tree then tends to reproduce by layering, or rooting the tips or undersides of its branches whenever they touch moist soil, thus increasing the size of the mat.

Krummholz occurs when the sun and the friction caused by moving air warm the needles and stimulate their stomata to open, resulting in desiccation. Deprived of their moisture and unable to replace it because of frozen roots, the tips of the affected branches die back. Larger trees with more water reserves stored in their trunks suffer less than smaller trees. Curiously, this phenomenon seems to be more prevalent in the East, suggesting that the boreal forest species do not fare as well in fierce, cold windy weather as do western species.

**Below** Subalpine forests in the Great Basin region host bristlecone pines, the oldest known living organisms on earth. The most ancient specimens exceed 4,600 years in age.

## Some common plants of western subalpine forests

### Trees and shrubs

| | |
|---|---|
| mountain hemlock | Engelmann spruce |
| subalpine fir | whitebark pine |
| lodgepole pine | foxtail pine |
| Douglas fir | Jeffrey pine |
| Pacific silver fir | subalpine larch |
| western hemlock | western redcedar |
| limber pine | bristlecone pine |
| alpine prickly currant | dwarf huckleberry |
| black spruce | bearberry |
| quaking aspen | western juniper |
| western serviceberry | red mountain heather |
| white mountain heather | creeping Oregon grape |
| shrubby cinquefoil | common snowberry |
| Rocky Mountain maple | mountain snowberry |

### Wildflowers

| | |
|---|---|
| beargrass | blue columbine |
| subalpine buttercup | pussypaws |
| pearly everlasting | red columbine |
| Lewis' monkeyflower | pipsissewa |
| queen's cup beadlily | fireweed |
| elephant head | glacier lily |
| avalanche lily | arrowhead groundsel |
| heartleaf arnica | mountain bluebell |
| orange agoseris | western monkshood |
| Parry primrose | subalpine Jacob's ladder |
| star gentian | rose crown |
| giant red paintbrush | tall chiming bells |
| balsamroot | mountain gentian |
| twinberry honeysuckle | thimbleberry |
| American bistort | ballhead sandwort |
| mountain death camas | silverleaf phacelia |
| yellow monkeyflower | brook saxifrage |
| pink pussytoes | globemallow |
| Rocky Mountain lily | fringed grass of parnassus |

**Left** Subalpine forests, which provide more shelter than alpine tundra, share many species with the vegetation zones of lower elevations. One of these, found in the herb layer, is blue columbine, the state flower of Colorado.

147

# BOTANY AND YOU
## WILD GARDENING

One of the most practical and rewarding ways to study botany is to start your own wild garden. A wild garden is not necessarily ground abandoned to follow its own course. More often, it is a carefully orchestrated re-creation of one or more specific habitats indigenous to your geographic locality, using native species. A homeowner in Illinois could convert the meadow behind the house into a replica of the tall-grass prairie that once covered his or her homesite, while in southern Arizona, a water-guzzling lawn could be replaced with the flora of the Sonoran desert.

In addition to being a pleasant and therapeutic pastime, wild gardening has low maintenance requirements. To be sure, there is occasional pruning, thinning, and transplanting to be done, but this is quite negligible compared to the attention required by the typical manicured garden. Lawns are, by definition, an early successional stage and a monoculture (a plant community composed primarily of one species), totally alien in the natural world, and therefore requiring a large expenditure of energy to maintain it.

Consider the large percentage of "free" time a homeowner spends mowing, raking, thatching, fertilizing, watering, and spraying the lawn, as well as clipping hedges, pruning shrubs, and weeding the garden. Add to this the cost, both financial and environmental, of the lawn mower or garden tractor, gas, oil, equipment maintenance, pesticides, herbicides, fertilizer, and water. At a point when both time and money are in short supply, it becomes increasingly difficult to justify the extravagance of a lush, manicured landscape.

In addition to the savings in terms of time and money, natural landscapes have other benefits. "Environment" is the buzzword of the nineties, and most people want to do their part. The native species in a wild garden can survive on the normal local precipitation, thus helping to conserve water. They require no pesticides because they have evolved defenses against most pests that plague domestic plants; a natural landscape also attracts wildlife, some of which provide natural pest control free of charge! Herbicides are out because a natural landscape is less susceptible to invasion by "weeds" than is a conventional garden; furthermore, a botanist will welcome most additions, whether intentional or not, and those unwelcome are easily removed by hand. Finally, a natural low-maintenance landscape may increase the value of your home as well as your enjoyment of it.

**Choosing a theme**
Natural ecosystems each have their own components, so to achieve a low-maintenance, healthy habitat, decide which habitat to copy and choose the appropriate plants. A hodge-podge of trees, shrubs, wildflowers, and lower plants thrown

**Left** and **right** Wild gardening, a concept spawned with the environmental movement of the seventies, has been steadily winning converts ever since. It involves the use of wild plants to achieve an attractive, natural-looking, low-maintenance landscape. If possible, it is often desirable to incorporate a water source, such as a pond or stream, into your wild garden for the sake of variety and the benefit of wildlife.

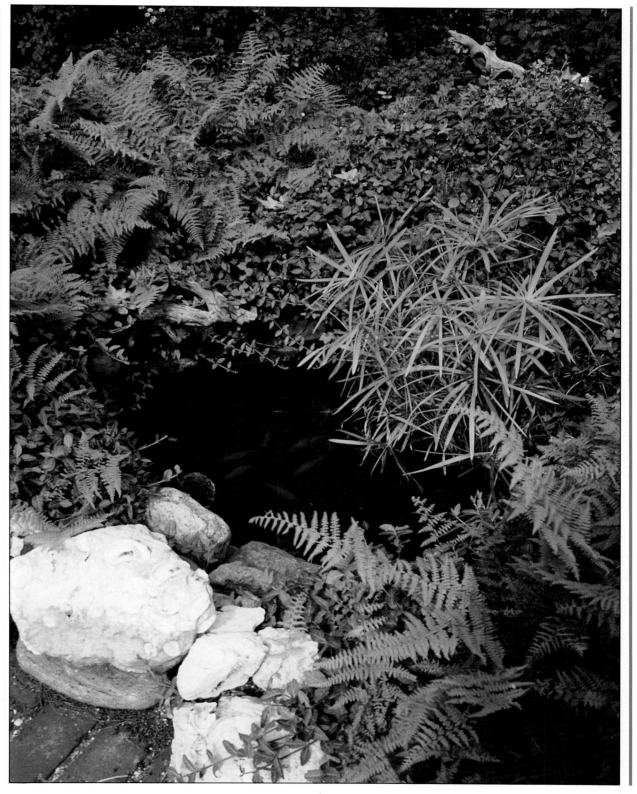

together on a whim is not likely to form a viable community and, in fact, you may lose many of your species in the first couple of growing seasons.

Always choose a wild-garden theme that is common to your area. Attempting a desert landscape in New England would be as fruitless as planting a tall-grass prairie high in the Rockies. Spend time researching local habitats through reading and especially through observation. Write down what grows where, which plants are frequently found together, which are never found together and the plants' maximum size, appearance, and life cycles.

### Elements of a wild garden

A wild garden should not just be a collection of plants. There are other elements, both living and non-living, that make up the natural ecosystem, and you should include them in your garden to break up the monotony of a mass of vegetation, create accents, and lend a touch of realism.

Rocks are a part of many natural habitats and their inert forms contrast effectively with the organic shapes of plants. Instead of posing an obstacle to your lawn mower, an exposed rock ledge or a boulder deposited by a long-ago glacier can become the centerpiece of your wild garden, with pockets of soil in cracks and depressions to host shallow-rooted plants. A stone wall of the type found throughout the northeast, though not natural, still makes an attractive feature and may also create a cool, moist, micro-habitat, especially on the north side, for mosses, liverworts and lichens to thrive; you may be surprised at the many different types that take up residence.

In a wooded area, standing dead trees, or snags, and fallen logs and branches are a natural part of the landscape, so resist the urge to clean them out of your garden. Not only do they look natural, but they host a myriad of fungi which help decompose them and enrich the soil, a natural cycle which you should encourage. Snags and fallen logs are also home to a surprising variety of wildlife. If too much debris accumulates, detracting from the garden's appearance, rent or buy a chipper and turn the excess into a mulch that can be spread over the garden to supply soil-building humus.

You are indeed fortunate if you have a stream or pond, for not only is the water an attractive feature, but the moist soil along its edge is ideal for a wetland habitat. A moist depression can be turned into a pseudo-marsh, fed perhaps by rainwater collected from the gutters on your roof. Use your imagination! Even if your land is dry, you may be able to construct a pond that looks natural, using a recirculating pump to prevent the water becoming stagnant. Many wild gardening books provide detailed instructions for building ponds.

Over-crowding your garden with large or showy species may diminish their appeal, and be detrimental to their health. Use ground covers, plants that spread by runners or rhizomes to form a fairly dense layer of low vegetation, or mosses that form solid cushions of greenery, between featured trees and shrubs. Flowering ground covers often have small blooms which, rather than dominating the scene, add just a tinge of background color. When planting a meadow, use a generous portion of native grass seed; the meadow then appears more authentic, and the grass supports weaker-stemmed wildflowers that would otherwise become scraggly and prostrate. In fact, many native grasses create attractive, subtle accents used on their own.

A well defined system of footpaths, though not a "natural" feature, provides access to various parts of the garden and minimizes traffic in sensitive areas. Natural materials such as pine-bark mulch or a medium-colored gravel, tend to blend in better than harshly colored or obviously man-made ones.

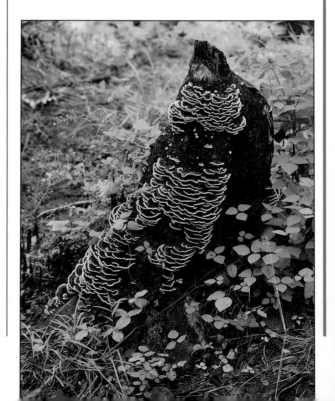

Paths that cross a body of water will require either a foot bridge (**right**) or stepping stones. Try to include all parts of the habitat you wish to recreate, such as rocks, stumps, and logs; rocks may provide anchors for lichens, and fallen logs and stumps will host many invertebrates and essential decomposers like fungi (**left**) and bacteria.

Install small footbridges for crossing streams and narrow boardwalks to provide access to marshy areas while protecting wetland plants. Benches and logs provide welcome rest areas for enjoying the surroundings.

### Obtaining seeds and native plants

Your first impulse may be to transplant plants from the wild. This is often the quickest and least expensive way of populating your garden, but it is seldom the best. Ethically, you should adopt the general rule of leaving plants where you find them. Even if you choose judiciously over a large area, the plants are part of a functioning ecosystem, and their absence leaves a void in that habitat. The main problem facing nature today is the encroachment of civilization and the accompanying loss or fouling of habitat, so habitats left relatively intact must be protected, to benefit future generations. Collecting plants removes not only that organism from that particular habitat, but all future generations that might have arisen from it, the food they would have produced, and the nutrients they would have returned to the soil. In addition, popular or rare plants may face extinction in the wild through well meaning collectors. Finally, many species do not transplant well, and some, not at all. Collecting them often just results in their death.

One instance where collecting plants from the wild may be justified and even encouraged is in areas slated for development. These plants are doomed anyway; better that they find a reprieve in your garden than be lost to the bulldozer's blade. Before staging plant rescue, you must obtain the landowner's permission, but most are cooperative.

Another method of obtaining plants from the wild is to collect ripe seeds, usually in late summer or fall. This has less impact on the habitat, because most species routinely produce many times more seeds than will ever grow into mature plants. To offset any negative effects, take only a few seeds from each plant, and collect from only a few plants in each location.

Most seeds have some form of germination inhibitor, a chemical that keeps them from sprouting at the wrong time. If you are storing seeds inside, these inhibitors must be deactivated, by a period of freezing that simulates winter, or by a certain amount of moisture, simulating melting snow or seasonal rains, before the seeds will germinate. From a nursery or library, obtain as much information as possible about the relevant species, to increase your chances of success.

The most ethical method of obtaining wild plants and seeds is to purchase them from nurseries. Many now specialize in native plants and offer mail-order service. Make sure, however, that the plants are nursery-raised and not collected from the wild; otherwise, you are paying someone else to negate your own good intentions.

# WHERE TO GO

## TALLGRASS PRAIRIE

**Illinois**
Belmont Prairie Preserve, Downers Grove; Fermi National Accelerator Laboratory; Gensburg-Markham Prairie, Markham; Goose Lake Prairie Nature Preserve, Morris; Illinois Beach State Park, Zion; James Woodworth Prairie Preserve, Chicago
**Indiana**
Hoosier Prairie Nature Preserve, Griffith
**Iowa**
Caylor Prairie, Spirit Lake
**Kansas**
Konza Prairie, Manhattan; Flint Hills Tallgrass Prairie, Rosalia
**Minnesota**
Minnesota Valley National Wildlife Refuge, Black Dog Unit, Bloomington; Malmberg Prairie, Polk County; Anna Gronseth Prairie, Wilkin County; Wahpeton Prairie, Walnut Grove
**Missouri**
Osage Prairie, Vernon County
**Nebraska**
Pawnee Prairie, Pawnee County
**South Dakota**
Sioux Prairie & Altamont Prairie, South Dakota State College, Brookings
**Wisconsin**
Scuppernong Springs Nature Area, Eagle; University of Wisconsin Arboretum, Madison

## MIXED GRASS PRAIRIE

**Kansas**
Quivera National Wildlife Refuge, Stafford; Kirwin National Wildlife Refuge, Kirwin
**Nebraska**
Fort Robinson State Park, Crawford; Valentine National Wildlife Refuge, Brownlee; Oglala National Grassland, Crawford
**North Dakota**
Theodore Roosevelt National Park, Medora; Lostwood National Wildlife Refuge, Lostwood; J. Clark Sayler National Wildlife Refuge, Upham; Little Missouri National Grassland, Grassy Butte
**Oklahoma**
Black Kettle National Grassland, Cheyenne; Great Salt Plains National Wildlife Refuge, Vining; Wichita Mountains National Wildlife Refuge, Indiahoma
**South Dakota**
Badlands National Park, Interior; Wind Cave National Park, Hot Springs; Buffalo Gap National Grassland, Edgemont; Fort Pierre National Grassland, Fort Pierre; Sand Lake National Wildlife Refuge, Hecla; Grand River National Grassland, Lodgepole
**Wyoming**
Thunder Basin National Grassland, Upton

## SHORTGRASS PRAIRIE

**Colorado**
Comanche National Grassland, Andrix; Pawnee National Grassland, Buckingham
**Kansas**
Cimarron National Grassland, Rolla
**Montana**
Red Rock Lakes National Wildlife Refuge, Lakeview; Charles M. Russell National Wildlife Refuge, Fort Peck; U. L. Bend National Wildlife Refuge, Valentine; Custer Battlefield National Monument, Crow Agency; Medicine Lake National Wildlife Refuge, Dagmar
**Nebraska**
Oglala National Grassland, Crawford; Crescent Lake National Wildlife Refuge, Oshkosh
**New Mexico**
Kiowa National Grassland, Clayton; Bitter Lake National Wildlife Refuge, Roswell
**Texas**
Rita Blanca National Grassland, Dalhart; Muleshoe National Wildlife Refuge, Needmore; Lake McClellan National Grassland Park, Alanreed

## INTERMOUNTAIN GRASSLANDS

**California**
Modoc National Forest, Alturas Clear Lake National Wildlife Refuge, Newell
**Colorado**
Dinosaur National Monument, Dinosaur
**Idaho**
Craters of the Moon National Monument, Arco; Curlew National Grassland, Holbrook; Caribou National Forest, Soda Springs; Sawtooth National Forest, Oakley; Camas National Wildlife Refuge, Camas
**Nevada**
Great Basin National Park, Baker; Charles Sheldon Wildlife Refuge, Denio Junction; Black Rock Desert, Sulphur; Humboldt National Forest, McDermitt; Humboldt National Forest, Mountain City; Humboldt National Forest and Ruby Lake; National Wildlife Refuge, Ruby Valley; Humboldt National Forest, Ely; Toiyabe National Forest, Austin; Smoke Creek Desert, Sand Pass
**Oregon**
Hart Mountain National Antelope Range, Plush; Malheur National Wildlife Refuge, Narrows; Malheur National Forest, Canyon City; Crooked River National Grassland, Madras; Ochoco National Forest, Mitchell
**Utah**
Bryce Canyon National Park, Bryce Canyon; Zion National Park, Springdale; Glen Canyon National Recreation Area, Ticaboo; Dixie National Forest, Cedar City

## BOREAL FOREST

**Alaska**
Denali National Park, McKinley Park
**Alberta**
Wood Buffalo National Park, Fort Fitzgerald
**Maine**
Acadia National Park, Bar Harbor; Baxter State Park, Millinocket; Moosehorn National Wildlife Refuge, Calais
**Manitoba**
Whiteshell Provincial Park, Westhawk Lake
**Michigan**
Isle Royale National Park, St. Ignace; Hiawatha National Forest, Eckerman; Ottawa National Forest, Bergland
**Minnesota**
Lake Itasca State Park, Lake Itasca; Boundary Waters Canoe Area; Voyageurs National Park, International Falls
**New Hampshire**
White Mountain National Forest
**New York**
Adirondack Forest Preserve
**Ontario**
Algonquin Provincial Park, Whitney
**Quebec**
La Verendrye Provincial Park, Mont-Laurier
**Saskatchewan**
Prince Albert National Park, Christopher Lake
**Tennessee**
Great Smoky Mountains National Park, Gatlinburg
**Vermont**
Green Mountain National Forest
**Virginia**
Shenandoah National Park, Front Royal

## NORTHERN HARDWOOD FOREST

**Maine**
Acadia National Park, Bar Harbor; Baxter State Park, Millinocket; Moosehorn National Wildlife Refuge, Calais
**Michigan**
Manistee National Forest, Big Rapids
**New Hampshire**
White Mountains National Forest
**New York**
Adirondack Forest Preserve
**North Carolina**
Pisgah National Forest, Asheville
**Ontario**
Algonquin Provincial Park, Whitney
**Pennsylvania**
Allegheny National Forest, Warren; Hickory Run State Park, White Haven; Rickett's Glen State Park, Red Rock; World's End State Park, Forksville
**Tennessee**
Great Smoky Mountains National Park, Gatlinburg
**Vermont**
Green Mountains National Forest
**Virginia**
Shenandoah National Park, Front Royal; George Washington National Forest; Jefferson National Forest

**West Virginia**
Monongahela National Forest
**Wisconsin**
Chequamegon National Forest, Ashland

## OAK-HICKORY FOREST

**Arkansas**
Hot Springs National Park, Hot Springs;
Ozark National Forest
**Georgia**
Chattahoochee National Forest
**Kentucky**
Mammoth Cave National Park, Mammoth
Cave; Daniel Boone National Forest
**Missouri**
Mark Twain National Forest
**New Jersey**
Stokes State Forest, Tuttle's Corner
**New York**
Bear Mountain State Park, Jones Point;
Harriman State Park, Willow Grove
**North Carolina**
Pisgah National Forest, Ashville
**Ohio**
Wayne National Forest
**Pennsylvania**
Hawk Mountain Sanctuary, Drehersville;
Delaware Water Gap National Recreation
Area, East Stroudsberg; Gettysburg
National Military Park, Gettysburg
**Tennessee**
Great Smoky Mountains National Park,
Gatlinburg; Cherokee National Forest
**Virginia**
Shenandoah National Park, Front Royal;
George Washington National Forest;
Jefferson National Forest
**West Virginia**
Monongahela National Forest

## SOUTHERN PINELANDS

**Alabama**
Conecuh National Forest, Andalusia;
Talladega National Forest, Tuscaloosa
**Florida**
Osceola National Forest, Lake City; Ocala
National Forest, Ocala; Appalachicola
National Forest, Tallahassee
**Georgia**
Oconee National Forest, Monticello;
Piedmont National Wildlife Refuge,
Macon; Laura S. Walker State Park,
Waycross; Cumberland Island National
Seashore
**Louisiana**
Kisatchie National Forest, Alexandria;
Tensas National Wildlife Refuge, Tallulah
**Mississippi**
DeSoto National Forest, Hattiesburg;
Homochitto National Forest, Meadville;
Noxubee National Wildlife Refuge,
Starkville
**New Jersey**
Wharton State Forest, Hammonton
**North Carolina**
Croatan National Forest, Havelock
**South Carolina**
Francis Marion National Forest, Goose
Creek; Carolina Sandhills National
Wildlife Refuge, Hartsville

**Texas**
Big Thicket National Preserve, Beaumont;
Sabine National Forest, San Augustine
**Virginia**
Chincoteague National Wildlife Refuge,
Chincoteague

## FLOODPLAIN FORESTS

Locations are too numerous to mention
here, but major river valleys, national
wildlife refuges, national parks and
forests, state parks and forests, Nature
Conservancy preserves, and Audubon
Society sanctuaries all offer excellent
opportunities to observe floodplain
forests.

## PONDEROSA PINE FORESTS

**Arizona**
Kaibob National Forest, Flagstaff
**Colorado**
Rocky Mountain National Park, Estes
Park; Pike National Forest, Colorado
Springs; Gunnison National Forest,
Gunnison
**Idaho**
Nez Perce National Forest, Grangeville
**Montana**
Glacier National Park, West Glacier;
Custer National Forest, Ashland
**New Mexico**
Sante Fe National Forest, Santa Fe
**South Dakota**
Custer State Park, Custer; Black Hills
National Forest, Rapid City
**Utah**
Ashley National Forest, Vernal; Fishlake
National Forest, Fishlake
**Wyoming**
Bighorn National Forest, Sheridan;
Medicine Bow National Forest, Laramie

## DOUGLAS FIR FOREST

**Alberta**
Banff National Park, Banff
Jasper National Park, Jasper
**Colorado**
Rocky Mountain National Park, Estes Park
**Idaho**
Boise National Forest, Boise
Nez Perce National Forest, Grangeville
**Montana**
Glacier National Park, West Glacier
Kootenai National Forest, Libby
Lolo National Forest, Missoula
**Wyoming**
Grand Teton National Park, Moose

## LODGEPOLE PINE FORESTS

**Alberta**
Banff National Park, Banff; Jasper
National Park, Jasper

**British Columbia**
Mount Revelstoke National Park, Revelstoke
**Colorado**
Rocky Mountain National Park, Estes
Park; Routt National Forest, Steamboat
Springs
**Idaho**
Salmon National Forest, Salmon;
Sawtooth National Recreation Area,
Stanley
**Montana**
Helena National Forest, Helena; Glacier
National Park, West Glacier
**Oregon**
Ochoco National Forest, Prineville
**Utah**
Ashley National Forest, Vernal
**Wyoming**
Bighorn National Forest; Yellowstone
National Park; Grand Teton National Park,
Moose; Bridger-Teton National Forest,
Jackson

## ASPEN FORESTS

**Alaska**
Denali National Park, McKinley Park
**Alberta**
Banff National Park, Banff; Jasper
National Park, Jasper
**Arizona**
Kaibob National Forest, Flagstaff
**Colorado**
Rocky Mountain National Park, Estes
Park; White River National Forest,
Glenwood Springs; Gunnison National
Forest, Gunnison
**Idaho**
Caribou National Forest, Soda Springs
**Montana**
Glacier National Park, West Glacier;
Lewis and Clark National Forest, White
Sulphur Springs
**New Mexico**
Cibola National Forest, Socorro
**Utah**
Cache National Forest, Ogden; Uinta
National Forest, Provo
**Wyoming**
Medicine Bow National Forest, Laramie;
Grand Teton National Park, Moose

## PACIFIC NORTHWEST COASTAL FORESTS

**Alaska**
Kenai Fjords National Park, Seward;
Glacier Bay National Park, Gustavus;
Tongass National Forest, Juneau
**British Columbia**
Pacific Rim National Park, Ucluelet;
Garibaldi Provincial Park, Whistler
**Oregon**
Wilamette National Forest, Oakridge;
Mount Hood National Forest, Portland;
Siskiyou National Forest, Grant's Pass
**Washington**
Olympic National Park, Port Angeles;
North Cascades National Park, Sedro
Woolley; Mount Rainier National Park,
Ashford

# REDWOOD FORESTS

**California**
Redwood National Park, Crescent City; Humboldt Redwoods State Park, South Fork; Muir Woods National Monument, Mill Valley; Grizzly Creek Redwoods State Park, Bridgeville; Jedediah Smith Redwoods State Park, Crescent City; Prairie Creek Redwoods State Park, Orick

# BOGS

**Connecticut**
Black Spruce Bog, Mohawk Forest, Goshen
**Maine**
Acadia National Park, Bar Harbor; Crystal Bog, Crystal; Appleton Bog, Appleton; Meddybemps Heath, Calais
**Massachusetts**
Black Pond Bog, Vinal Nature Preserve, Cohasset; Thoreau's Bog, Concord
**Michigan**
Isle Royale National Park, Houghton
**Minnesota**
Voyaguers National Park, International Falls
**New Hampshire**
Wapack National Wildlife Refuge, Greenfield
**New Jersey**
High Point State Park, Sussex; Wharton State Forest, Hammonton
**New York**
Moss Lake Bog, Houghton; McLean Bogs, McLean
**Ontario**
Algonquin Provincial Park, Whitney
**Pennsylvania**
Tannersville Cranberry Bog Preserve, Tannersville
**Rhode Island**
Diamond Bog, Woodville
**Vermont**
Peacham Bog, Groton State Forest, Marshfield; Snake Mountain Bog, Weybridge
**West Virginia**
Cranberry Glades, Monongahela National Forest

# MARSHES

There are too many sites to list. For directories contact:

National Wildlife Refuges: National Wetlands Inventory, U.S. Fish & Wildlife Service, Department of the Interior, 1730 K St., N.W., Washington, D.C. 20240, (202) 653-8726.
Nature Conservancy Preserves: The Nature Conservancy, 1800 North Kent St., Arlington, VA 22209.

# EVERGLADES

**Florida**
Everglades National Park, Homestead; Loxahatchee National Wildlife Refuge, Loxahatchee; Big Cypress National Preserve, Monroe

# CYPRESS SWAMPS AND SOUTHERN HARDWOOD SWAMPS

**Arkansas**
White River National Wildlife Refuge, St. Charles
**Delaware**
Pocomoke River Swamp, Gumboro
**Florida**
Blackwater River State Forest, Munson; Appalachicoloa National Forest, Tallahassee; Corkscrew Swamp Sanctuary, Immokalee; Big Cypress National Preserve, Monroe
**Georgia**
Okefenokee National Wildlife Refuge, Edith
**Louisiana**
Atchafalaya Swamp, Donner
**North Carolina**
Alligator River National Wildlife Refuge, East Lake; Merchants Mill Pond State Park, Sunbury
**South Carolina**
Four Holes Swamp, Harleyville; Congaree Swamp National Monument, Gadsden
**Tennessee**
Reelfoot National Wildlife Refuge, Walnut Log
**Texas**
Big Thicket National Preserve, Evadale
**Virginia**
Great Dismal Swamp National Wildlife Refuge, Suffolk

# SAND DUNES

**Florida**
Canaveral National Seashore, Titusville; Gulf Islands National Seashore, Pensacola
**Georgia**
Cumberland Island National Seashore, St. Marys
**Louisiana**
Delta National Wildlife Refuge, Pilottown
**Maryland**
Assateague Island National Seashore, Berlin
**Massachusetts**
Cape Cod National Seashore, South Wellfleet; Parker River National Wildlife Refuge, Newburyport
**New Jersey**
Gateway National Recreation Area, Highlands; Island Beach State Park, Seaside Heights
**New York**
Fire Island National Seashore, Oak Beach
**North Carolina**
Cape Hatteras National Seashore, Manteo; Cape Lookout National Seashore, Beaufort

**Oregon**
Oregon Dunes National Recreation Area, Reedsport
**Rhode Island**
Ninigret National Wildlife Refuge, Charlestown
**South Carolina**
Cape Romain National Wildlife Refuge, McClellanville
**Texas**
Padre Island National Seashore, Corpus Christi
**Virginia**
Chincoteague National Wildlife Refuge, Chincoteague

# ROCKY SHORES

**Alaska**
Glacier Bay National Park, Gustavus
**British Columbia**
Pacific Rim National Park, Ucluelet
**California**
Point Reyes National Seashore, Point Reyes Station; King Range National Conservation Area, Redway; Redwood National Park, Crescent City; Channel Islands National Park, Ventura; Cabrillo National Monument, San Diego
**Maine**
Acadia National Park, Bar Harbor
**New Brunswick**
Fundy National Park, Alma
**Nova Scotia**
Cape Breton Highlands National Park, Cheticamp
**Oregon**
Oregon Islands National Wildlife Refuge, Brookings; Three Arch Rock National Wildlife Refuge, Cape Meares
**Washington**
North Cascades National Park, Sedro Woolley; Olympic National Park, Port Angeles; Willapa National Wildlife Refuge, Naselle; San Juan National Wildlife Refuge, Shaw Island

# SALT MARSHES – ATLANTIC COAST

**Connecticut**
Salt Meadow National Wildlife Refuge, Grove Beach
**Delaware**
Bombay Hook National Wildlife Refuge, Smyrna
**Florida**
Merritt Island National Wildlife Refuge, Titusville
**Maine**
Rachel Carson National Wildlife Refuge, Wells; Scarborough Marsh, Falmouth
**Maryland**
Assateague Island National Seashore, Berlin; Blackwater National Wildlife Refuge, Church Creek
**Massachusetts**
Cape Cod National Seashore, South Wellfleet; Parker River National Wildlife Refuge, Newburyport

**New Brunswick**
Kouchibouguac National Park,
Kouchibouguac
**New Jersey**
Edwin B. Forsythe National Wildlife
Refuge, Brigantine
**North Carolina**
Alligator River National Wildlife Refuge,
East Lake; Cape Hatteras National
Seashore, Manteo
**Prince Edward Island**
Prince Edward Island National Park,
Covehead
**South Carolina**
Cape Romain National Wildlife Refuge,
Awendaw; Santee Coastal Reserve,
McLellanville
**Virginia**
Chincoteague National Wildlife Refuge,
Chincoteague

## SALT MARSHES – GULF COAST

**Florida**
St. Marks National Wildlife Refuge, St.
Marks; Gulf Islands National Seashore,
Pensacola
**Louisiana**
Sabine National Wildlife Refuge,
Hackberry; Rockefeller National Wildlife
Refuge, Grand Chenier
**Texas**
Aransas National Wildlife Refuge,
Austwell

## SALT MARSHES – PACIFIC COAST

**California**
San Francisco Bay National Wildlife
Refuge, Newark; Elkhorn Slough
Estuarine Sanctuary; Salinas River
Wildlife Management Area, Salinas; San
Pablo Bay National Wildlife Refuge, San
Pablo
**Oregon**
South Slough Estuarine Sanctuary
**Washington**
Willapa National Wildlife Refuge,
Naselle; Dungeness National Wildlife
Refuge, Dungeness; Nisqualla National
Wildlife Refuge, Olympia; Grays Harbor
National Wildlife Refuge, Olympia

## MANGROVES AND TROPICAL FOREST

**Florida**
Everglades National Park, Homestead;
Biscayne National Park, Homestead; J.N.
"Ding" Darling National Wildlife Refuge,
Sanibel; Great White Heron National
Wildlife Refuge, Big Pine Key;
Chassahowitzka National Wildlife
Refuge, Chassahowitzka; Merritt Island
National Wildlife Refuge, Titusville

## GREAT BASIN DESERT

**California**
Modoc National Forest, Altura
**Colorado**
Dinosaur National Monument, Dinosaur
**Idaho**
Camas National Wildlife Refuge, Hamer;
Curlew National Grasslands, Holbrook;
Minidoka National Wildlife Refuge,
Minidoka; Sawtooth National Forest
**Nevada**
Black Rock Desert, Sulphur; Great Basin
National Park, Baker; Charles Sheldon
National Antelope Refuge, Denio
Junction; Humboldt National Forest;
Toiyabe National Forest
**Oregon**
Hart Mountain National Antelope Refuge,
Plush; Malheur National Wildlife Refuge,
Narrows; Ochoo National Forest, Seneca
**Utah**
Bryce Canyon National Park, Bryce
Canyon; Zion National Park, Springdale;
Dixie National Forest, Panguitch; Glen
Canyon National Recreation Area,
Ticaboo

## MOHAVE DESERT

**Arizona**
Hualapai Mountain State Park, Kingman
**California**
Joshua Tree National Monument,
Twentynine Palms; California Poppy
Reserve, Lancaster; Death Valley National
Monument, Death Valley
**Nevada**
Desert National Wildlife Refuge, Indian
Springs; Pharanagat National Wildlife
Refuge, Alamo; Lake Meade National
Recreation Area, Boulder City

## SONORAN DESERT

**Arizona**
Desert Foothills Drive, Phoenix; South
Mountain Park, Phoenix; Picacho Peak
State Park, Picacho; Saguaro National
Monument, Tuscon; Arizona-Sonoran
Desert Museum, Tuscon; Organ Pipe
Cactus National Monument, Ajo; Boyce
Thompson Southwestern Arboretum,
Superior
**California**
Anza-Borrego Desert State Park, Borrego
Springs; Coachella Valley Preserve, Indio

## CHIHUAHUAN DESERT

**New Mexico**
Living Desert State Park, Carlsbad;
Carlsbad Caverns National Park,
Carlsbad; White Sands National
Monument, Alamagordo
**Texas**
Big Bend National Park

## SUBALPINE FOREST AND ALPINE TUNDRA

**California**
Yosemite National Park; Kings Canyon
National Park, Three Rivers; Sequoia
National Park, Three Rivers; Klamath
National Forest, Yreka
**Colorado**
Rocky Mountain National Park, Estes
Park; Pike National Forest, Colorado
Springs; Gunnison National Forest,
Gunnison
**Idaho**
Salmon National Forest, Salmon
**Maine**
Mt. Katahdin, Baxter State Park,
Millinocket; Cadillac Mountain, Acadia
National Park, Bar Harbor
**Montana**
Glacier National Park, West Glacier;
Bitterroot National Forest, Missoula
**New Hampshire**
The Presidential Range, esp. Mt.
Washington, White Mountain National
Forest
**New York**
Mt. Marcy, Lake Placid
**Oregon**
Mt. Hood National Forest, Cherryville
**Utah**
Uinta National Forest, Provo
**Vermont**
Mt. Mansfield, Mt. Mansfield State Forest,
Stowe
**Washington**
Camel's Hump State Park, Ashford;
Olympic National Park, Port Angeles;
North Cascades National Park, Sedro
Woolley
**Wyoming**
Grand Teton National Park, Moose;
Yellowstone National Park

# GLOSSARY

**Abscission:** the shedding of leaves, flowers, or fruits through the formation of an abscission zone at the point of attachment to the plant.

**Adventitious roots:** roots that develop along an above-ground stem or on leaves.

**Aerobic respiration:** the cellular breakdown of sugar or other food requiring oxygen and resulting in the release of energy.

**Alternate:** leaf arrangement of one leaf per node.

**Anaerobic respiration:** the cellular breakdown of sugar or other food that does not require oxygen but results in the release of energy.

**Annual:** a plant needing only one growing season to complete its life cycle.

**Annulus:** a membranous ring around the stem of a mushroom.

**Anther:** the pollen-bearing portion of a stamen.

**Aperture:** the adjustable opening of a camera lens which determines the amount of light passing through in a given time.

**Apical meristem:** the region of actively growing cells at the tip of a root or shoot.

**Auxins:** growth-regulating substances produced by plants.

**Biennial:** a plant requiring two growing seasons to complete its life cycle.

**Bilateral symmetry:** having two identical halves; symmetrical about one plane only.

**Blade:** the broad, flattened portion of a leaf.

**Bulb:** food-storage organ consisting of fleshy, modified leaves or leaf bases packed tightly around a small stem.

**Calyx:** the outer, protective part of a flower, made of sepals fused together to form a funnel, bowl or trumpet-shaped structure.

**Chlorophyll:** the green pigment present in the chloroplasts of plants and responsible for photosynthesis.

**Chloroplasts:** small granules within plants' cells which contain chlorophyll and other compounds active in photosynthesis.

**Climax community:** the stable, self-perpetuating community of vegetation at the culmination of ecological succession.

**Compound:** describing a leaf, flower or fruit divided into smaller, separate but similar units.

**Corolla:** inner protective part of a flower, composed of completely or partly fused petals.

**Corm:** an underground food-storage organ composed of a thickened stem usually covered by papery skin.

**Cotyledon:** an embryonic leaf within a seed, and the first to appear on germination.

**Cross-pollination:** the transfer of pollen from one plant to another of the same species.

**Deciduous:** a plant, especially a tree or shrub, which sheds all its leaves annually, at the end of the growing season.

**Dicot:** a class of flowering plants whose seeds have two cotyledons.

**Desiccant:** a drying agent.

**Digestion:** the enzyme-controlled conversion of complex, insoluble food molecules into simple, soluble molecules.

**Entire:** describing leaves or petals with smooth margins.

**Fibrous roots:** a spreading root system continuously branching into fine, hair-like structures.

**Filament:** the stalk of a stamen, bearing two anther lobes.

**Frond:** the leaf-like, spore-bearing organ of ferns and some other non-flowering plants.

**Herbarium:** a systematically arranged collection of dried, pressed, mounted, and labeled plant specimens.

**Humus:** the organic component of soil derived from decomposing plant or animal matter.

**Hydrosere:** the primary succession in a wet environment.

**Hyphae:** tubular, thread-like filaments of fungi.

**Lanceolate:** describing lance-shaped leaves, broad at the base and tapering to a point.

**Lateral bud:** a bud formed between a twig and the petiole of a leaf.

**Leaflet:** the sub-unit of a compound leaf.

**Leaf scar:** the scar left on a twig after the leaf is shed through abscission.

**Lignin:** the strengthening or stiffening substance that impregnates the cell walls of plants to varying degrees.

**Linear:** describing long, narrow leaves, bracts or petals, having parallel margins.

**Margin:** the edge of a leaf.

**Midrib:** the central vein of a pinnately-veined leaf from which lateral veins branch.

**Monocot:** the class of flowering plants whose seeds have one cotyledon.

**Mycelium:** the collective term for the hyphae of a fungus.

**Node:** the stem joint from which buds, side shoots and leaves form.

**Opposite:** describing a leaf arrangement in which two leaves are attached to the stem at the same point.

**Ovary:** the enlarged base of a pistil containing the ovules, which ultimately develop into seeds.

**Ovate:** describing egg-shaped leaves, bracts or petals, which are broadest at the base.

**Ovules:** immature seeds in the ovary containing the eggs.

**Palmate:** describing hand-shaped leaves, with deep lobes radiating from a single point.

**Peduncle:** the stalk of a flower or flower cluster.
**Pedicel:** the stalk of an individual flower within a flower cluster.
**Perennial:** a plant, usually herbaceous, whose life cycle exceeds two years.
**Perianth:** the collective term for the sepals and petals of a flower, in which the two structures are indistinguishable from one another.
**Petal:** the basic, flattened unit of the corolla, often brightly colored.
**Petiole:** the stalk of a leaf.
**Phloem:** tube-like conductive tissue which transports food up or down in vascular plants.
**Pinnae:** the primary sub-units of a deeply divided leaf or frond.
**Pinnate:** describing opposite leaflets or veins branching from both sides of a common axis.
**Pioneers:** the first plants in any successional stage to become established.
**Pistil:** the central, female organ of a flower consisting of a stigma, a style, and an ovary.
**Pollen:** the male reproductive cells of a plant, formed in the anthers.
**Pollen tube:** a structure that develops from a pollen grain and conducts the male cells from the stigma through the style to an ovule.
**Pollination:** the transfer of pollen from an anther to a stigma.
**Primary succession:** the ecological succession beginning in an area devoid of soil.
**Prothallus:** the initial stage of a fern's life cycle.
**Protoplasm:** the living, translucent liquid substance of a cell including cytoplasm and the nucleus.
**Rachis:** the central axis of a compound leaf or raceme or spike on which flowers or leaflets are carried.
**Radial symmetry:** having identical halves divisible by an infinite number of planes.
**Receptacle:** the swollen tip of a stem to which all of the flower parts are attached.
**Rhizoids:** tiny, root-like structures of certain non-vascular plants that function as anchors.
**Rhizome:** a horizontal, underground stem acting as a food storage organ.
**Respiration:** the cellular breakdown of sugars and other foods resulting in the release of energy.
**Secondary succession:** ecological succession in an area where soil has already formed.
**Sepal:** the primary leaf- or petal-like unit of the calyx whose major function is to protect the unopened flower bud.
**Seral stage:** one stage in the process of ecological succession.
**Sere:** the entire process of ecological succession.
**Serrate:** describing leaves with forward pointing, saw-like teeth on the margins.

**Simple leaf:** the opposite of compound; a broad, undivided leaf.
**Sori:** the spore-bearing structures of ferns.
**Stamen:** the male reproductive organ of a flower consisting of a filament and an anther.
**Stigma:** the sticky tip of the pistil which receives the pollen grains.
**Stolon:** a prostrate, creeping stem growing along the surface of the ground, and rooting from the nodes, producing fuller stems or plantlets.
**Stoma:** a minute pore, usually on the underside of a leaf, which opens and closes to regulate transpiration and gas exchange.
**Strobili:** the catkin-like, spore-bearing flower spikes of conifers.
**Sucker:** a shoot arising from below ground, usually from the roots and remote from the main stem.
**Style:** that portion of the pistil connecting the stigma with the ovary in a female flower.
**Taproot:** the main anchoring root of a plant, especially a tree, often reaching deep into the ground.
**Tendril:** a slender, modified leaf or stem that coils around a support on contact and aids climbing.
**Terminal bud:** the topmost bud at the end of a twig.
**Transpiration:** the loss of water vapor, through stomata, from leaf and stem surfaces.
**Tuber:** a swollen, starchy underground stem or thickened, fleshy root functioning as a food storage organ, and a means of surviving drought or cold.
**Undulate:** describing a leaf, sepal or petal with a wavy or crimped margin.
**Veins:** strands of tissue which support a leaf and consist of xylem and phloem, the internal conducting elements of a leaf.
**Weathering:** the chemical or physical breakdown of rock into its smallest units, which form the inorganic portion of soil.
**Whorl:** describing three or more leaves attached at a single point on the stem, like the spokes of a wheel.
**Xerosere:** ecological succession occurring in a relatively dry environment.
**Xylem:** tube-like vascular tissue that forms the wood, and conducts water and dissolved substances upward in a plant.

# CONTACTS

## NATIONAL BOTANICAL ORGANIZATIONS

**Environmental Defense Fund,** 1616 P St., NW Suite 150, Washington, D.C. 20009.
**The Nature Conservancy,** 1800 N. Kent St., Suite 800, Arlington, VA 22209.
**American Horticultural Society,** P.O. Box 0105, Mt. Vernon, VA 22301.
**The Garden Club of America,** 598 Madison Ave, New York City, NY 10461.
**National Arbor Day Foundation,** 100 Arbor Ave, Nebraska City, NE 68410.
**Canadian Wildflower Society,** 35 Bauer Crescent, Unionville, Ontario L3R 4H3.
**Royal Botanical Gardens Members Association,** Box 339, Hamilton, Ontario L8N 3H8.
**Canadian Botanical Association,** Department of Botany, University of British Columbia, Vancouver, British Columbia V6T 2B1.
**National Council of State Garden Clubs, Inc.,** Operation Wildflower, P.O. Box 860, Pocasset, MA 02559.
**National Council of State Garden Clubs, Inc.,** 4401 Magnolia Ave, St. Louis, MO 63110.

## SOURCES OF NATIVE PLANTS AND SEEDS

**Baldwin Seed Company of Alaska,** Box 3127, Kenai, AK 99611.
**Bill Dodd's Rare Plants,** P.O. Box Drawer 377, Semmes, AL 36575.
**Alberta Nurseries & Seeds, Ltd,** Box 20, Bowden, Alberta T0M 0K0.
**Beaverlodge Nursery, Ltd,** Box 127, Beaverlodge, Alberta T0H 0C0.
**Izard Ozark Natives,** P.O. Box 32, Berryville, AR 72616.
**Southwestern Native Seeds,** Box 50503, Tucson, AZ 85703.
**Alpenglow Gardens,** 13328 King George Highway, North Surrey, British Columbia V3T 2T6.
**British Columbia Nursery Trades Association,** Suite #101·A, 15290-103A Ave, Surrey, British Columbia V3R 7A2.
**The Plant Man Yes,** 1017 2nd St, Santa Rosa, CA 95405.
**Wildwood Farm,** 10300 Sonoma Hwy. Kenwood, CA 95452.
**Dean Swift Seed Co,** P.O. Box B, Jaroso, CO 81138.
**Salter Tree Farm,** Rt. 2, Box 1332, Madison, FL 32340.
**Wildflowers From Nature's Way,** R.R. #1, Box 62, Woodburn, IA 50257.
**Northplan Seed Producers,** P.O. Box 9107, Moscow, ID 83843.
**Windrift Prairie Shop and Nursery,** R.D. #2, Oregon, IL 61061.
**Sharp Bros. Seed Co,** P.O. Box 140, Healy, KS 67850.
**Louisiana Nature and Science Center,** 11000 Lake Forest Blvd, New Orleans, LA 70127.
**Manitoba Nursery & Landscape Association,** 104 Parkside Dr, Winnipeg, Manitoba R3J 3P8.

**Environmental Concern Inc,** 210 West Chew Ave, P.O. Box P, St. Michaels, MD 21663.
**Far North Gardens,** 16785 Harrison, Livonia, MI 48154.
**Prairie Restorations, Inc,** P.O. Box 327. Princeton, MN 55371.
**Missouri Wildflowers Nursery,** Rt. 2, Box 373, Jefferson City, MO 65101.
**Lawyer Nursery, Inc,** 950 Hwy. 200 West, Plains, MT 59859.
**Niche Gardens,** Rt. 1, Box 290, Chapel Hill, NC 27514.
**Stock Seed Farms, Inc,** R.R. #1, Box 112, Murdock, NE 68407.
**Plants of the Southwest,** 1812 2nd St, Santa Fe. NM 87501.
**Atlantic Provinces Nursery Trades Association,** 130 Bluewater Rd, Bedford, Nova Scotia B4A 1G7.
**Downham Nursery, Inc,** 626 Victoria St, Strathroy, Ontario N7G 3C1.
**Woodland Nurseries,** 2151 Camilla Rd, Mississauga, Ontario L5A 2K1.
**Sheridan Nurseries,** 1116 Winston Churchill Blvd, Oakville, Ontario L6J 4Z2.
**Canadian Nursery Trades Association,** 1293 Matheson Blvd. Mississauga, Ontario L4W 1R1.
**Northwest Biological Enterprises,** 23351 SW Basky Dell Lane, West Linn, OR 97068.
**Appalachian Wildflower Nursery,** Rt. 1, Box 275A, Reedsville, PA 17084.
**Wildflower Patch,** 442 RC Brookside Dr., Walnutport, PA 18088.
**Greenhedges,** 650 Montee de Liesse, Montreal, Quebec H4T 1N8.
**Saskatchewan Nursery Trades Association,** Box 460, Carnduff, Saskcatchewan S0C 0S0.
**Oak Hill Farm,** 240 Pressley St, Clover, SC 29710.
**Woodlanders, Inc.,** 1128 Colleton Ave, Aiken, SC 29801.
**Echinational Plant Products,** 602 Jefferson St, Vermillion, SD 57069.
**Native Gardens,** Rt. 1, Box 494, Fisher Lane, Greenback, TN 37742.
**Sunlight Gardens, Inc,** Rt. 3, Box 286TX, London, TN 37774.
**Green Horizons,** 218 Quinlan, Suite 571, Kerrville, TX 78028.
**Gunsight Mountain Ranch & Nursery,** P.O. Box 86, Tarpley, TX 78883.
**Bambert Seed Co,** Rt. 3, Box 1120, Muleshoe, TX 79347.
**Mid-Atlantic Wildflowers,** S/R Box 226, Gloucester Point, VA 23062.
**Frosty Hollow Nursery,** Box 53, Langely, WA 98260.
**Little Valley Farm,** R.R. 1, Box 287, Richland Center, WI 53581.

# ACKNOWLEDGMENTS

Quarto would like to thank Rick Imes and Photo/Nats for providing photographs and for permission to reproduce copyright material. With the exception of Rick Imes and Moira Clinch, all the photographers credited are represented by Photo/Nats.

Key: bl = bottom left; br = bottom right; tr = top right; tl = top left; l = left; r = right; t = top; c = center; b = bottom

Liz Ball 74
Jean Baxter 126bl
Philip Beaurline 49bl; 49br; 81b; 84t; 84b; 84c; 107; 133; 134t; 137cr
Louis Borie 221; 32b; 72; 95t
Paul M. Brown 26c; 78; 116tl; 137cl; 139r; 144
Gay Bumgarner 77b; 148
Al. Bussewitz 125b
Priscilla Connell 77t; 79l; 121t; 139br
Greg Crisci 44
Deborah Crowell 62
Betsy Fuchs 110
Michael Goodman 90t; 104
Carl Hanninen 6; 23t; 64t; 73; 92t
Edward S. Hodgson 18; 139bl
Valorie Hodgson 32t; 41c; 41b; 47t; 50tl; 50tr; 51tl; 51tr; 71t; 123; 130; 131tr
Hal Horwitz 26t; 93t; 99; 115t; 115b; 129tl; 131br
Don Johnston Photos 20t; 28; 47bl; 47br; 48; 63;68b; 94t; 102b; 106; 111; 112t; 112b; 113; 143
Sydney Karp 29; 136
Dorothy Long 87
John A. Lynch 23b; 24br; 24t; 26b; 30b; 37; 60t; 61b; 66t; 86; 116b; 127r; 151
Robert E. Lyons 17r; 25; 49t; 79r;
Stephen G. Maka 19; 34; 118; 119r; 120
Jeff March 24bl; 51b; 68t; 83t; 105; 147l; 147r
A. Peter Margosian 42; 138t; 138b; 140
Iuan Massar 53
Mary A. Mather 8br; 57; 90b
Herbert B. Parsons 8tr; 121b
Ann Reilly 54; 141; 149
John J. Smith 13; 14; 171; 59c; 59b; 60l; 92bl; 92br; 94b; 100; 108; 117; 125t; 126t; 126bc; 128; 129b; 132; 134b; 137t
David M. Stone 27; 36; 38; 41t; 56; 67c; 67b; 71b; 81t; 95bl; 97t; 98r; 109; 116tr; 119l; 124; 129tr; 137b
Eugene H. Walker 65b; 70
Mrs. Eugene H. Walker 52; 80b; 142; 145t; 145b
Muriel V. Williams 31; 35t; 58
Marilyn Wood 11; 22r; 96; 122; 135

Moira Clinch 3
Rick Imes 20b; 21; 30t; 59t; 64b; 80t; 82b; 91; 93b; 95br; 97b; 98l; 101t; 101b; 102t; 103; 146; 150